A SPY IN PLAIN SIGHT

A SPY IN
PLAIN SIGHT

THE INSIDE STORY OF THE FBI AND ROBERT HANSSEN—
AMERICA'S MOST DAMAGING RUSSIAN SPY

LIS WIEHL

PEGASUS BOOKS
NEW YORK LONDON

A SPY IN PLAIN SIGHT

Pegasus Books, Ltd.
148 West 37th Street, 13th Floor
New York, NY 10018

Copyright © 2022 by Lis Wiehl

First Pegasus Books cloth edition May 2022

Interior design by Maria Fernandez

Library of Congress Cataloging-in-Publication Data is available.

ISBN: 978-1-63936-171-7

10 9 8 7 6 5 4 3 2 1

Printed in the United States of America
Distributed by Simon & Schuster
www.pegasusbooks.com

For Dani and Jacob. I love you to the moon and back.

—Mom

CONTENTS

AUTHOR'S NOTE

Dear Reader,

As the daughter of an FBI agent and a third-generation federal prosecutor, I grew up believing the men and women of the FBI were always the good guys, combating crime and working hard toward the ultimate goal of keeping us all safe. My father was that kind of FBI agent, and so were the people I worked with.

But all the while my father and other FBI agents were working to keep Americans safe, Robert Hanssen was working just as hard to betray the agency he had sworn allegiance to and the people and country he had sworn to protect. His selling of national secrets to the Russians cost lives and gutted operations critical to national security. In the process, he also besmirched the reputation of the FBI and branded it in ways that echo still—as an agency under siege, one unable to regulate itself from within.

I was compelled to dig deeper into the Robert Hanssen story because I believed that there were secrets yet to be uncovered. What's more, I believed that the uncovering of those new details would further a richer understanding of the facts behind the story and a more robust discussion of how we can assure the FBI never again cultivates another treasonous character like Robert Hanssen within its ranks.

After more than twenty years of selling America out to the Soviets and later Russians, Robert Hanssen was finally arrested on February 18, 2001.

He was still being processed when reporters began digging into his past and barely behind bars before book deals were being signed. Before the year was out, Adrian Havill (*The Spy Who Stayed Out in the Cold*) and David A. Vise (*The Bureau and the Mole*) had brought their accounts to market, followed the next year by Ann Blackman and Elaine Shannon (*The Spy Next Door*), Lawrence Schiller (*Into the Mirror*), and David Wise (*Spy: The Inside Story . . .*). Schiller's book, written with Norman Mailer, is the outlier in this crowd—a blend of fact and speculation. The others are all solid journalistic accounts that do their authors proud. Wise's *Spy* is even better than that.

But all these early books struggled to a greater or lesser degree to put Hanssen's actions into the context of the organization he so egregiously betrayed. The March 2002 report by the Commission for the Review of FBI Security Programs—commonly known as the Webster Commission after its chairman, former FBI and CIA director William Webster—helped a bit with that and was available to some of the later authors. But the full examination of how Hanssen was able to hide in plain sight arrived in August 14, 2003, when the Justice Department's Office of the Inspector General issued its *Review of the FBI's Performance in Deterring, Detecting, and Investigating the Espionage Activities of Robert Philip Hanssen*. That document was devastating to the Bureau and incredibly enlightening for those trying to understand how such a traitor could have been in operation all those years. The report also enraged some of those closest to the Hanssen case and has gradually loosened their tongues in the decades since.

Victor Cherkashin's 2004 memoir *Spy Handler* threw an entirely new perspective into the mix. A Washington-based KGB agent, Cherkashin was Hanssen's handler. In theory, the book was a rare chance to see America's star traitor through the eyes of his Soviet master, and the book is occasionally revealing if not always trustworthy. At least two FBI agents I interviewed told me they thought Cherkashin's memoir was part of a disinformation campaign, and I have been wary of it accordingly.

The most recent print addition to the Hanssen library—Eric O'Neill's *Gray Day* (2019)—focuses on a thin slice of the story. O'Neill was sent undercover to be Hanssen's office assistant for the six weeks before his arrest, and he recounts his experience in lively detail that centers around his own contribution. More valuable but far harder to access is David Wise's second crack at telling the story. *The Seven Million Dollar Spy* (2018) provides rich detail on Hanssen's eventual takedown, but Wise took ill while working on it, and his book was published posthumously and is available only as an audio book.

Meanwhile, the fifteen years between Cherkashin's questionable account and O'Neill's narrow one have been filled with revealing bits and pieces of this incredibly complex story, and I have tried to take full advantage of them all. Mike Rochford, the FBI agent most responsible for running Hanssen to ground; David Major, Hanssen's champion at the Bureau for much of his career; and David Charney, the psychologist who has spent more time with Hanssen post-arrest than any other mental-health professional, have all spoken at great length about the case in appearances at the International Spy Museum in downtown Washington, DC, and elsewhere. I've followed up on those talks with extensive interviews, especially with Rochford and Charney.

Bonnie Hanssen, still Bob Hanssen's wife, although he languishes in a federal prison from which he will never be released, refuses to meet with writers and reporters, but I have spent numerous hours communicating with her brother Mark Wauck, also an FBI agent. Mark granted me access to extensive email communications with the now-deceased Brian Kelley, the CIA officer who was psychologically brutalized by the CIA while under suspicion for the crimes Hanssen committed. Kelley's son, Barry, and widow, Patricia McCarthy, also opened up in heartbreaking ways and led me to explore in detail the full scope of collateral damage that accompanies crimes as heinous as Hanssen's.

Maybe most hauntingly, Hanssen's best friend since high school, Jack Hoschouer, laid himself bare for this account—an act of raw courage for which I will be forever grateful and a kind of expiation for actions that Jack is still struggling to understand.

Where feasible I've given many of these principal characters space to tell key parts of the story in their own words. They were there and deserve to be heard.

Bob Hanssen is where he should be, in jail for the rest of his life, but still at large are questions about his motives, his psyche, and the damage he caused; whether the FBI has blinded itself to the lessons it should have learned; and whether we are any better protected today from a new Bob Hanssen than we were from the actual one who ripped the guts out of America's secrets. That's where this book ends. But Hanssen's story will continue to wind through American history for years to come.

Even in a mature democracy, the rule of law can hang by a slim thread. An FBI that fails to police itself adequately or allows its mission to become subverted or its vast investigative powers to be abused could be the only difference between government of, by, and for the people and government by a tyrannous few.

—Lis Wiehl

STRANGE ENCOUNTER

December 2000

For FBI director Louis Freeh, this evening's keynote address should be sheer pleasure. The event is almost a family affair, the annual father-son banquet at his son's school. Justin, the youngest of the Freehs' four children, is by his side.

The venue is a friendly one, too. Located in a nicely wooded campus just off busy Seven Locks Road, in Potomac, Maryland, the Heights School lacks the panache of more established DC-area private schools such as St. Albans, Georgetown Preparatory, and Sidwell Friends, but the Heights has a unique value proposition that fits comfortably with Louie and Marilyn Freeh's own beliefs. The all-male school, grades 3 through 12, was founded in 1969 by a group of Catholic laymen associated with Opus Dei.

In his mega-best-selling novel *The Da Vinci Code*, Dan Brown portrays Opus Dei as an almost Satanic rear-guard cult within the Church. That was fiction, but Opus Dei members do take the deep traditions of their faith very seriously. The prelature of Opus Dei oversees the school, and thus the Heights, its student body, and the school family reflect some of the most old guard strains within Catholicism.

Mass and prayer are integral parts of school life, decorum is stressed, and boys at the Heights are expected to dress the part. The school handbook spells out explicitly the requirements for eighth graders through high school seniors: sport coat with dress trousers, dress shirt, tie, belt, dress shoes, and socks. Trousers must be able to hold a crease: no jeans, no denim of any kind, no cargo pants or fatigues, either. Shirts must have a collar. Dress shoes do *not* include any kind of athletic footwear. "Loud" clothing generally is forbidden. Also ear studs, any sort of bling, and hair that hangs in the eyes or over the collar.

"The Heights School," the handbook says, "is a training ground for adult responsibility and for a professional sense of work." End of story.

No surprise, the all-male faculty is drawn heavily from the ranks of Roman Catholic colleges and universities and includes anywhere from ten to fifteen teachers who are themselves members of Opus Dei. As also befits a school tied to a prelature in which about a third of lay members are numeraries—voluntary lifelong celibates who also practice mortification of the flesh—boys at the Heights are urged to be abstinent until marriage. No condom education allowed, or presumably needed.

While academic issues, discipline, financial concerns, and the like are left to a board of directors and an administrative council, "the spiritual direction of the Heights School is entrusted to Opus Dei," the handbook states, and Opus Dei priests are available to provide counsel to the entire school family.

The Freehs aren't the only parents who drive twenty-five miles round-trip through crippling traffic to deliver their sons to the school's door, nor the only ones who are hard-pressed to meet an annual tuition that today stands at about $30,000. Heights parents want and expect their sons to be steeped in church teaching. They are paying top dollar for the sort of intense moral education not available in the otherwise excellent public schools found in the wealthy Virginia and Maryland suburbs. The Heights unabashedly, even enthusiastically, teaches values, proper behavior, high moral standards, patriotism, and good citizenship. Parents, in turn, make the financial sacrifice of tuition because they expect the school to send good, moral, well-behaved citizens out into the world.

All of which makes this evening's encounter most strange.

The subject of Louie Freeh's keynote talk, suggested by Headmaster Richard McPherson, is ethics and integrity in government, and that, too, is right up the FBI director's alley.

For starters, Freeh is a fierce protector of his own reputation for integrity, and easily offended by perceived failures of integrity in others. His well-publicized struggles with Bill Clinton, who appointed him FBI director in 1993, have multiple roots but foremost among them perhaps is Freeh's personal revulsion over the Monica Lewinsky affair. Freeh's steely look and hard-set jaw aren't for show. He's a zero-tolerance guy, a grown-up altar boy who lives by a strict moral and ethical code.

Freeh is also a fierce protector of the FBI's reputation for integrity, and as the fathers and sons settle into their seats in front of him, that reputation hangs in the balance, along with multiple questions within the US intelligence community about the Bureau's basic investigative competency.

After more than seven years at the FBI's helm and a quarter century in the public sector—as a special agent and US attorney before becoming director—Louie Freeh is ready to cash in on his résumé. But a gaping security breach that has equally plagued the FBI and the CIA across the Potomac River has finally come to a head. For more than a decade, both agencies have been searching for the Russian mole buried deep within one or the other of them and doing irreparable harm to the nation's intelligence capacity overseas, especially in dealing with the Russians.

The mole has a code name—GRAYSUIT—and according to a joint special investigative unit led by the FBI, the mole has an almost certain home: the CIA. By the late 1990s, suspicion has focused brutally and resolutely on counterintelligence officer Brian Kelley. His family members are grilled ruthlessly; his house secretly searched. Kelley himself is stripped of his entry badge and placed under a semi house arrest.

To drive the last nail into Kelley's coffin, FBI special agent Mike Rochford launches a bizarre global search that eventually nets an ex-KGB officer on the lam from a Russian mobster and willing to sell out GRAYSUIT for $7 million. But the evidence, when it arrives in November 2000, writes a different end to the story: the mole isn't Brian Kelley. The real GRAYSUIT has been hiding out in the FBI all along, and in more than one way, he's Louie Freeh's doppelgänger.

Like Freeh, GRAYSUIT is a devout Catholic. Both men joined the Bureau within a year of each other. Both took an oath to "support and defend the Constitution of the United States against all enemies, foreign and domestic" and "bear true faith and allegiance to the same." Both have also signed the FBI Pledge for Law Enforcement Officers, accepting the obligation to "consider the information coming into my knowledge by virtue of my position as a sacred trust." Freeh and GRAYSUIT live within easy driving distance of each other in the Virginia suburbs; they regularly attend the same church—St. Catherine of Siena, in Great Falls—with long strings of children in tow on either side. Like Freeh's brother, John, but not the director himself, GRAYSUIT is also a member of Opus Dei.

Shortly after GRAYSUIT is identified, the FBI buys a house in his immediate neighborhood and installs an additional thirty telephone lines to turn it into a surveillance center. His car is tailed everywhere. Within a few weeks, he will be moved into a new office on the ninth floor of the FBI's headquarters—the J. Edgar Hoover Building—ostensibly as a reward for faithful service as he nears retirement, but his promotion is to a non-job, his new office will be bugged and videoed to a fare-thee-well, and the lowly agent assigned to be his aide-de-camp will in fact be the Bureau's eyes and ears inside GRAYSUIT's new and rapidly shrinking world.

GRAYSUIT, in short, is under round-the-clock watch—at home, at work, and in between—but this evening, in this bastion of patriotism and conservative Catholicism, GRAYSUIT needs no additional surveillance. He's part of the welcoming committee that greets Louie Freeh upon his arrival, and now, as Freeh prepares to speak about ethics and integrity, the most successful Russian mole in American history is in the front row, and GRAYSUIT's *own son is sitting beside him.*

"There I was on that small stage, waiting to start my talk and knowing the man right in front of me had sold his nation down the river," Freeh recalls. "And there GRAYSUIT was, not having any idea that we had finally cracked his cover wide open. I don't think I ever showed it that evening, but the longer I sat there, the angrier I got. It wasn't just that he had betrayed America for money or that he had smeared the Bureau and violated his own oath of office, although all that was certainly part of it. He had also betrayed his family, and very soon his crimes were going to come crashing down on the head of that unsuspecting boy sitting with him along with his wife and rest of his family. To me, that was almost as unforgivable as the espionage itself."[1]

How hard those crimes will crash down, though, is still an open question. Even today, the value of the secrets GRAYSUIT turned over to America's mortal enemy remains almost inestimable. Because of them, operations vital to national security have been gutted. Blood has been spilled in the prisons of Moscow; bodies are in the ground because GRAYSUIT has revealed identities, knowing for certain what the outcome will be. If the Bureau can catch GRAYSUIT in the act of espionage—making a drop to the Russians, picking up yet another pack of crisp $100 bills that regularly come in bundles of $30,000 or more—he might be executed; at the least, he's certain to spend the rest of his life in jail.

But espionage also has a high threshold of proof, and GRAYSUIT is less than five months away from mandatory retirement. What if this worst spy in American history gives it up and walks free—never sins again and rides off into the golden sunshine of a government-funded pension? That's the nightmare scenario, the possibility that has the small handful of people at the Bureau who have been fully read into GRAYSUIT's case staring at the ceiling at 3:00 in the morning, night after restless night.

And GRAYSUIT, sitting there in row one with his long horse face set in its perpetually dour expression, does he have any sense of what lies ahead? Maybe. After two decades of on-and-off cocksure communication with his spymaster handlers, a frantic tone has begun to slip into the notes he leaves with the stacks of documents and encoded disks chock-full of America's deepest secrets.

Does GRAYSUIT care, though? That's maybe the better question. Or does he even in some dark chamber of his psyche welcome what might lie ahead? His name is Robert Philip Hanssen, and the thing about being the best mole ever is that nobody knows it until you are caught.

PART I

CHAPTER 1

TOPHAT

The video lasts only sixty-four seconds, but it's almost impossible to pull your eyes away from the quiet malice in front of you. Four younger men in tight-fitting suits—agents for the KGB, the Soviet state intelligence service—surround a fifth older man in a small room, lit by a window covered by a dingy café curtain. One of the younger men has his right arm locked around the older man's neck. The others are methodically stripping him of his shirt. By twenty-two seconds, the older man's chest is exposed. Soon, he's naked from the waist up. From behind, fingers grab hold of his chin and turn his face directly toward the camera. What do we see? Resignation, for sure. A silent dignity. But no fear, and no apparent regrets. It's a grandfather's face, shockingly calm given what he knows lies ahead.

Dmitri Polyakov—the older man in the video just described—is a name mostly lost to history, but he deserves a better place in modern memory. Polyakov is both a Soviet military officer and an intelligence officer. In the former capacity, he has access to a vast range of information about missiles, tanks, biological and chemical weapons, nuclear strategy, general military planning, and the like. As a member of the GRU, the Soviet Union's military intelligence wing (it is a Russian acronym for Main Intelligence Directorate), he also is up to date on agents and the where and why of Soviet espionage operations. As he rises in rank to become a general, Polyakov further becomes deeply versed in Kremlin foreign and economic policy. Beginning in 1962, at the critical height of the Cold War, Dmitri Polyakov is also an American intel asset—known to the FBI as TOPHAT—and a volunteer, unpaid asset at that.

"The reasons Polyakov decided to work for us were not terribly complex," according to Sandy Grimes, a veteran member of the CIA Clandestine Services with a special focus on the Soviets. "He was rather a simple man with simple tastes, but he was also a man who was very principled and loved his country. He was a Russian first and foremost, and he was always going to be a Russian, and he loved his people. What he didn't love were the leaders of his country . . .

"I think Polyakov had such a distrust of the Soviet leadership that he was fearful they might take any action. It was something he couldn't predict. That, combined with his perception of the United States—that we were weak, that we wouldn't face up to the Soviets—frightened him. He truly believed that this was a war. We weren't shooting at one another, but it certainly could come to that, and his role was to assist us in any way he could, not just assist the United States . . . but assist the western world in countering the Soviet leadership and where he saw his country going."[1]

How valuable is the intelligence Polyakov/TOPHAT passed on to the Americans? Grimes's answer is unequivocal: "Polyakov was our crown jewel, the best source at least to my knowledge that American intelligence has ever had and I would submit the best source that any intelligence service has ever had. There was really no one to compare him to, because he worked for us for so many years and he achieved such a rank that rather than us looking at an organization through the eyes of one of our sources [. . .] from the bottom up, with Polyakov, we were able to look at the GRU, his organization, from the top down, as well as look at the KGB and the Soviet Ministry of Foreign Affairs and the Communist Party apparatus, again through Polyakov's eyes, from the top to the tops of the other organizations, and it's very unique."[2]

Beyond doubt, TOPHAT's intel affects the balance of power between the Soviets and the United States at a critical time during the Cold War and across multiple decades. Arguably, Polyakov prevents the massive loss of life on both sides. Doubtless, too, passing secrets to his American counterparts places him in almost constant and dire peril.

"He knew that if he were caught, he would be sentenced to die," Grimes says. "He would be taken into the room, asked to kneel down and be shot in the head."[3]

And indeed that's more or less what happens on March 15, 1988, half a decade after Polyakov retires, more than a quarter century after he first starts feeding intel to his American counterparts, and almost two years after the video of his arrest is made.

Polyakov is "working on his dacha" when the KGB comes for him, Grimes says. He is "playing with his grandchildren. [. . .] It should have gone down in history as the greatest spy story of all time."[4]

It doesn't, though. Instead it goes down as one of the saddest.

As befits an asset of such vital importance, Dmitri Polyakov has the distinction of being ratted out not once but twice to the KGB by members in good standing of the US intelligence community: In 1985 by CIA intelligence officer Aldrich Ames, who will emerge as the most notorious spy in modern US history with his arrest in 1993; and five years earlier by the man who will replace Ames at the pinnacle of America's espionage hall of shame, with his own arrest in 2001. In 1980, FBI special agent Bob Hanssen sells TOPHAT to Polyakov's own agency, the GRU, for basically chump change: a figure generally placed at $30,000, although we have only Hanssen's word to go on this, and that comes more than twenty years after the fact. Between them, the CIA and FBI will eventually pay 233 times that for Hanssen's own identity.

The KGB, it should be noted, does make another video starring Dmitri Polyakov. In this one he's lying naked on a metal tabletop, still alive after his torturers have extracted every last secret they can from him. As the video rolls, the tabletop is slowly elevated at one end until TOPHAT slides off the lower end into a roaring fire. The KGB shows it as a cautionary tale to new recruits.

CHAPTER 2

SPYING 1.0

Bob Hanssen has left an indelible stain on the FBI, a toxic cloud that haunts it still, but his entry into the Bureau is the same as that of thousands of agents before him and thousands since. After completing the twenty-week basic training at the FBI Academy in Quantico, Virginia, new agent Hanssen is assigned in January 1976 to the Indianapolis field office and farmed out to the Gary, Indiana, resident agency to work white-collar crime.

The posting is predictable. Hanssen has an MBA from Northwestern University. He's done a tour as a junior auditor of the Chicago branch of Touche Ross (now Deloitte & Touche), and touts a CPA license earned while working as a Chicago cop. The Bureau also seems to have gone out of its way to make the posting convenient. The Hanssens—Bob and Bernadette, known as Bonnie—both grew up in Chicago and have friends and family nearby. And Bob clearly performs well because his next transfer, in August 1978, is to the high-profile New York City field office.

The transfer, however, presents the growing Hanssen family with a trade-off all too familiar to young FBI careerists. The most high-profile field offices—New York, Los Angeles, Chicago, Miami, Washington, and the like—are also found in cities with the highest housing costs, and the Bureau provides no cost-of-living adjustments. In, say, the Boise, Idaho, field office, a standard FBI salary allows an agent to house his family in comfort relatively near his workplace. Working in the New York field office, for most agents, means either substandard housing fairly close by or, much more commonly, a long daily commute from the distant suburbs.

The Hanssens halve the dilemma by buying one of the more modest three-bedroom houses in the upscale, relatively close-in suburb of Scarsdale in Westchester County. For Bob, the purchase means a shorter commute than many of his coworkers. For Bonnie and their three children, the neighborhood is safe and green. But no house in Scarsdale sells cheap, and the financial pressure of the mortgage is ever-present.

Jack Hoschouer, Bob Hanssen's best friend beginning in high school and forevermore, returns to the States in the fall of 1979 from Germany, where he has been stationed with the army, and stays several nights with Bob and Bonnie in their new Scarsdale home. "Bonnie," Hoschouer tells me, "was a little desperate because they didn't have the money to pay the doctor bills for the girls."[1]

Having proved his chops as an accountant in Gary, Indiana, Hanssen is initially assigned to similar work in New York—bigger crimes, bigger money, bigger everything in the Big Apple—but poring over numbers day after day bores him silly. His big break, though, is just around the corner.

In March 1979, Hanssen is detailed to the Soviet counterintelligence division within the New York office. The plum jobs there are the cloak-and-dagger ones: surveillance, recruiting spies, busting networks, street work, the stuff movies are made from, indeed the kind of role Hanssen seems to have been dreaming of since his teenage years. Real life, though, is different, and Bob Hanssen is definitely not a kick-the-door-in type or someone who's going to charm a potential Soviet target over a quart or two of vodka. For his future career as a mole, though, he gets something even better: a place on the team assigned to create an automated national counterintelligence database for the FBI.

The work is important. The FBI has always been and long will remain a paper place: endless 302 forms memorializing interviews, banged out in triplicate on trusty Remingtons. The automated database Hanssen is assigned to work on is one of the early first steps in dragging the Bureau into the computer age. Thanks to his Touche Ross background and his computer-nerd proclivities, Hanssen is uniquely positioned to help with that—and will remain so throughout his almost twenty-five-year FBI career—and New York City is just the place to begin the database.

For the Soviet Bloc, the Big Apple, not Washington, DC, is spying's ground zero. The KGB is based at the Soviet (later Russian) Mission to the United Nations—a den of spies hiding behind diplomatic immunity. TASS, the Soviet news agency with a heavy New York presence, is also basically a wholly owned subsidiary of the KGB, with its spies doubling as thinly disguised journalists. The GRU has a separate base—Amtorg, the Soviet commercial trading agency—and separate personnel, but it's just as thick on the ground as the KGB. Additionally, the Hungarians, the Czechs, and other Eastern European spy services are nicely represented in the inner workings of the United Nations itself. Hanssen's work launching the new intel database gives him a godlike picture of all this: who is who, what is what, where all the players can be found, and, critically, who has flipped—which Soviets were working with, not against, the Americans.

For Bob Hanssen, the New York field office should be a little piece of heaven: a plum assignment near the onset of his career. But there's a problem here, too. As he would for the rest of his time with the Bureau, Hanssen is having trouble fitting in with the dominant culture of the FBI. The New York field office is happy to benefit from his tech expertise, but as far as most of the office is concerned, Bob is dancing to the beat of a different drum.

Bob's brother-in-law and fellow FBI agent, Mark Wauck, gets a taste of this a few years later when he's transferred to New York shortly after Bob follows the Bureau musical chairs to Washington. Bob has pulled some strings to get Mark assigned to his old Soviet unit, and his former colleagues are waiting with a surprise on Mark's first day.

"I sit down at my desk, open the drawer, and there's a three-card in there—one of those old cards we had to fill out every single day with all our ins and outs, our destinations, and the cases we had worked on," Wauck says. "This one purported to be from Robert Hanssen, and for destination they put 'Allen Belt,' the radiation belt that surrounds the Earth. They were telling me that Bob is a space cadet."[2]

Worse, Space Cadet Hanssen can't stop himself from trying to remake the New York field office in his own overearnest image, according to Jack Hoschouer.

"He told me later that when he was in New York for the first time, their job was to keep a watch on the Soviet delegation to the UN. They had figured out that the Soviets did their drops and serviced the drops on Sundays because all the FBI agents were in church or at home with their families. So Bob set up a plan to get all the agents to cover all the possible dead-drops on a Sunday morning.

"He's in the office, and he's talking to all these guys, and they're all assuring him, 'Yeah, I'm in place. I'm in place.' And they are all home having ham and eggs with the kids.

"If it's true—and it probably is—that was one of his 'aha' moments about his disappointment with the professionalism of his fellow agents. They had failed him in his plan to catch the Russians in the act. Add that to his monetary problems, and we're starting to get to a motivation that goes beyond just filthy lucre."[3]

But filthy lucre can't be ignored. Bob's transfer to the New York field office has placed him in close proximity to the principal players, and the mortgage on his Scarsdale house and those kids' doctor bills are shouting ever louder in his ear. To Hanssen, the answer to the latter problem must seem obvious.

As Hanssen three decades later will explain to the Webster Commission formed to look into his treachery, "I could have been a devastating spy, I think, but I didn't want to be a devastating spy. I wanted to get a little money and to get out of it."[4] Note that there's at least a bit of false modesty baked into that quote. By the time he says this, he has already been outed as a very devastating spy indeed. Note, too, that the evidence will show that Bob Hanssen spends the rest of his FBI career simultaneously convinced that he has fallen in among simpletons and benefiting mightily in his own mind by existing among them. He is not a simple man.

Bob Hanssen is still in his first year on the new database assignment when he walks into the Amtorg headquarters in Manhattan, asks to speak with a GRU official, and volunteers to spy for the Soviets, for money of course. In all, it is a sloppy approach—Hanssen even lets on that he is an FBI agent—but the Soviets couldn't care less. They are about to buy a gold mine on the very cheap.

Hanssen's first offering is a teaser: news that the FBI has bugged one of the Soviet's residential complexes. (The bigger news might have been if they *hadn't* bugged it.) Later offerings are much better, including the names of Soviet intel officers who, if not yet turned, are at least in contact with their American counterparts. That one opens the door for Hanssen, and soon he is communicating with the GRU through encoded radio bursts and unbreakable codes and state-of-the-art gizmos that bring immense joy to his techie heart. But Hanssen's big gift—and it was practically a gift, given what the Soviets pay for it—is TOPHAT.

Hanssen can probably be excused for undervaluing his asset. He's new to the game. He has a name to sell but perhaps no clear sense of its market value, and his mortgage is due the first of the month, month after month after month.

What Hanssen does know, though, is that if he is going to continue doing business with the GRU, Dmitri Polyakov is the one American asset placed highly enough in the Soviet intelligence services to uncover his identity. Maybe Hanssen has undersold TOPHAT, but given the certain outcome of the sale, he has protected his own market value immensely.

From a business point of view, selling TOPHAT to the GRU is pretty much a no-brainer. Reduce Dmitri Polyakov to a commodity, not a human life, and any MBA would back the deal. Flipping him to the Soviets is also, very nearly, the beginning and end of what might have been Bob Hanssen's very minor spy career.

CHAPTER 3

"WHAT ARE YOU HIDING?"

Bernadette "Bonnie" Hanssen is Catholic through and through. Her father, Leroy, descended from Polish Catholics, trained for two years for the priesthood before settling on psychiatry as his calling. Her mother, Frances, was raised in an Irish Catholic family. Bonnie's schooling has been all Catholic. Her uncle on her mother's side is a monsignor. John Paul, the youngest of her eight siblings and one of two brothers to join Opus Dei, will eventually become a professor at the prelature's Rome stronghold, the Pontifical University of the Holy Cross. Inevitably, perhaps, Bonnie's husband drifts that way, as well. Bob has been raised Lutheran, although not with any great devotion. Eight years into their marriage, he follows Bonnie into the Church, and two years after that, in 1978, he is accepted into Opus Dei—practically a family obligation. Bonnie's brother Mark happens to be looking directly at Bob during the ceremony when he mouths three words to his wife: "I love you."

The scene is touching. Bonnie, though, might be forgiven for wondering exactly what those three words mean, coming from her husband's mouth.

Bob and Bonnie have been married less than a week when a woman with whom Hanssen is having an ongoing affair calls Bonnie to tell her that she and Bob had just made love and that she is the one he really wanted to marry. Hanssen repents when his wife confronts him—he's good at repentance—and vows this will never happen again. But the flesh is weak, memory is strong, and this is a wound that occasionally gets rubbed raw, according to what Jack Hoschouer tells me.

"Bonnie told me in Scarsdale that she went to pick Bob up at the train station. It was raining like crazy, and he was standing there under an umbrella with one of his arms wrapped around a woman, maybe a secretary in the office."[1]

Bonnie might have both incidents in mind and maybe others when she happens upon Bob in late 1980 in the basement of their Scarsdale home, pen in hand, hunched over some kind of document.

Details are sketchy and will stay hidden for more than two decades, but we know Bonnie has a feisty side. We know from his life's story that Bob is deft at deception and quick to cover his tracks. And this is a common enough domestic scene to allow us to fill in the empty spaces.

"What are you up to?" Bonnie asks, but instead of answering, Bob tries to conceal the paper completely.

"What are you hiding? Are you having an affair?" she demands.

No, he insists, but Bonnie doesn't back off. Finally, he tells her the truth, or his version of it: He's writing a letter to his GRU handlers.

"GRU? Are those Russians, Bob?"

"Not Russians, Bonnie. Soviets. There's a difference."

"But—"

"Okay. I've been selling presumed American intelligence to the Soviets, Bonnie, but *presumed* is the word to focus on. None of it is real."

Bob goes on to explain that he's running a scam on America's mortal enemies, a con game that has thus far netted him—*them*—$30,000 (or maybe $20,000, the number has never been confirmed one way or the other), money they desperately need to finance the house, pay the medical bills, and make up for the other insane shortfalls of an agent's salary in a place as expensive as New York. But he is through with that, he assures Bonnie. Lesson learned.

Game played out. Besides, their finances are back on safe ground thanks to the risk he has taken, and as ever, he is remorseful beyond all expression.

Does she buy it? Entirely? Maybe or maybe not—living with Bob requires a certain amount of ongoing self-delusion—but Bonnie's answer in any event is not to contact authorities and least of all the FBI itself. Her answer is to go to the highest authorities she recognizes: the Church, God, and the organization sanctioned by the Pope himself to do God's work on Earth—*Opus Dei*.

The paid obituary for the Rev. Msgr. Robert P. Bucciarelli that runs in the *Boston Globe* February 26–28, 2016, paints a priest both highly educated and highly successful within his chosen calling. Bucciarelli is born in New Canaan, Connecticut, in September 1935 and educated at New Canaan High School and Harvard, graduating in 1956. From there he goes on to earn a doctorate in sacred theology at the Pontifical Lateran University in Rome, and in August 1960, Bucciarelli is ordained a priest for the Prelature of Opus Dei.

As a priest, he serves in Chicago, Milwaukee, Washington, DC, New York City, Rome, and Dublin, but his duties extend well beyond his ministry. He's Vicar of Opus Dei for the United States for a decade, from 1966 to 1976. From 1988 to 1992, he lives in Rome and works at the prelature's central offices, where he almost certainly crosses paths with Bonnie's brother John Paul. A decade later, in 2003, Bucciarelli begins another tour as a vicar, this time of Ireland, but illness and age appear to cut short that work. In 2012, he returns to the United States, to Chestnut Hill, just outside of Boston, where he continues providing spiritual direction to lay people and priests until his death from Parkinson's disease on February 24, 2016.

From other sources, we know that Father Bucciarelli is also an ardent tennis player with a unique motion that makes his serves hard to return. He is, in short, a sophisticated man, a scholar. From the tennis, one might even suspect he's a kind of priestly bon vivant—one of those cheerful clerics at home in the confessional or the country club. Nowhere in his obituary, though, is there mention of his key footnote role in the history of spying. Bucciarelli is the Opus Dei priest Bonnie Hanssen insists her Bobby see to confess his sins.

The late 1980 meeting takes place in New Rochelle, New York, where Bucciarelli lives. Officially, it's a counseling session—the priest in conference with Bonnie and Bob—not a confession that he hears. But for the rest of his life, Bucciarelli maintains that what transpired in those sessions is nonetheless covered by the rules of the confessional and thus never to be revealed.

The broad outlines of his advice, though, are well established. Go to the authorities, the priest tells Bob. Fessing up, making a clean breast of things is the only way to get right with God. Perhaps Bucciarelli is simply a law-and-order guy—you do wrong, you pay your debt to society. Much more likely, Hanssen tells him the same story he told Bonnie: It was a scam, phony stuff; I was pulling the Soviets' leg. They got nothing real, nothing actionable. Even so, for Bob Hanssen the priest's solutions must be fearsome advice. He knows what he has actually sold to the other side. There's nothing penny-ante or phony about it, and there will be nothing soft and cuddly about the punishment to be meted out.

Sleep comes hard for Hanssen back in Scarsdale, but the morning brings far better news. Father Bucciarelli has prayed on the matter overnight and now has a better idea: go to God instead of the FBI. Bob can atone for his sins through prayer and by feeding his ill-gotten gains back to charity, bit by bit so as not to attract too much notice. And that's what Bob Hanssen does—feeds as much as $30,000 over the course of the next four years to Mother Teresa's Missionaries of Charity. Or so he claims. It's always hard to believe a man whose entire public life is a lie.

As for Father Bucciarelli, in his quest to save Bob's soul, he green-lights the rest of Hanssen's spying career, with dire consequences for America's security and with further loss of life among US assets within the Soviet intelligence services. Bucciarelli also unknowingly adds his own signature to the death warrant Hanssen has already issued for Dmitri Polyakov.

The GRU acts quickly after Hanssen reveals TOPHAT. Polyakov is recalled from his posting in India and given a Moscow office job, but they don't let the KGB in on the secret for several years for fear of staining their own reputation within the constantly warring bureaucracies of Soviet espionage. There's a window of opportunity there. If forewarned that TOPHAT has been betrayed, American intelligence services might well have been able to spirit him out of the country. At the least, his US connections could have alerted him to the danger he faced so that he can make his own run for it, before he ends up on that metal slab slowly being tilted into a fiery hell.

Hanssen's silence, Bonnie's tacit assent to it, and Bucciarelli's ecclesiastical endorsement close that window of opportunity and impose a cone of secrecy that will last more than twenty years. No one in or out of the US intelligence community will have any idea of Bob Hanssen's first spying career until Bonnie tells this story while being interviewed after Hanssen's arrest—the first breach of Bucciarelli's expansive understanding of the sanctity of a confessional.

CHAPTER 4

GROOMING A MOLE

I f the decades immediately after World War II give birth to the Cold War and its shadow war of espionage, the 1980s and 1990s are the decades of cashing in on it. The 2003 Webster Commission tallies 117 instances between 1945 and 1990 in which American citizens are either prosecuted for espionage or clearly guilty of it even if insufficient evidence exists to move to trial, but this is a building tide. Reported espionage cases double from the 1950s to the 1970s, then double again in the 1980s. Spies, moles, traitors—whatever you want to call them—sometimes seem to be a dime a dozen within America's intelligence community.

Some are shockingly inept and settle for paltry rewards. In the late 1970s, William Kampiles, a watch officer in the CIA Operations Center, smuggles out a KH-11 satellite technical manual, sells it to the Soviets for a measly $3,000, covers his tracks about as successfully as a bull in a china shop, and earns a forty-year prison sentence for his troubles.

Other spies spin their treachery into generational family affairs. John Walker, a US Navy communications specialist with a "top secret crypto" clearance, starts out as a solo act, peddling navy secrets to the Soviets, then convinces a friend with a similar clearance to do likewise, and eventually adds his own brother Arthur, a navy lieutenant commander, and his son, Michael, then a recent navy recruit, as his espionage start-up matures into an eighteen-year enterprise. John Walker tries to bring his daughter into the fold, too, but she alone resists. Armed with the Walker ring's cryptomaterial, the Soviets receive and decode more than one million communications, essentially living inside and following in real time US naval warfare planning.

Walker might have the simplest explanation for his spying, once he is finally caught and imprisoned: "We let the Russians read our mail just like we read their mail. That's it. That's all. The United States monitors every international telephone call and open circuit in the world. All I did was sell those poor bastards the same access."[1] Well, not exactly.

The Soviets are not the only beneficiary of this pilfering. American secrets are highly valued in the global spy market even among the nation's supposed allies. From June 1984 until his arrest just before Thanksgiving 1985, Jonathan Pollard pinches almost two thousand intelligence documents and cables—all classified—from the Central Intelligence Agency, the National Security Agency, the Defense Intelligence Agency, and elsewhere, a smorgasbord of intel for his Israeli handlers. Business consultant Katrina Leung spends more than twenty years, beginning in 1982, in the secret employ of Chinese counterintelligence.

Most of this American spy product, though, is destined for Moscow, and it continues unabated after 1991 when the Soviet Union collapses back into Russia and the lead foreign-intel portfolio passes from the KGB (Soviet intelligence) to the SVR (Russian intelligence). CIA counterintelligence officer Aldrich ("Rick") Ames, for one, glides right through glasnost and the Soviet collapse. From 1985 until his arrest in February 1994, Ames banks an estimated $4.6 million for passing the Soviets information that compromises more than a hundred American intelligence operations.

Another CIA officer, Harold James Nicholson, picks up the slack after Ames's arrest, selling more of his agency's secrets to the GRU until he himself is nabbed in 1996. Among Nicholson's betrayals are the identities of many newly hired CIA agents whom he has come to know as a senior faculty member at a CIA training facility, in some ways an even deeper violation of trust.

Other American spies from the same broad era bear mention as well: FBI agent Earl Pitts, who, like Hanssen, starts out spying for the Soviets and ends up a Russian asset and earns almost a quarter million dollars; Ronald Pelton, the NSA intel analyst who tips the Soviets to a joint NSA-US Navy operation wiretapping undersea cables; Frank Terpil, who sells his country out to the Cubans; Jeffrey Carney, in the sub-rosa employ of the East Germans; Edward Lee Howard, yet another CIA agent from the mid-1980s who feeds America's secrets to the Soviets (unlike the others, though, Howard manages to escape to the Motherland); and on and on.

"The United States was penetrated very broadly but not very deeply," according to David Major, a counterintelligence expert with both the FBI and National Security Council. "Lots of agencies were losing secrets, but they didn't have huge penetrations."[2]

Clearly, though, two moles stand out against such a broad backdrop of shallow betrayal: Rick Ames and Bob Hanssen. Even Ames, though, must take a back seat to Robert Philip Hanssen. Only Katrina Leung spies longer than Hanssen—at least that we know about today. No one at all burrows more deeply or broadly into the national intelligence community's vault of top secrets. And no one gives America's superpower archenemy more to work with or intelligence of greater value. Victor Cherkashin, who will soon become Hanssen's KGB handler, estimates the total value of Hanssen's espionage to the Soviets to have been $10 *billion*, secrets they got for nano-pennies on the dollar.

But with the exception of Dmitri Polyakov, all that value is in the future. In the late summer of 1985, Bob Hanssen is just a dark storm gathered on the horizon.

Hanssen has already shown he has no more scruples than his fellow moles. Almost certainly if Bonnie had not come across him in their basement preparing to communicate with the GRU, he would have been spying for the Soviets continuously since 1979, but fortunately for him, his previous spying had been discovered by the one person on earth most likely to believe his cover story and forgiven by a priest more attuned to the power of prayer than the rule of secular law. Even better, while Hanssen is doing his penance, his employer has been doing its very unintentional best to make him the perfectly groomed mole should he want to get back in the game.

Hanssen's work in New York developing the national database has given him a pilot's cockpit view of the Cold War—spies and counterspies from 35,000 feet up. His next assignment, after he is transferred to the Washington, DC, headquarters in January 1981, is just the opposite. As now a supervisory special agent detailed to the FBI Budget Unit, Hanssen is responsible for formulating and executing the budget for the FBI's counterintelligence program, including overseeing the presentation of the budget request to the relevant House and Senate committees and preparing the director to testify in its support.

As ever, the easiest way to do this is to wow the Hill with the down-and-dirty of specific FBI counterintelligence operations—who is doing what to whom when, how, and why, at the granular level.

"In order to justify future expenditures, you have tell them what you've done in the past, and the past is always a list of successes," explains Jim Ohlson, who precedes Hanssen in the role and spends several months breaking him into the work. "The budget request doesn't name informants, but it gives you a real good indication of where crucial success has taken place. If the Russians had access to the current budget cycles, they could make those kind of analyses—determine, for example, that something's going on in New York or in San Francisco and double their efforts to find a leak there."[3]

Preparing the counterintelligence budget also gives Hanssen a kind of division-wide carte blanche, according to Ohlson: "He could poke around in all the operational units, finding more information to justify his budget write-up."[4]

Hanssen now has invaluable information and access for multiple purposes, and information he never would have had access to if the Bureau had allowed him to fulfill his dream of becoming a cloak-and-dagger FBI operative.

"Nobody wants to go to the Budget Unit," says David Major, who supervised the unit while Hanssen was there, "but the people in the Budget Unit know everything. Hanssen was put in charge of moderating a dedicated technical program. He understood tech, and that gave him further special access."[5]

Two years later, in 1983, Hanssen is reassigned once more, this time as a supervisory special agent with the Soviet Analytical Unit, another important step forward in the education of a spy. In the Budget Unit, Hanssen was down in the weeds, dissecting specific operations to justify their costs. In the Analytical Unit, he can merge that with a broader view of the Bureau's counterintelligence successes and failures in dealing with the Soviets. Maybe even more important, with the new assignment his clearance is boosted to above top secret.

"The Analytical Unit," Major explains to me, "is filled with PhDs, very smart people. We were trying to pull together what we knew about the Russians, their recruits, and so on, and put all that on a stand-alone computer. You have to have someone who knows how to do that, and Bob did. Think about that. He knew everything about what we had gotten from defectors over time and from recruitments-in-place. For a period of time, he had that kind of access. The point is there were just a few of us who knew all this, and he was one of those guys."[6]

Hanssen revels in his almost unlimited access once he gets to the Analytical Unit. His brother-in-law Mark Wauck remembers Bob telling him he has landed the best job in the entire Bureau. "When he went to that unit, he was elated. He told me it was the perfect job because you knew *everything* that was going on. As he described it, all he did was come in in the morning and start reading a stack of teletypes from all over. He described it as the best job possible."[7]

Whether Hanssen has simply fallen into this career path or has engineered his way to this vital information node is an open question. But Dave Szady, who served as assistant director of the FBI's Counterintelligence Division, votes for the latter.

"If you look at where Hanssen positioned himself, he was very smart," said Szady. "What he did was, he put himself in two areas that were brand-new for the FBI, relatively speaking. One was the analytical effort of the FBI. The FBI was just developing its analytical program, and it really didn't grow into maturity until after 9/11. But we were creating analytical units within the FBI at the time, and if you have analysts, all information is going to flow through those people eventually or at least they will have access to it. Hanssen put himself into the middle of that, as a supervisor. That's number one.

"And then, number two, he made himself a computer expert. Now, this is back when computers and laptops were really just coming into being within the FBI. So, obviously, the beer-drinking, cigar-smoking, door-kicking agents don't know anything about this. But Hanssen put himself in a position where he could become kind of a driving force within that environment, and both situations gave him access to the information he needed to provide to the KGB or that he wanted to provide to it—information that was extremely sensitive.

"Another thing, the protocols for protecting information within this computer network environment were just then being developed. They weren't as stringent as they are now, and they were never monitored as much as they are now. If Hanssen was on a computer, there always seemed to be a good reason why he was pulling up information. He's the guy who knows what he's doing!

"I maintain he knew very well what he was doing at that time. In putting himself in those positions, he could access information without causing a great deal of suspicion. And that's what he did."[8]

Then, in September 1985, having accumulated all this knowledge thanks to his extraordinary access to the Bureau's Soviet secrets, Hanssen is transferred back to New York, again to the Soviet counterintelligence division but now in a field supervisory position, and finds himself faced with the same old dilemma and the same temptations.

Appearances are important to Bob Hanssen. The Scarsdale house was mostly Bob's idea—he enjoys living a notch above most of his fellow workers even if he has to strain the budget to do so.

"The house," Jack Hoschouer says, "was a prestige thing for him. He put a lot of stock in the appearance of being well-off. He liked to show up with a beautiful woman on his arm—the visuals of being important, of being envied. That was part of his initial attraction to Bonnie. He could walk into a room with Bonnie on his arm, and she would stop the traffic. The trouble is Bonnie's idea of a great Christmas or birthday present is a new vacuum cleaner. She knows she's beautiful, but she hesitated to play that role."[9]

This time around Bonnie puts her foot down. Scarsdale is a mistake not to be repeated. Look what it drove you to do, she tells Bob. Instead they find a cheaper house farther out from the city—in Yorktown, as things turn out. Bob will just have to deal with the longer daily commute to and from the office.

But the bills are still coming in, the family is growing, nothing is getting cheaper, and the FBI pay scale continues to be so rigid that Hanssen's new boss, Tom Sheer, complains to headquarters that beginning agents in his office are making less than New York City trash collectors. A financially hard-pressed agent, he warns, is ripe for Soviet picking. Someone, of course, who has already tested those waters and lived to tell the tale is even more ripe. Robert Philip Hanssen, for example. And it takes Hanssen all of nine days after he first reports to the New York field office to make his move.

Hanssen's first crack at spying four years earlier was bush-league—a walk-in. He even let drop that he was with the FBI. No more. This time around Bob Hanssen has a plan, and everyone is going to dance to *his* tune.

CHAPTER 5

SPYING 2.0

Hanssen relaunches his spy career with a letter within a letter, postmarked October 4, 1985, and sent from New York. The package itself is addressed to Viktor Degtyar, a KGB colonel and press secretary at the Soviet embassy, but sent to his residence in Alexandria, Virginia, just across the Potomac from Washington, DC, and hard by the Pentagon. But Degtyar is only the conduit. Inside is an envelope that reads: "Do not open. Take this letter to Victor I. Cherkashin."

For Hanssen, Cherkashin is an easy choice. He's widely known within the American intelligence community as the KGB's man at the Soviet embassy—the tip of the spear of the USSR's counterintelligence efforts in Washington—and has been so since the late 1970s. What Hanssen has no way of knowing, though, is that Cherkashin is already handling CIA mole Rick Ames, who volunteered his own services six months earlier. In fact, the resident KGB spy chief initially wonders if Hanssen's letter hasn't come from Ames—a second front of sorts to protect his own identity. Instead, Cherkashin has been handed a two-headed spy team unequalled in the history of espionage.

Hanssen's letter to Cherkashin gets straight to the point:

> Soon, I will send a box of documents to Mr. Degtyar. They are
> from certain of the most sensitive and highly compartmented
> projects of the US intelligence community. All are originals to aid
> in verifying their authenticity. Please recognize for our long-term
> interests that there are a limited number of persons with this array
> of clearances. As a collection they point to me. I trust that an officer
> of your experience will handle them appropriately. I believe they
> are sufficient to justify a $100,000 payment to me. [1]

As a further tease—both to bolster his bona fides and, as with TOPHAT, to
eliminate those who might eventually be able to identify him—Hanssen provides Cherkashin with the names of three Soviet intel officers working for the
Americans. Two are KGB officers stationed in Washington, DC. Lieutenant
Colonel Valery Martynov is charged with gathering up scientific and technical
secrets. He and his wife, Natalia, arrive in DC in late 1980. Five years later,
when Hanssen rats him out, Martynov's hearing-challenged twelve-year-old
son is attending junior high school in Alexandria, Virginia, and his five-year-
old daughter is in preschool. Martynov is considered such an important asset
that he is handled, on the FBI side, by Jim Holt, a top counterintelligence
specialist, and for the CIA by Rodney Carlson, who has previously handled
Oleg Penkovsky, the GRU mole who helps defuse the Cuban Missile Crisis.
The other DC-based KGB agent, Major Sergei Motorin, also has two children,
but he's less of a family man. In addition to a favorite prostitute, he's having
an affair with the wife of a Soviet diplomat. The third person Hanssen names
is Boris Yuzhin, also a KGB officer who poses as a TASS correspondent in San
Francisco and secretly copies KGB documents with a CIA-provided camera
disguised as a cigarette lighter.

The ability to finger all three men sends a strong message to the Soviets
that their new benefactor draws his information from multiple sources within
the intelligence community. Six months after his initial letter to the KGB,
Hanssen expands on his unsolicited gift of the three US assets and burnishes
his own résumé while doing so:

I cannot provide documentary substantiating evidence without arousing suspicion at this time. Nevertheless, it is from my own knowledge as a member of the community effort to capitalize on the information from which I speak. I have seen videotapes of debriefings and physically saw the last, though we were not introduced. The names were provided to me as part of my duties as one of the few who needed to know. You have some avenues of inquiry. Substantial funds were provided in excess of what could have been skimmed from their agents. The active one has always (in the past) used a concealment device—a bag with bank notes sewn in the base during home leaves.[2]

Motorin and Martynov have already been fingered by Rick Ames. With Hanssen's corroboration, what passes for the wheels of justice within the Soviet Union swing into motion, in this instance with considerable flair and with no apparent concern on Hanssen's part that he is condemning to almost certain death a valuable American asset and the father of two.

"Martynov is the one with the secret compartment in his briefcase," explains Mike Rochford, who will eventually play a central role in bringing Bob Hanssen to justice. "When Vitaly Yurchenko [a Soviet defector who redefected to Moscow in November 1985, three months after arriving in the United States] goes home, Cherkashin puts Martynov in charge of taking him back. The plane is full of KGB agents. When it lands in Moscow, the militia gets on the plane, bypasses Yurchenko, and goes straight to Martynov.

"'I'm here to get my medal, I guess,' Martynov says to the guy in charge. He has no idea what's coming.

"And the guy says, 'Bullshit, you're a spy!' He dramatically slices open the briefcase, and there's the money and his instructions."[3]

The trial that follows is pro forma—for Motorin, too—and the executions that follow the trials are inevitable. Yuzhin manages to get off with a fifteen-year prison sentence.

Almost simultaneously, Ames corroborates Hanssen's information delivered a half decade earlier that TOPHAT is an American asset and seals his fate, as well. In some ways, the two moles are a wrestling match tag team, but Cherkashin is effectively in charge of the undisciplined Ames. Hanssen isn't going to let that happen to him.

In his first letter to Cherkashin via Degtyar on October 4, 1985, Hanssen lays out the boundaries on how communication will be carried out without dictating the entire process: "I am open to communications suggestions but want no specialized tradecraft. I will add 6 (you subtract 6) from stated months, days, and times in both directions of our future communications."[4]

His second mailing—this one a package sent a week and a half later, on October 15, again to Degtyar's home—contains the promised treasure trove of classified documents. The next morning, at 8:35 A.M., the permanent FBI surveillance team assigned to the Soviet embassy notes as "unusual" the fact that the KGB colonel has come to work hauling something in a large black canvas bag, but the report is never followed up, the beginning of a low-attention pattern that will favor Hanssen for the next fifteen years.

In his third mailing, posted October 24, Hanssen—whom the Soviets by then are referring to internally simply as "B," after the "Mr. Baker" that Hanssen uses for the fictitious return addresses on his mailings—wades into the infrastructure of the espionage trade: payments, tradecraft, and dead-drop sites.

DROP LOCATION

Please leave your package for me under the corner (nearest the street) of the wooden footbridge located just west of the entrance to Nottoway Park. (ADC Northern Virginia Street Map, #14, D3)

PACKAGE PREPARATION

Use a green or brown plastic trash bag and trash to cover a waterproofed package.

SIGNAL LOCATION

Signal site will be the pictorial "pedestrian-crossing" signpost just west of the main Nottoway Park entrance on Old Courthouse Road. (The sign is the one nearest the bridge just mentioned.)

SIGNALS

My signal to you: One vertical mark of white adhesive tape meaning I am ready to receive your package.

Your signal to me: One horizontal mark of white adhesive tape meaning drop filled.

My signal to you: One vertical mark of white adhesive tape meaning I have received your package.

(Remove old tape before leaving signal.)[5]

"The Source," Cherkashin would write in his memoir, "was calling the shots. The KGB almost always designated dead-drop and signal sites for our agents and did most of the preparatory work. This time the tables were turned. All we had to do was drop our package and mark a signal."[6]

Hanssen is also serving his own convenience. Nottoway State Park is known territory—a short walk from the home on Whitecedar Court where Bob, Bonnie, and their children lived before his 1985 transfer back to New York and a quick drive from the home on Talisman Drive that the Hanssens will buy when they return to the DC area in 1987.

Cherkashin does push back, without much success. He proposes several different drop sites, ones his people are familiar with, and he pushes for the kind of communications equipment that (unknown to the Soviet spymaster) Hanssen was introduced to five years earlier—burst transmitters and the like—along with a meeting between the two men somewhere outside the United States, just as Cherkashin has already had with Rick Ames. But Hanssen nixes them all.

In part, this is Hanssen's well-honed instinct for self-preservation at work. Not only is he in a position within the FBI to have vital secrets to sell, he also has access to all the operational mistakes the Soviets have made in running their own agents. And he has structured the dead-drops and pickups so that he is handling the vast bulk of the work, not them. By normal terms, this is labor-intensive spying, but it puts Hanssen in charge of the process, sufficient reward for him to justify the added burden and greater risk.

As David Major puts it: "Bob had four or five operational acts and the Russian had one. Read and then fill, clear, go home, and the next day come out and see if the signal had been set to show it had been cleared. That minimized the [Soviet] officer's action and maximized the agent's action. No one else spies like that."[7]

Victor Cherkashin's only line in the sand is money. His benchmark for first payments is $50,000, exactly what Ames received. Hanssen won't get a penny more. Accordingly on Friday, November 1, 1985, Cherkashin hand-counts five hundred $100 bills taken from a safe in his embassy office—the first of the roughly six thousand $100 bills he will eventually count out for his new superagent—places them in a plastic bag, and hands it to an embassy official, Aleksandr Fefelov, for delivery the next morning to the dead-drop site at Nottoway State Park. After stowing the money beneath the footbridge, Fefelov replaces the white vertical strip on the pedestrian crossing with a horizontal one. When he returns to check later that day—still driving a car that has never before been used in a similar operation—the white strip has returned to vertical.

Six days later, on November 8, 1985, Hanssen sends his thanks to Cherkashin via Degtyar and makes it clear that he is in this for the long run:

Thank you for the 50,000.

I also appreciate your courage and perseverance in the face of generically reported bureaucratic obstacles. I would not have contacted you if it were not reported that you were held in esteem within your organization, an organization I have studied for years. I did expect some communication plan in your response. I viewed the postal delivery as a necessary risk and do not wish to trust again that channel with valuable material. I did this only because I had to so you would take my offer seriously, that there be no misunderstanding as to my long-term value, and to obtain appropriate security for our relationship from the start.[8]

As smoothly as that first operation went, Hanssen still isn't beyond getting spooked. He also turns out to be correct in insulating himself as much as possible from Soviet ineptitude.

The next planned dead-drop is to take place at the beginning of March 1986. The Soviets do their part—loading the site in Nottoway Park with cash on March 3—but Hanssen never shows. Almost four months later, on June 30, he explains why in a letter meant for Degtyar: "During routine questioning of a Soviet defector, FBI agents asked if the defector knew Victor Cherkashin"[9]—information conveyed in a March 4 classified FBI debriefing report that Hanssen has obviously seen.

"I thought this unusual," Hanssen writes to Degtyar. "I had seen no report indicating that Victor Cherkashin was handling an important agent, and heretofore he was looked at with the usual lethargy awarded Line Chiefs. The question came to mind, are they somehow able to monitor funds, i.e., to know that Victor Cherkashin received a large amount of money for an agent? I am unaware of any such ability, but I might not know that type of source reporting."[10]

Hanssen's fears, though, are obviously allayed because he is ready to get back to work, once again absolutely on his own terms.

If you wish to continue our discussions, please have someone run an advertisement in the *Washington Times* during the week of 1/12/87 or 1/19/87 [code for July 6, 1986, or July 13, 1986], for sale, "Dodge Diplomat, 1971, needs engine work, $1000." Give a phone number and time-of-day in the advertisement where I can call. I will call and leave a phone number where a recorded message can be left for me in one hour. I will say, "Hello, my name is Ramon. I am calling about the car you offered for sale in the *Times*." You will respond, "I'm sorry, but the man with the car is not here. Can I get your number?" The number will be in Area Code 212. I will not specify that Area Code on the line.[11]

The letter is signed "Ramon"—Hanssen's first use of what will become his *nom de espionnage*: Ramon Garcia.

A few weeks later, the ad runs as specified in the *Washington Times*. Hanssen calls a public telephone somewhere near the Old Keene Mill Shopping Center in suburban Virginia, Aleksandr Fefelov answers, and an hour later Fefelov calls the 212 number Hanssen provides and leaves a message that the KGB has loaded the Nottoway Park dead-drop site, and all is well. But not quite. The crack Russian spy team has indeed loaded the package but under the wrong corner of the specified wooden footbridge.

All of which leads to what might be, under other circumstances, a fairly hilarious and entirely oblique August 18, 1986, telephone conversation between Hanssen and Fefelov. Ultimately, however, these few minutes of sound recorded by Fefelov will go a long way toward sealing the case against Hanssen.

Fefelov: Uh, yeah, and the car is still available for you, and as we have agreed last time, I prepared all the papers and I left them on the same table. You didn't find them because I put them in another corner of the table.

B [Hanssen]: I see.

Fefelov: You shouldn't worry, everything is okay. The papers are with me now.

B: Good.

Fefelov: I believe under these circumstances, mmmm, it's not necessary to make any changes concerning the place and the time.

Our company is reliable, and we are ready to give you a substantial discount which will be enclosed in the papers. . . . You see. After you receive the papers, you will send the letter confirming it and signing it, as usual. Okay?

B: Excellent.

Fefelov: I hope you remember the address . . . If everything is okay.

B: I believe it should be fine and thank you very much.

Fefelov: Heh-heh. Not at all. Not at all. Nice job. For both of us. Uh, have a nice evening, sir.

B: Do svidaniya. ["Goodbye"—Hanssen is showing off his college Russian.]

Fefelov: Bye-bye. [12]

The next day, Fefelov and team load the dead-drop site—the right site, this time—with $10,000 and proposals for additional dead-drop sites, an emergency communication plan for Hanssen to personally contact KGB personnel in Vienna, Austria, and other espionage arcana.

Hanssen, of course, rejects the new plans in two "Dear Friends" letters, just as he rejected Cherkashin's earlier efforts to tilt the balance of power in the spymaster's favor.

On September 8, Hanssen writes: "No, I have decided. It must be on my original terms or not at all. I will not meet abroad or here. I will not maintain lists of sites or modified equipment. I will help you when I can, and in time we will develop methods of efficient communication." [13]

Hanssen, though, is careful to bait this letter with promises of glad tidings to come before he lays it all on the line: my way or the highway.

"Unless I see an abort signal on our post from you by 3/16, I will mail my contact a valuable package timed to arrive on 3/18. I will await your signal and package to be in place before 1:00 p.m. on 3/22 or alternately the following three weeks, same day and time. If my terms are unacceptable, then place no signals and withdraw my contact."[14] (By the code earlier established, the actual dates above are September 10, 12, and 16.)

Two weeks later, thanking the Soviets for another $10,000 payment, he reinforces his objection: "I am not a young man [he was 42 at the time], and the commitments on my time prevent using distant drops such as you suggest. I know in this I am moving you out of your set modes of doing business, but my experience tells me that we can be actually more secure in easier modes."[15]

In mid-November, he is back in groan-and-moan mode again, chiding his handlers for their penchant for multiple dead-drop sites in not always convenient locations: "Unable to locate AN based on your description at night. Recognize that I am dressed in business suit and cannot slog around in inch-deep mud. I suggest we use once again original site. I will place my urgent material there at next AN times. Replace it with your package. I will select some few sites good for me and pass them to you."[16]

In a less productive relationship, this litany of complaints might be too much to bear for both sides, but by the fall of 1987, the money is rolling in and America's secrets are beginning to fly out as they have never taken wing before.

CHAPTER 6

"HOLY SHIT!"

Mike Rochford recruits spies for the FBI, men and women who are willing, almost always for hard cash, to be America's eyes and ears within the enemy's intelligence community—mirror images of Bob Hanssen, in short—but once he has signed them up, he doesn't necessarily keep track of their progress or monitor how effectively they are performing. Thus, as the decade of the 1980s draws to a close, he is shocked to discover how perilously few of the human assets he signed up are still operational.

"In 1989, I recruited an Afghan intelligence officer who had been cooperating with the Russians," Rochford tells me. "Later that year, I'm back in Washington, and the chief of the Soviet Analytical Unit calls me over and says, 'Mike, do you realize this is the only in-place intelligence officer we have in the whole Eastern Bloc—Russia, China, any place even close to there? It's the *only* intelligence officer we have in place who's still alive.'

"I go, 'Holy shit! I didn't realize that.'

"And he says, 'Yeah, we got an issue.'

"It's hard to explain, but you don't expect that to happen, right?"[1]

In retrospect, of course, it's not hard to explain in the least. Many of those in-place assets and the operations they were involved in have been transformed by the wonderful alchemy of espionage into either crisp $100 bills bundled by Victor Cherkashin and distributed out of the Soviet embassy in Washington, DC, or designated transfers within the Soviet banking system.

On September 29, 1987, for example, the KGB deposits $100,000 into an escrow account set up for B in a Moscow-based bank. Later that same year, Hanssen removes from one of his dead-drop sites $20,000 in cash along with word that another $100,000 has been deposited in the Moscow bank at between 6 and 7 percent interest.

In return, the KGB receives "top secret" documents from the National Security Council, the US National Intelligence Program for 1987, and just to put a knife in his own employer, a top secret FBI review that is a backdoor window into multiple years of Bureau counterintelligence efforts, kicked off by this warning:

> In view of the extreme sensitivity of this document, the utmost caution must be exercised in its handling. The contents include a comprehensive review of sensitive source allegations and investigations of penetration of the FBI by the Soviet intelligence services, the disclosure of which would compromise highly sensitive counterintelligence operations and methods. Access should be limited to a strict need-to-know basis.[2]

Hanssen's need-to-know basis, one hopes, is different than that of other agents made privy to the study, but for him it is good for another 250 of those ever-mounting $100 bills.

Then there is the technical document describing COINS-II, an acronym for the then-current version of the US Community On-Line Intelligence System—basically, an invitation to the Soviets to listen in on a classified, community-wide intranet, a huge advantage in the struggle for global superpower dominance. Not to mention betraying the continuing-operations plan for evacuating America's political and military leadership in the event of nuclear attack at a time when paranoid elements within the crumbling Soviet Union are fearful of an American first strike and contemplating one of their own.

Should the Soviets actually launch that first strike, they won't have to worry about catching the American president and the Joint Chiefs of Staff asleep in a well-defended Washington, DC. They can simply let them scurry off to the "secret" southern Shenandoah Valley stronghold near the famed Greenbrier resort or the closer redoubt inside Mount Weather on the eastern slope of the Blue Ridge Mountains, and then take them out with a submarine-launched nuclear missile once they arrive. Easy peasy, at least relatively so.

"Polymath," from the Greek *polus* (much) and *manthanein* (learning), refers to a person of wide-ranging knowledge. Benjamin Franklin—adept in science, politics, diplomacy, education, and much more—was a classic polymath. Hanssen is a classic polymole. He steals and sells to the Soviets and later the Russians a huge treasure trove of secrets drawn from all across the US intelligence community, and because he is an invaluable techie and information-systems guru in the FBI's IT backwater, Hanssen is also able to gather his golden eggs almost regardless of his official status.

Hanssen's first, brief turn as a spy is closely tied to his rookie status with the New York field office's Soviet Analytical Unit in 1979. He takes advantage of what amounts to low-hanging fruit, including TOPHAT's identity, and parlays it into thirty grand. When Hanssen resumes spying in 1985, he is still assigned to the unit, but now he is a supervisory special agent with the Headquarters-based Intelligence Branch, a far bigger and more varied pond to fish in.

In September 1987, for example, Hanssen passes to the KGB top-secret documents from the White House–based National Security Council. Eleven days later, he sends along a document that the Soviet's log in as "National Intelligence Program for 87." In November he's back again, this time with a cable report about a meeting the previous month with a valuable source within the Soviet intelligence community, a survey of information provided by the Soviet defector Vitaly Yurchenko during his brief American sojourn, and the technical document previously mentioned that gives the KGB a backdoor into the US intelligence community's intranet.

In the early spring of 1988, Hanssen is able to streamline his operation and upgrade security by moving to diskettes programmed in the "40-track mode"—a way of reformatting computer diskettes to conceal data on specific tracks. Without access to decryption codes, the diskettes appear to be blank.

On one of his new diskettes, Hanssen hands over the FBI's "Double Agent Program" and a document the KGB titled "Stealth Orientation" that originates in the office of then CIA director William Webster—the same William Webster who will lead the commission that eventually looks into Hanssen's spying and the FBI's security shortcomings.

The CIA is back on Hanssen's hit list in a July 1988 handover that includes information on US nuclear programs; a "Compendium of Future Intelligence Requirements" that also originates in the CIA director's office; a counterintelligence staff study that focuses on KGB recruitment operations against the CIA; and, for balance, a top-secret FBI historical study that identifies Soviet recruits and defectors with great specificity, including particular information they have provided. The balance is by intent: someone looking at Hanssen's espionage product in the aggregate will be hard-pressed to determine whether it most likely came from the FBI or the CIA, and the CIA has historically been the larger hotbed of spies flipped by the Soviets.

That same month—July 1988—Hanssen suffers another bollixed handoff and feels obliged to remind the KGB of both the risks he endures on its behalf and the value he brings to the relationship.

> I found the site empty. Possibly I had the time wrong. I work from memory. My recollection was for you to fill before 1:00 a.m. I believe Viktor Degtyar was in the church driveway off Rt. 123 [in McLean, Virginia], but I did not know how he would react to an approach. My schedule was tight to make this at all. Because of my work, I had to synchronize explanations and flights while not

leaving a pattern of absence or travel that could later be correlated with communication times. This is difficult and expensive. . . .

My security concerns may seem excessive. I believe experience has shown them to be necessary. I am much safer if you know little about me. Neither of us are children about these things. Over time, I can cut your losses rather than become one.[3]

And so it goes straight up to the summer of 1990 when Supervisory Special Agent Hanssen is promoted to the headquarters Inspection Division as an inspector's aide. Hanssen slips the KGB the CIA's National Measurement and Signature Intelligence Program for fiscal year 1991. He also tips them to the FBI's investigation of US Foreign Service Officer Felix Bloch, a betrayal that ultimately comes back to haunt him and lands an innocent man square in the FBI's crosshairs once the Bureau sets out in earnest to find the man they will come to know as GRAYSUIT.

In this same rough time frame, Hanssen also passes along documents that compromise a US technical operation so highly sensitive and ultra-top-secret that the charging affidavit in his case will delicately describe it only as "a program of enormous value, expense, and importance to the United States." That's almost an understatement given what the operation actually is.

When the Soviets set out to build a new embassy in Washington, DC, they make none of the same mistakes the United States has made with its new Moscow embassy. The US embassy was constructed in a hollow surrounded by Soviet listening stations, using construction materials embedded with listening bugs. The Soviets, having gone to school on their own chicanery, choose for their new embassy site an elevated location known locally as Mount Alto, just west of Wisconsin Avenue, not far below the neo-Gothic Washington National Cathedral at the intersection of Wisconsin and Massachusetts Avenues NW, and they monitor the construction materials with great care.

There is, however, one vulnerability—not above or around the new embassy, but beneath it. To exploit it, the FBI purchases a North Georgetown townhouse to serve as the headquarters of a mining operation that has been tunneling toward the Mount Alto edifice for years at huge effort and enormous expense in pursuit of invaluable rewards to be reaped by an NSA listening station manned round the clock right at the boiling heart of the KGB's secrets. So proud is the Bureau of its mining operation as it nears completion that it begins giving top-secret tours to select members of the congressional intelligence committees, high-ranking visitors from the British intelligence services, and senior officials of the CIA. By the time Louie Freeh becomes FBI director in 1993, the digging is almost done.

The operation has an ambitious code name—MONOPOLY—but even that is so secret that Freeh isn't immediately allowed to know it. He is, though, read into the project by his staff after only a few months in office.

"They told me they were right under the code room," Freeh recalls. "'Just a little farther and we'll be in it.'

"'Great!' I told them. 'Dig on.'

"'Well, there's a problem,' they said.

"'Problem?'

"'If we dig any closer, we think their instrumentation will detect us.'

"'How much have we spent on this?'

"'Millions.'

"'And now we're almost there, but can't get there?'

"'Right. We think it would be best if we filled in the tunnel.'

"'How much?'

"'Millions.'

"'How long?'

"'Years.'"[4]

Freeh declines an offer to tour the tunnel before it ceases to be, and the Bureau eventually un-engineers the tunnel, if only to keep the townhouses above it from collapsing into an FBI-made sinkhole, but the entire exchange is basically academic. The strategic value of the tunnel had been compromised four years before Freeh ever hears of it. Hanssen gets wind of a massive off-the-books FBI operation as far back as 1981 when he is first assigned to the Budget Unit, but he doesn't have the deliverable goods on the tunnel until September 1989 when he sells the whole operation out for another $30,000. For the past four years, the Soviets have been listening to the FBI tiptoeing toward them.

By the end of the decade, the KGB deliveries and payments are becoming so numerous that Hanssen and Cherkashin, et al., begin adding new dead-drop sites—one in Foxstone Park, a short walk from the original Nottoway Park site and, like it, under a footbridge spanning Wolftrap Creek; another under a footbridge in Lewinsville Park, in McLean, Virginia, not far from CIA headquarters; still another in DC, under a footbridge in Rock Creek Park; and elsewhere. Studying the ever-growing dead-drop sites, one begins to wonder if espionage could exist at all without sylvan parks and footbridges to hide packages and payments under.

In his ongoing communications with his handlers, Bob Hanssen is worried that his one-year stint with the inspector's staff, which requires both domestic travel and longer trips to FBI legal attaché offices in embassies worldwide, will hamper his espionage production and put a dent in communication. He expresses concern, too, about the rocky state of the USSR and the vulnerabilities inherent in the Soviet system. Will he even have a shadow employer when he is again at liberty to roam through the Bureau's secrets?

His handlers, though, are quick to reassure him on both fronts. (Note the almost consistent capitalization of "You" and "Your." In formal Russian, such pronouns are normally uppercase, but capitalizing them also provides ego support for an aching self-image.)

> We appreciate Your sympathy for some difficulties our people face—Your friendship and understanding are very important to us. Of course, You are right, no system is perfect, and we do understand this.
>
> Speaking about the systems. We don't see any problem for the system of our future communications in regard to this new circumstance of Yours. Though we can't but regret that our contacts may be not so regular as before, like You said.[5]

That feels a little like whistling into the wind. Things are far from rosy for the USSR in the summer of 1990, but Hanssen's new position and the Soviets' crumbling system seem to put hardly a dent in his throughput or slow his momentum. Between July 1990 and June 1991, Hanssen delivers three more diskettes to the KGB, and his handlers reward him with three payments totaling $60,000.

Hanssen returns to Headquarters at the beginning of July 1991 as program manager in a unit responsible for countering the KGB's efforts to acquire American scientific and technical intel and gets right to work, although not on the FBI's behalf. He has been in his new position only two weeks when he sends the KGB diskette 23, this one containing a hodgepodge of 284 pages that reveal, among other information, the details of a joint FBI-CIA operation, other FBI documents, human-intelligence plans, and documents tied to nuclear-weapons proliferation. "I . . . grabbed the first thing I could lay my hands on," he explains to the KGB in a cover note. There soon follow diskettes 24 (classified technical and operation matters), 25 ("The US Double-Agent Program Management Review and Policy Recommendations," etc.), and 26, accompanied by the current FBI congressional budget justifications, detailing the activities and resource needs of the foreign counterintelligence program.

By now, the situation in Mother Russia has clearly become more than a little unsettling and seems to have been driving information requests from the KGB. Hanssen must mention all this in some lost note to Cherkashin, including still more concerns about his security, because in a July 15, 1991, reply, his handler takes on the whole smorgasbord of his concerns:

> Actually, Your information greatly assisted us in seeing more clearly many issues, and we are not ashamed to correct our notions if we have some. So, thank You for Your help. But if some of our requests seem a bit strange to You, please try to believe us there were sufficient reasons to put them and that what we wanted was to sort them out with Your help.

In regard to our "memo" on Your security, just one more remark. If our natural wish to capitalize on Your information confronts in any way Your security interests, we will definitely cut down our thirst for profit and choose Your security. The same goes for any other aspect of Your case. That's why we say Your security goes first.[6]

Despite the chilling possibilities inherent in "capitalize on Your information" (or maybe because of them), Hanssen is heartened by the reply. A month later, on August 19, he even dares to lecture his KGB "friends" on just how the Soviets should handle the domestic unrest then rocking Moscow and the entire USSR. Hanssen's advice: "Go to school on the no-nonsense way Mayor Richard Daley handled the turmoil that rocked Chicago in the late 1960s."

Seven weeks later, the KGB responds with considerably more wit than Hanssen had mustered in making his recommendation: "The magical history tour to Chicago was mysteriously well timed. Have You ever thought of foretelling things? After Your retirement for instance in some sort of Your own 'Crystal Ball and Intelligence Agency' (CBIA)? There are always so many people in this world eager to get a glimpse of the future."[7]

Predicting the future, however, might not be Bob Hanssen's forte. In a December 16, 1991, note to the KGB, Hanssen proposes a new communications system. He is going to set up an office somewhere in the District of Columbia or its environs that will be free from electronic surveillance. Then he and his handlers can communicate directly via computers specially fitted with certain advanced technology. By mid-December 1991, though, there is barely any KGB at all. (As we'll see later, this plan also dovetails with another to set up: a love nest for a woman who might or might not be his lover.)

A month later, in January 1992, Hanssen is promoted to be chief of the National Security Threat List Unit, under the Intelligence Branch, responsible for realigning US counterintelligence activities to comport with new geopolitical realities. By then, one can make a reasonable argument that Hanssen belongs on such a list, perhaps near or at the top. The only thing that ultimately halts his prolific treason is the collapse of the Soviet Union back into ancient Russia, but in both instances, that turns out to be only a stall.

By some measures, Bob Hanssen is well on his way to becoming the most dangerous man in America, among the most destabilizing people in the world, and absolutely no one knows for sure who he really is—maybe not even Hanssen himself.

PART II

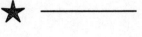

CHAPTER 7

WHO IS ROBERT HANSSEN?

Robert Hanssen is frequently described by those who knew him as a fringe person, someone who stands at the edge of gatherings, who never manages to get in the spirit of things, a guy who never quite fits in. Joe Navarro, an FBI agent and counterintelligence expert, served for a time in the Intelligence Branch with Hanssen. He recalls being with him at a Bureau gathering in Dallas.

"We had been in meetings all day, and by the time we came back from dinner, we were all just tired out and cold from the walk. The place we were staying had an indoor-outdoor pool with a Jacuzzi, and as we were passing by, somebody in our group said, 'Wouldn't it be great to get in a hot Jacuzzi?' And everyone said, 'Yeah, that's a great idea!' We all went up to our rooms and changed, and we were back in a few minutes.

"So we're having beers, sitting around telling stories, mostly guys, having a nice time, except for Hanssen. He was just sitting there, outside the Jacuzzi, still wearing his overcoat.

"We said, 'Hey, Bobby, go change and come on in,' and he was like, 'No, I'm okay.' 'Okay,' we said, 'if you just want to sit there and protect us.' It was like he wanted to participate, but he didn't know how."[1]

Navarro says he found this "odd." In fact, *odd* pops up in one form or another in just about every account of Hanssen's behavior.

Like Joe Navarro, Jim Ohlson has a snapshot memory of Bob Hanssen that seems to encapsulate his character—in this case, an actual snapshot: "It was St. Patrick's Day 1985, I think. We all went to this Irish pub. And in the photograph, we're all there having fun. But Hanssen's standing off to the right—there's a slight air gap between the rest of the group and him. He's wearing a black suit, white shirt and tie, and all of us are casual."[2]

Jim Ohlson is something of a rarity among FBI agents—he's someone who still admits to getting along famously with Bob Hanssen way back in the day. Their paths first cross in 1981 in the Budget Unit when Ohlson hands his job off to Hanssen over a several-month transition. Both are from the same general Chicago neighborhood with a mutual interest in new technologies. They even attended the same high school, although Ohlson was several grades behind Hanssen.

"I liked the guy," Ohlson says. "I liked his analytical way of thinking about things. I liked the way he solved problems. We hit it off. We were both interested in computing, and we both had early Apple II computers. He was very adept at using automation to solve a broad brush of problems in the FBI, and I really enjoyed working with him on those kinds of projects. We also were both members of what was called the Washington Apple Pi Group, basically centering around Apple computer games.

"I often describe people in the FBI as concentric circles around Hanssen. The closest-in circle may have had ten people in it, and I was one of those. We actually liked the guy, and we liked solving problems with him. We got along, and we tolerated his eccentricities, which were predominantly the result of weak interpersonal skills.

"The next, larger circle around him consisted of people who appreciated his work but didn't really care for him personally. A lot of his bosses were that way. They knew he did a good job. Being a CPA, he could analyze problems much more deeply and come up with a taxonomy of a problem that really helped you get a solution.

"And then there was the outer ring of people who knew Hanssen and didn't like him, who thought he was weird. And that's hundreds of people."[3]

Did Ohlson see any red flags back then? Hanssen, after all, had already sold TOPHAT to the Soviets and had landed in a very handy crossroads for his avocation.

"If I'd had more familiarity then with psychopathic personalities, I think I would have been able to label him psychopathic," Ohlson tells me, "but I didn't have the terminology or the experience at the time to recognize that. The main thing he did, and I see this now, is that he compartmented aspects of his life.

"I was in a friendship with him in one compartment. He had his family in another, and his church relationship in still another. And he had other friends in other compartments—for example Jack Hoschouer. I actually remembered Jack from high school. I wasn't a good friend of his, but Bob always told me, after the fact, 'Oh, Jim, Jack was in town last week.' He never told me ahead of time, though, so that I could go out with the two of them. I just wasn't in that compartment. At the time I wrote it off as, all right, he's just not interested.

"Another thing, I was really close with him at work, but that never spun off into a dinner with our wives joining. That was another compartment, too."[4]

When David Major moves from the White House National Security Council in September 1987 to become deputy director of the FBI's C13 Section, charged with Soviet analysis, he inherits Bob Hanssen as his deputy chief. Hanssen, Major says, has a disconcerting way of slipping quietly into his office and then waiting to be noticed. Other sources tell the Webster Commission that Hanssen habitually walks into meetings uninvited when classified material is being discussed. In conversation, he tends to whisper as if to emphasize the secrecy of whatever is being discussed.[5]

Dave Brown, who works with Hanssen on the technical side of several counterintelligence issues, remembers calling him "Whispering Bob because of his habit of talking in a very quiet and superior voice. . . . He was an arrogant jerk, always fully confident that he was not only the smartest guy in the room but also a vastly superior person in every way."[6]

Hanssen also seems to have an instinctive feel for who controls the secrets and who doesn't. He's the first person to greet Major on his first day in the job, but he almost never exercises or plays basketball with his fellow special agents at the downstairs gym in the Headquarters building. Nor does he have any real capacity for light conversation. Banter about the latest Redskins game means nothing to him. Colleagues who stop by his various FBI offices over his final fourteen years in Washington are more likely to be treated to a monologue on Catholicism or godless communism. Even office politics, the common language of bureaucracies, seems to hold no interest for him.

Rather than turn off David Major, these qualities endear Hanssen to him. In time, he will become Bob's biggest champion within the FBI's Soviet counterintelligence division.

"This is strange to say," Major tells me, "but we had a professional respect for each other. Bob had a very high IQ. If he walked into my office, I knew I was going to have an interesting conversation. We had some very deep talks about the Russians—how to beat them, how they were organized.

"We weren't drinking partners, but we did go to company parties together, he and his wife, me and my wife. Bonnie is a very attractive woman. I knew Bob well enough that the first [time] I met her, I could say to him, 'That's *your* wife? How the hell did you do that?'"[7]

Others who work with Hanssen over the years are far more annoyed by his standoffishness and his tendency to wear his religion on his sleeve, especially after he joins Opus Dei. With a convert's zeal, Hanssen latches on to the many causes that come with conservative Catholicism. *Roe v. Wade* and its fallout is what really animates him. Over the years, Bob and Bonnie will march in pro-life demonstrations, and the family minivan will come to sport multiple right-to-life stickers. At work, no one, no matter how lowly, is exempt from his proselytizing.

"He was like someone who quits drinking or smoking and becomes obnoxious about it around people who still do," Mike Rochford tells me.

"He found out a couple of ladies at Headquarters were living with their boyfriends, and he didn't approve of it, so he started lecturing them on birth control ideas, the rhythm method, all that stuff. That left a number of them unimpressed."[8]

"Unimpressed" doesn't begin to capture how I. C. Smith feels about Hanssen. Hanssen reports to Smith when he is detailed to the Budget Unit and later works beside him when Smith is overseeing the Chinese side of the Counterintelligence Division.

"Frankly, I found Hanssen just a loathsome individual," Smith says. "His demeanor, the whole dark-knight thing with the black suits he always wore. I can't think of a single Bureau employee who was disliked as much as Hanssen."[9]

Hanssen, Smith says, works hard at appearing to be a superior intellect—a step above the common herd at the Bureau. In reality, according to Smith, he is nothing like that. "I base that not only on conversations with him, but also on having seen his work. . . . He was not viewed as one who could be promoted to higher rank, an assessment I completely agreed with."

Hanssen's last posting of any length—he's detailed to the State Department as the FBI's liaison to foreign missions—"is not without responsibility," Smith says, "but this is not a person they are looking at as a future unit chief."[10]

Ironically, what Smith calls Hanssen's "mediocrity" at his day job sets him up beautifully for his night mole work: while other agents are being transferred to this place and that as they ascend through the ranks to the Bureau's senior executive service, the agents who are never destined to get there can burrow their way ever deeper into where they are stationed. For every cloud, a silver lining.

Still another agent, Jerry Doyle, describes Hanssen as having an almost macabre appearance and personality. "He reminded you of Ichabod Crane. If you saw him on a Halloween night, he'd scare you."[11] Inspired by both his behavior and his preference for black suits, colleagues take to calling Hanssen "The Mortician" and "Dr. Death." If they could see Hanssen at night, they might double down on the nicknames: he slept exclusively in black pajamas.

Maybe Bob Hanssen sees himself as a kind of ninja warrior carving out a space between two superpowers bent on global domination. The black pajamas bring that to mind. Maybe, as one of his colleagues suggests, he's enamored of the mid-century G-man look—black suits, white shirts, and ties, right off the set of 1959's *The FBI Story*. But black is also the color magicians and illusionists favor, masters of sleight-of-hand and cat burglars, as well as judges, executioners, and priests for that matter. And there is some of all that in Hanssen. He's the Man Behind the Curtain, the one you never see but who is watching you all the time.

"My perception is that he very much liked to see himself as a puppet master, pulling the strings on other people and getting them to do what he wanted them to do," his brother-in-law Mark Wauck says. "If I would ask him a simple question about some kind of configuration issue involving my Lynx, he would often frame his reply in terms of 'Do this . . . now do this,' and so on, instead of explaining to me what I needed to know. He wanted me to be in the position of following his instructions rather than understanding the issue. That was very much a part of him. He pulls the strings. He controls what's going on."[12]

At one level, Bob Hanssen is an even more enigmatic figure to his Soviet and later Russian handlers and paymasters. His bosses, his colleagues, his underlings at the FBI at least know his name and what he looks like, even what he sounds like. They can tell you he is tall, that there's a techie geekiness to him, that he has terrible taste in the ties that are mandatory wear for FBI agents at every level except undercover.

Victor Cherkashin, Viktor Degtyar, Aleksandr Fefelov, and others familiar with and abetting Hanssen's treachery know none of that. The only name they know him by—other than Mr. Baker or simply B—is the one he has begun signing his communications with: Ramon Garcia. Years later, once he is incarcerated, Hanssen will claim that the last name—especially its final three letters: "cia"—has been carefully chosen to further obscure his identity. Maybe so—again, we're talking about a lifetime liar here. "Ramon" also might be a nuanced way of suggesting Hanssen's hardcore dedication to the

Soviet cause: Ramón Mercader spent two decades in a Mexican prison for assassinating Leon Trotsky, but while he was jailed, Joseph Stalin rewarded him in absentia with the prized Order of Lenin. Hanssen might deserve an Order of Lenin, too.

To be sure, Cherkashin et al. are deeply familiar with the part of Hanssen that his brother- in-law describes just above: the puppet master who wants to be certain you are following his instructions, not the other way around. Hanssen has made that clear on first contact: he is picking the dead-drop sites and dictating the communication protocols. All the Soviets really have to go on in painting their own portrait of the Man Behind the Curtain are the text and subtext of his communications, but those, it turns out, tell them plenty.

In his FBI life, Hanssen is frequently at pains to remind colleagues that he is the smartest person in the room. Jack Thompson, who will help launch the process that eventually runs Hanssen to ground, sees this quality time and again. "In conversations or in section meetings among unit chiefs, Hanssen would occasionally say something that implied he knew more than the rest of us, or he would smirk if he disagreed with something. He was quite full of himself." [13]

The Soviets can't see the smirk or the eye rolls, but they get more than a taste of this side of Hanssen as well—remember how he lectured these seasoned spy professionals in his early letters on the value of keeping the tradecraft simple? But rather than resent it, Cherkashin and his colleagues frequently compliment their source on his "sharp-as-a-razor mind."

At Bureau headquarters on Pennsylvania Avenue, Hanssen is often the only one laughing at the jokes he tries to slip into office conversation. Again, not so with the Soviets. They not only praise Bob's "superb sense of humor" but even respond with some lighthearted doggerel of their own when they sense their ace spy is burning the candle too hard at both ends. "What's our life / If full of care / You have no time / To stop and stare." [14]

That entire communication, in fact, is such a superb example of the manipulator being manipulated by his handlers that's it worth quoting the rest in full:

You've managed to slow down the speed of Your running life to send us a message. And we appreciate it.

We hope You're OK and Your family is fine too. We are sure You're doing great at Your job. As before, we'll keep staying alert to respond to any call from You whenever You need it.

We acknowledge receiving one disk through CHARLIE [one of several new dead-drop sites mentioned in the missive]. One disk of mystery and intrigue. Thank you.

Not much a business letter this time. Just formalities. We consider Site-9 cancelled. And we are sure You remember: our next contact is due at ELLIS.

Frankly, we are looking forward to JUNE. Every new season brings new expectations.

Enclosed in today's package, please find $10,000. Thank You for Your friendship and help.

We attach some information requests. We hope You'll be able to assist us on them.

Take care and good luck. Sincerely,

Your friends[15]

A disk of "mystery and intrigue"? What could be more satisfying to a mole who early fell in love with espionage tales piled high with spies of mystery and intrigue?

"Your friendship"? Solace for a largely friendless man, at least in his professional life. Sometimes the best tradecraft is the right words, filling the right needs at the right times.

On December 25, 1989, Cherkashin and associates go as far as breaking ranks with the official atheism of their homeland to wish Secret Agent Bob a Merry Christmas. Hanssen must feel as if he has been welcomed into a workplace family much warmer than that of the Hoover Building in downtown DC—a Marxist-Stalinist rendering of a Norman Rockwell holiday setting.

At FBI headquarters, his high-and-mighty manner makes Hanssen, for the most part, persona non grata. Few people want to work with him even though he brings valuable technical skills to the table. While Hanssen's career path is generally unblemished—he is promoted steadily up the line and given ever-greater clearances and access as he goes along—he and everyone else know what I. C. Smith knows: there's not a chance in a million that he will ever enter the inner circle of management at the Bureau. He is smart, yes, but he's too strange, and the mortuary attire doesn't help a bit.

The Soviets have no idea Hanssen dresses like an undertaker, but they can sense his need—and frequently fill it. Cherkashin assures him that the documents he is providing are being read at the "very top" of the KGB, by director Vladimir Kryuchkov himself. The director is impressed again when Hanssen turns over the package of purloined documents that reveal, among other secrets, the COINS-II specs.

It isn't long before Hanssen is not only basking in Kryuchkov's attention but also aiming his documents directly his way. Hanssen's cover note with another batch of America's secrets reads: "Send to the Center [meaning KGB headquarters in Moscow] right way. This might be useful."[16] To accentuate the importance, Hanssen bypasses his usual dead-drop zone, employing instead an emergency signal at a site just off the busy Dupont Circle in downtown DC. The next communication back from the Soviets is more music to Hanssen's ears, and of course, just what his handlers want him to hear: "The Chairman of our organization in Moscow sends his congratulations to you for the latest material sent to the Center. We thank you for your last exceptionally interesting document."[17]

In an October 1989 response, Cherkashin et al. stroke Hanssen's ego still further, again conveying regards from the KGB chairman and asking their man inside the FBI to please in future deliveries indicate which materials should be opened by the KGB in Washington and which should go to the Center for delivery. That point made, the note moves on to extensive requests for targeted information about US intelligence activities.

They are back at work again in May 1990, all but offering to partner with their "Dear Friend"—and being careful to frame the offer with a request for still more secrets and another fat bundle of $100 bills:

> We attach some information requests which we ask Your kind assistance for. We are very cautious about using Your info and materials so that none of our actions in any way cause harm to Your security. With this on our mind we are asking that sensitive materials and information (especially hot and demanding some actions) be accompanied by some sort of Your comments or some guidance on how we may or may not use it with regard to Your security.
>
> We wish You good luck and enclose $35,000. Thank you.
>
> Sincerely,
>
> Your friends.[18]

When Hanssen is promoted in June 1990 to the Headquarters Inspection Division, his Soviet handlers have reason to be concerned about his continuing value, at least in the short term. Rather than having ready access to the Bureau's deepest secrets, Hanssen will be traveling extensively—to FBI field offices, resident agencies, and legal attaché offices at US embassies abroad. But instead of urging him to refuse the promotion, Cherkashin and others congratulate their "dear friend," wish him the "very best in Your life and career," and advise him to "do Your new job, make Your trips, take Your time." Once again, the capitalization of "Your" seems to be intentional as well as formal—an effort to underline Hanssen's importance.

"The KGB did a wonderful job of dealing with a person they never met, a masterful job of dealing with what they had, which was one of the best spies they ever had in their history," says David Major, who equally admires how Hanssen handled the KGB. "Both sides accomplished what they wanted."[19]

Bob Hanssen gets to spy by his rules. He clips identifying headers and footers off every document he passes to the KGB. Cherkashin, et al., really do have no way of knowing for sure where within the US intelligence community their mole is burrowed, which means they also have no way of knowing for sure the legitimacy of the product he is selling them. His handlers will learn his actual name the same way everyone else in the world does, except for a precious few within the FBI and CIA: splashed across headlines worldwide after his arrest. But at a deeper level, the KGB knows Hanssen inside out and upside down, almost certainly far better than he knows himself.

"The KGB was willing to look at his production and say, 'You know what—we don't care what his identity is,'" Mike Rochford says. "They could follow him around. They could set him up. But they instructed their officers who were leaving the drops, 'Don't do that. You'll make him mad. If he discovers you're lingering, we will have inactivity from a highly productive source, and we can't afford that.' So they were willing to go with the preponderance of the evidence he gave them and say, 'It's okay. It's bona fide. Who cares?' They were willing to throw $50,000 at a drop and live with it."[20]

Odds are, too, that even if the Soviet KGB or later the Russian SVR is able to secure Hanssen's identity and dig deep into his background, they will be surprised—maybe even disappointed—by just how conventional it seems, at least on the surface.

CHAPTER 8

ALL-AMERICAN BOY

Robert Philip Hanssen is born in Chicago on April 18, 1944, just at the dawn of the Cold War. Not long after he turns nine, Julius Rosenberg, an engineer with the US Army Signal Corps, and his wife, Ethel, are executed by electric chair for supposedly passing atomic secrets to the Soviets—the first and only Americans ever put to death in peacetime for espionage. The next year, Red-baiting Wisconsin senator Joe McCarthy launches his infamous televised hearings into whether the US Army as a whole is soft on Communism. Three years after that, on October 4, 1957—Bobby Hanssen is now in junior high—the Soviets launch *Sputnik 1* into a low elliptical orbit around the Earth. As *Sputnik* blinks its way across the night sky, Americans dream of nuclear warheads raining down on them from outer space.

The United States and the Soviets aren't just in an arms race; they are in what seems an existential struggle for survival itself. Knowledge is power; and knowledge that really matters is hard won and often stolen. Spies, moles, double and triple agents are everywhere—in real life and in popular culture.

In 1952, the radio serial titled *I Was a Communist for the FBI* launches. That's followed two years later by an early TV serial, *I Led Three Lives*. Both are based loosely on the real-life adventures of Boston advertising executive Herbert Philbrick, who infiltrated the US Communist Party on behalf of the FBI. The TV series, starring Richard Carlson as Philbrick, runs through the beginning of 1956, 117 episodes in all. By then, the boldest, most dapper, and unflappable fictional spy of them all is well on his way to immortality: Ian Fleming's James Bond makes his first literary appearance in April 1953 in *Casino Royale*.

In case children wonder what's at stake in this global struggle between the two emergent postwar superpowers, grade schools in "first-strike" targets—Chicago is one—regularly stage emergency drills. First, the community air-raid siren sounds. Then, if a schoolroom has a bank of windows, the fastest, most sure-handed boy rushes to pull down the shades so shattering glass won't shred his classmates. Next it's under the desk or, if there's time, a dash to a basement shelter with the sweltering boilers, imagining destruction until the all-clear signal follows.

Nevil Shute's 1957 novel *On the Beach* lays out, at least in fiction, the worst-case scenario: the aftermath of a nuclear conflagration so total that Australia is the last, doomed hope for the preservation of the species. Stanley Kramer's haunting 1959 film version of the novel makes the horror tangible. Death looms imminent and triumphant as the dwindling Aussie survivors gather on the beach to await extinction. And then, in October 1962, what fiction has posited almost becomes real: the Cuban Missile Crisis, a fourteen-day, eye-to-eye superpower showdown that brings the world closer to nuclear war than it has ever been before or since.

Few people realized at the time that the United States had a secret weapon in confronting the Soviets over Cuba. American intelligence officials had solid reason to believe that the Russian's long-range-missile capacity was far more limited than advertised, and they knew exactly how long it will take Russian missiles based in Cuba to arrive on the US mainland should they be launched. All that comes courtesy of Oleg Penkovsky, a Soviet intelligence officer who volunteered his services to the British a year earlier—a double agent, the mole who might have saved mankind.

Hanssen is a month into his first semester away from home, at Knox College in Galesburg, Illinois, when the Cuban Missile Crisis explodes across the network news broadcasts. He is just starting to see the world and figure out how he will fit into it.

In America, the antidote to all this nuclear gloom and doom is the family sitcom: *The Adventures of Ozzie and Harriet, Leave It to Beaver, My Three Sons, The Andy Griffith Show*. Perky mothers, wise fathers, mischievous sons, happy leafy settings—the formula doesn't vary much from show to show. The outside world in which superpowers roar at each other and spies creep nervously down blackened alleys to make dead-drops is a million miles away.

Norwood Park, the sixteen-acre North Side Chicago community where Bobby Hanssen is raised, isn't literally the suburbs, but it's often described as a kind of suburb within the city. Many of the homes have lawns. Sometimes curving streets are nicely shaded. June, Ward, Wally, and the Beav would have felt right at home there. Like Opie's father, Bobby Hanssen's dad is in law enforcement—a Chicago cop to Andy Taylor's rural North Carolina sheriff. But any similarity between the sitcom world and the Hanssen household ends there.

Howard Hanssen, Bobby's father, has a foot in the Red Scare himself. He's part of a special team within the Chicago police force formed to root out Communist influence in the private and public sectors. Howard also has a penchant for racehorses, including part ownership in one, and uncanny luck at the track—although according to Mike Rochford, it's rumored that the winnings he regularly brings home are more courtesy of the longshoremen's union than the thoroughbreds running at Arlington Park.

One other thing Howard has: a massive mean streak, at least as far as his son is concerned. When Bobby is six or seven, his dad wraps him in blankets and spins him around and around until he gets so dizzy he vomits. One account of that incident has Howard forcing his son's face into the mess afterward. On another similar occasion, Howard grabs one of his son's legs, yanks it up high, and holds it there until Bobby urinates all over himself. In still another grim vignette—they pile up quickly—Bob is somewhere between ten and twelve years old when his dad wraps him in a rug mostly for the sheer joy of watching his son suffer.

Vivian Hanssen, Bobby's mother, later says her son shows virtually no emotion after these incidents. Instead of howling or breaking into sobs and tears, he goes silently to his bedroom, closes the door, and reads about comic-book heroes who right the wrongs of the world: Batman; Superman; the Phantom, who travels the civilized world disguised as Mr. Walker—"the Ghost Who Walks." For lighter fare, he leans toward *Mad* magazine, a satiric staple of the 1950s with its jaundiced view of the adult world, with features like "Spy vs. Spy" and the magazine's ever-amiable "What, Me Worry?" mascot, Alfred E. Neuman. As Hanssen gets older, he graduates to more worldly tales about a subject that has captivated the nation: espionage.

Jack Hoschouer, Bob's best friend from the beginning of high school onward, says much the same thing about Hanssen and his father. It wasn't a close father-son relationship, but Bob showed no visible wounds from his abuse.

"I didn't get any sense of anger. The things he said about his dad had more to do with his part ownership in the racehorse. Bob and I were in and out of each other's houses all the time, but my own interactions with his dad were limited. He'd be sitting on the couch reading the *Racing Form* and we might exchange a few words. That's all.

"I remember one time we were cruising around in my car, and I got pulled over by some cops. The guy's looking at my driver's license, asking, 'What are you doing cruising around here?'—that kind of thing. Bob got out of the car, went back and talked to the other cop, and the other one hollered up to my cop, 'Hey, this guy's dad is Howard Hanssen. He's a good guy. Let the kid go.'

"But apart from that kind of vicarious use, I could tell his relationship with his dad was not close. His grandmother was a different story. She lived upstairs, and he was close to her. He'd holler up the stairs and talk to her, and she just doted on him. The whole time he was in college, he would package up his laundry and send it to her, and she'd wash it and mail it back to him. Frankly, I thought that was a little strange."[1]

Meanwhile, even though his son won't rise overtly to the bait, Howard Hanssen doesn't give up on making Bob's life as difficult as he can. When he isn't physically abusing his son, Howard bad-mouths him far and wide and engineers humiliating failures to taunt his only offspring.

"My mom used to run into Bob's dad shopping at the grocery store, probably once a week," Hoschouer recalls, "and my mom always said Bob's dad put him down, made fun of him all the time."[2]

Others say the same. Howard Hanssen tells anyone willing to listen that his son will never amount to a hill of beans, and he keeps it up even while Bob is in graduate school. Through his police connections, Howard also arranges for Bobby to fail his driving test the first time around. Who knows what effect these incidents have on the future course of Bob Hanssen's life, but Hoschouer's mother doesn't have a moment's doubt.

"I was visiting my folks out in Arizona when we heard that Bob had been arrested," Hoschouer says. "The first words out of my mother's mouth were, 'That's his father.'"[3] Given the speed of that response, she has likely been carrying that thought around in her head for the better part of forty years, since she knew Bob as a teenager.

In a letter to his Soviet handlers, Bob Hanssen will later claim that he was fourteen when he read *My Silent War*, Kim Philby's best-selling memoir about spying for the KGB while deep within a British intelligence establishment. If he wasn't simply lying, Hanssen clearly misremembered the date—Philby's book was published in 1968, when Bob was twenty-four, not fourteen—but he seems to have gone to school on Philby's life. Three decades later, Hanssen will ask his own Russian handlers to arrange an escape route to Moscow, where, like Kim Philby, he can live out his years and take advantage of the $800,000 supposedly deposited in his name in a Russian bank.

But even if Hanssen did get the date wrong on Philby's memoir, he is still steeping himself in spy literature from an early age, according to Hoschouer. "He read everything he could about espionage, anything that purported to be about 'Here's my life as a spy.'"[4] And it isn't just spy literature that catches Hanssen's eye and stokes his imagination.

Bob had just turned sixteen when Ursula Andress walks out of the Caribbean wearing a slim white bikini in the very first James Bond movie and captures the attention of high-school boys everywhere, Hoschouer included.

"We went to see the opening of *Dr. No*," Hoschouer says, "and after that we went together to the opening of every James Bond movie. Here's this cool guy with gorgeous women who drives like a maniac. All that stuff. What guy doesn't want to go to a party with a gorgeous woman?"[5]

Or drive an Aston Martin DB5? Or have ready at hand Bond's favorite sidearm, the Walther PPK? Hanssen could afford the DB5 once his spy career takes off, but he knows better than to stretch credulity on an agent's salary. He does, however, count two Walther PPKs among his extensive and less visible gun collection. Eventually, he will have fourteen firearms in his house, some from his dad but also an Uzi semiautomatic.

"What else did James Bond do?" Hoschouer continues. "He rescues women in distress, and that went through Bob almost as long as I've known him.

"One day we went to the beach in Lake Michigan. We were lying there in the sun, and there were these two girls ten to fifteen feet away from us, and these two guys, probably high schoolers too, started running around the girls and throwing balls over them. Bob went over and said to one of the girls, 'Miss, are these guys bothering you?' And it was pretty clear these the girls were quite happy to be bothered."[6]

If that sounds a bit out of touch and geeky, Hoschouer won't disagree. "Bob was a ham-radio guy, and we hung around with some of his ham-radio friends. After a movie one time, we were sitting around having milkshakes with some girls and the guys started talking to each other in Morse code. One guy said 'What now?' and Bob took a napkin and started writing F-U-C- in Morse code. It wasn't meant in a literal sense, but one of the girls grabbed the napkin, took it home, and looked up what he was spelling. He didn't get in trouble for that, but he never got a date with that girl.

"Bob had a reputation of being kind of nerdy, verging in the direction of creepy. A girl in my church who also went to our high school told me she thought his social demeanor was very strange.

"'You have this friend who's really weird,' she would say.

"I would tell her, 'You're basically misunderstanding him,' but I recognized also he was a little awkward socially. That doesn't mean he was evil. Neither of us were cool guys. We were both sort of nerdy."[7]

The event nearly everyone familiar with Hanssen in those early years agrees is formative happens in sixth grade. During the school day, his close friend Paul Steinbachner gets knocked down by a ball in a playground game, normal recess mayhem. But that afternoon, when Hanssen goes over to Paul's house to play, his friend complains of a headache, goes into the bathroom, and minutes later drops dead of a brain hemorrhage. Bobby hears him fall.

Maybe it's that experience that makes it so hard for Hanssen to form friendships as an adult. Why bother if they are just going to die? Maybe also, it's what binds him so closely to Jack Hoschouer in the decades ahead. True friends are precious, hold them close. But Hanssen resists easy pigeonholing and dime-store diagnoses.

As cautious as he is in personal relationships, risk-taking and a kind of callous arrogance seem to be hardwired into his personality and they sometimes emerge in spectacular ways. Hanssen does finally get his driver's license, his dad not withstanding; and once he has it, he does what teenage boys have been doing since the beginning of the automotive age: drives the family sedan—a 1962 Dodge Dart in this instance—way too fast through the shaded streets of Norwood Park and beyond. But as often seems to be the case with Hanssen, he takes it one step further.

"Bob and I developed an interest in racing cars," Hoschouer says. "We went for two or three years to the Road America June Sprints at Elkhart Lake, Wisconsin. In the parking lot, all these different manufacturers had their hot cars on display, and there would be attractive women standing by them. We'd watch cars race around, and Bob would get car magazines—*Road & Track*, that kind of thing—and study how to go through the curves to get maximum advantage in a road race. Then we would go out and see if a slower car could win by taking the turns better than a faster car. We'd challenge guys to race, but not drag races. We'd pick these twisty, turning streets and challenge someone to follow us through them. Then we would zoom around as fast as we could. We did that fairly often, actually. Sometimes, one of the cars we were racing would end up in the middle of some guy's front yard."[8]

Again, fairly typical teenage-boy stuff, even if taken to an extreme, but according to Hoschouer, there are times when his best friend crosses the line and doesn't even seem to realize it.

"Bob had these compartmented places in his mind—smart places and dumb places. One of the dumb ones was down in my basement when my folks were upstairs, watching TV. My dad had bought my brother and me .22 rifles, and we had a bullet trap. You could shoot into it, and the bullets would drop down into the bottom.

"Well, Bob decided he could shoot into the trap from his hip. I told him, 'Don't do this.' But I didn't want to wrestle with a guy with a loaded gun. So he shot from the hip, and he was in line with the target but about a foot above it. The bullet clunked into the concrete wall of the basement and made a big bang. For some reason, my parents never asked what happened, but there was a chip the size of a quarter out of the wall. He would do stuff like that.

"Another time when I was back from Germany—this was years later—I was visiting Bob and Bonnie. I had retired from the army not long before and had to bring some of my rifles back to the States, and Bob was keeping them for me. Well, he took one of them, went out on the deck in his Virginia suburb, and just shot it off—at a steep angle, but that had to come down some place. In my mind that was incredibly careless, but Bob didn't give a damn about other people in some ways."[9]

Maybe, in fact, in many ways.

At Knox College, Hanssen mostly flies beneath the radar. "Introverted" and "nondescript" pop up frequently in classmates' memories, if there are any memories at all. During a 2006 fortieth reunion of Hanssen's class, Knox political science professor Robert Seibert corrals three of Bob's dorm mates and asks what they remember about what is by then one of the college's most infamous alumni ever.

According to Seibert, the classmates "had nothing to say about him. He apparently lived here with very little interaction with his peers and teachers."[10]

College seniors often inflate their accomplishments for their final yearbook listings: clubs joined, honors won, positions held. Not Hanssen. The activities under his 1966 yearbook photo are limited to a single word: "intramurals." Basketball to be exact—Hanssen grows to a skinny six-foot-three while at Knox. From his first day there, though, he seems to want to be remembered as the Man No One Really Knew. More than four decades later, that will essentially be the reaction of just about everyone in his life, especially after its dark sides are laid bare.

The only solid memory that emerges from those college years is the time Hanssen walks out of a Western Civilization final exam almost immediately after it begins—he doesn't like the first question—and spends the next two-and-half hours practicing left-handed layups in the gym. From a grade point average, it isn't a smart move, but even then, Hanssen has a Plan B ready. On more than one occasion, he purportedly makes up for inattention to his studies and a cavalier attitude toward tests by breaking into the school offices late at night and changing his grades. Maybe spying is what he was really preparing for all along during those four years at Knox College.

As critical as he is of his son, Howard Hanssen still has big plans for him. He wants him to be a dentist, not a cop—white-collar, not blue—and Bob buys into the plan, or succumbs to his father's wishes, albeit somewhat grudgingly. After graduating from Knox College in 1966, where he majors in chemistry, Hanssen applies for a job as a cryptographer with the National Security Agency. (He has also taken a few undergraduate courses in Russian.) When that doesn't pan out, he enrolls in the Northwestern University Dental School. There, unlike Knox College, Hanssen does manage to leave some lasting impressions behind.

His dorm roommate, Jerry Takesono, vividly recalls Hanssen's daily wardrobe, what will become a signature look for the whole of his working life: black suit, white shirt, and tie. At dental school, Hanssen wears it everywhere, not even taking the suit jacket off when he works on cadavers.

"The suit smelled of formaldehyde, and he was hanging it up each night in our room," Takesono says. "Our place reeked of the cadaver. I finally had to ask him to get it dry-cleaned."[11]

Another classmate, Marty Ziegner, recalls a professor's long-winded lecture on tooth structure. Everyone is madly taking notes, except Hanssen. He writes a single word on a sheet of paper—"bicuspid"—and then accompanies it with a sketch of a nude woman.

"The professor walked around the room as he talked," Ziegner remembers. "It was hard for him to miss Bob's naked lady. He came over to Bob's desk and just lost it. He began reaming Bob out. It was something about how Northwestern was a professional school and how he was lucky to get in. Bob sat there and I could see he was pissed off. Finally, Bob couldn't take it anymore and interrupted the tirade.

"He told the professor he had accused him of not listening and didn't appreciate it. He said, 'Why don't you go back up to the front of the class and start over and I'll pick it up from there.' When the professor began, Bob interrupted and began repeating his lecture word for word. It was like he had a tape recorder in his brain. [Afterward he told me,] 'I can remember every conversation I have ever had.'"[12]

Actual fact or a throwaway boast? There's no real way of knowing or ever finding out. But for a future mole, a man who will rise to lasting infamy by burrowing tunnels through the darkness, a photographic memory is an invaluable resource. What can be said for certain, though, is that for the rest of his life, Hanssen's intellect and arrogance will travel hand in hand.

Summers during his time as a dental student are spent working at the Chicago State Hospital, a psychiatric facility, filling in for the regular staff on weekends and as needed. The second year he convinces his best friend to join him, reeling him in with promises of attractive student nurses.

"My job," Hoschouer says, "was to interact with the patients, play cards, tell stories, take them out and play softball. Bob during this time developed a fascination with one of the therapists, two or three years older than him, maybe more. He became convinced her husband was not being nice to her and decided he was going to look after her. I don't think there was anything real about it. This was another of his damsel-in-distress fantasies.

"He never even mentioned her first name. Her last name was Ohler, and he always called her Mrs. Ohler. He ended up giving her a lavaliere from the college as a token of his esteem."[13]

The hospital is also where he meets Bonnie. She's a sociology major at Jesuit-affiliated Loyola University in Chicago, working a summer job as a nurse, a position she lands through her father, a Loyola faculty member. A psychiatric facility might not seem the best place for romance to flourish, but Bob has expanded his pickup repertoire beyond dirty words in Morse code. For the amusement of Bonnie and others, maybe most of all himself, he begins playing doctor—psychiatric doctor, that is, conducting one-on-one interviews with the facility's patients, with himself in the starring role as a fully qualified clinician.

John Sullivan, a Northwestern classmate also working part time at the hospital, sees a dark side to these playing-doctor moments: "[Hanssen] loved showing people the control he had over the patients. They were mostly bonkers, but he would perform for his friends, putting the patients through their paces. He wasn't mean; he just quietly interrogated them."[14]

Bonnie, though, clearly is not offended by Bob's clinical antics. Far from it, in fact. She is taken almost immediately by his creativity, his imagination, and his brain. Not long after they start dating, she brings him home to meet her parents. The new beau is "tall, dark, and handsome," her mother will later say. "He seemed to adore my daughter, he had good credentials in education—that was important to us—and treated her like a queen. That was enough for me."[15]

For his part, Bob is impressed by the Waucks' upscale lifestyle. They live in Park Ridge, the same high-end suburb where Hillary Rodham (later Clinton) grows up. The family also summers on a Wisconsin lake. It's all a far cry from the Hanssens' bungalow back in Norwood Park.

The two have been dating about a year when Bonnie graduates from college. Two months later, on August 9, 1968, they are married at Mary, Seat of Wisdom Catholic Church in Park Ridge, home also to the parish school Bonnie attended. She is twenty-one; Bob, twenty-four. Bonnie's brother Mark remembers how quiet Bob is at the ceremony and receptions afterward, as if in a way he wasn't at his own wedding. Quiet will become another of Hanssen's hallmarks.

That fall, the newlyweds set up house in an apartment hard by the railroad tracks on Chicago's North Side. To make ends meet, Bonnie teaches grade school. But Bob's future course is not quite set yet. Before the academic year is out, he will drop out of dental school.

Bob Hanssen's next and final stop on the academic circuit, in the fall of 1969, is the two-year MBA program at Northwestern's School of Business, and this time he sticks, emerging in 1971 with a master's degree in accounting and information systems, and quickly landing a job as a junior auditor in the Chicago office of Touche Ross & Company. It isn't dentistry, but the pay is good and the future promising—Hanssen starts at $10,000 a year, equivalent to almost $67,000 annually today. Adult life has begun.

Perhaps comforted that his son has at least married up in the world, Howard Hanssen retires from the Chicago police force in July 1972. In short order, he and Vivian sell their two-story white house on North Neva Avenue to Bob and Bonnie and take off for the eternal sunshine of Florida. Two months later, Bob does exactly what his father doesn't want him to do: quits his accounting job to become a Chicago cop, just as Howard Hanssen was, and soon ends up doing what must have been from his father's point of view the very worst kind of policing possible.

"Bob didn't like to go out in uniform," Jack Hoschouer explains. "He called it 'clown duty.'"

Nor does Hanssen like the people you commonly deal with on street patrol. "He called them 'mokes'—vagrants, homeless people," Hoschouer says. "He had no sympathy for people."[16]

To escape the "mokes," he joins the much-despised C-5 Unit, undercover cops scattered throughout the department, tasked with rooting out not Commies, nor gangsters, nor crime lords but internal corruption. Had he joined six months earlier, his own father might have been one of his targets, if Mike Rochford's rumor about Howard Hanssen and the Longshoremen's

Union is on the mark. From their fellow cops' perspective, the C-5 people are rats, stoolies—in short, spies. Part of the training—done off-site in a storefront school disguised as a TV repair shop—entails installing what is then high-tech surveillance equipment. Bob Hanssen has found his calling and received his first lessons in tradecraft on the Chicago Police Department's dime.

Not only does defying his father's wishes prep him for his future work as a Soviet mole, it also ironically points him toward the place where he will ultimately practice his craft. If anything, Hanssen is too intense in his undercover role. He asks too many leading questions, spends too much time hanging quietly around, eavesdropping on the idle chatter of his fellow police. Before long, John Clarke—the boss he has been detailed to, and one of those he is secretly assigned to pry into—has Hanssen pretty much figured out.

"He was brilliant, and he looked like an altar boy," Clarke will later say. "But I always thought he was a spy, a counterspy, when he worked for us. I thought he was working for the police brass who wanted to know what we were doing. I always felt something was wrong, so we held Hanssen on a short leash. I even thought at one point he might be working for the feds because he was so inquisitive about Mayor Daley."[17]

Finally, to get Hanssen off his back, Clarke suggests he apply for a job with the FBI. Hanssen does just that. Turns out, an accountant with police experience, an advanced business degree, and expertise in information systems is just the trifecta the Bureau is looking for. The fox is in the henhouse.

CHAPTER 9

BLACK IS WHITE/ GOOD IS EVIL

Does anyone ever really know Bob Hanssen? Certainly, lots of people know parts about him—the Opus Dei side, the patriotic FBI agent, the loyal husband and father, the ever-reliable mole, the nerdy techie, the go-to guy for a damsel-in-distress, and on and on. But does anyone really know the whole Hanssen?

If anyone should be able to sense a mole in the hole, it's James Bamford. For four decades as an author, documentary producer, and investigative reporter, Bamford has been burrowing into American intelligence entities and their secrets. His 1982 book about the National Security Agency, *The Puzzle Palace*, is widely considered one of the gold standards of such work. His subsequent books—*Body of Secrets*, also about the NSA, and *A Pretext for War: 9/11, Iraq, and the Abuse of America's Intelligence Agencies*—have both been *New York Times* best sellers. In 2014, Bamford burnished his résumé even further by spending three days in Moscow interviewing the famous (or infamous) NSA whistleblower Edward Snowden.

Bamford has been tight with some of America's foremost secret keepers. He has interviewed, written about, and filmed a who's who of spooks and their handlers. On the side, he has circumnavigated the globe by land and sea, partly on his own sixty-foot motor yacht neatly named for the subject of so much of his work: *Safehouse*, where spooks hang out.

Bamford and Hanssen first meet in 1992, brought together on Bamford's yacht by a mutual acquaintance, Bart Borrasca. Bamford is just getting started on his second NSA book, and Borrasca, a CIA officer and Bamford's lifelong friend, thinks it might be useful for him to talk with a senior FBI agent then serving as chief of the National Security Threat List Unit and an expert in Russian efforts to place moles within the US government. In retrospect, irony abounds, but the two strangers hit it off from the get-go. Hanssen breaks the mold.

"He was different from the younger street agents and supervisors I knew," Bamford writes in a March 18, 2001, piece for the *New York Times*, four weeks after Hanssen's arrest. "He would much rather talk about the immorality of abortion and the dangers of Planned Parenthood than the latest draft picks. He was also old school. In his low voice, little more than a loud whisper, he spoke in reverential terms of 'Mr. Hoover.' That day, Hanssen came across as a fierce anti-Communist out of the 1950s' Red Scare mold. In the years that I knew him, he often encouraged me to do stories on the dangers of Russian subversion."[1]

In the near decade to come, Hanssen and Bamford grow ever more tight. They fly together to a gun show in Virginia Beach, in a private plane piloted by Borrasca. Bonnie and Bob are guests at Bamford's wedding. After Hanssen is detailed to the Department of State in February 1995, the two men—"spy writer" and "spy catcher," as Bamford put it—often lunch in the State Department cafeteria or simply jaw together in Hanssen's office suite. Hanssen's job title by now is huge—senior representative to the Office of Foreign Missions, in which he functions as head of an interagency counterintelligence group with the State Department and as FBI liaison to the State Department's Bureau of Intelligence and Research—but in fact he has almost nothing to do, and no work product seems to be required of him. Bamford helps fill his time in the best possible way.

In 1995, Bamford scores a rare interview with Victor Cherkashin, then back in Moscow. When the writer returns to Washington, Hanssen is so "hungry for details" that he even asks to see a transcript of the meeting. Little wonder, Bamford has done the one thing Hanssen will never do: meet his handler face-to-face. If anyone is ever going to be able to supply the FBI with clues that will lead to Hanssen, that person is most likely to be Cherkashin as well, if he can ever be flipped into cooperating with the Americans.

This, of course, is a subject that can never be discussed in part or full between the two men, for obvious reasons. Nor can Felix Bloch. Bloch is another of Bamford's journalistic coups. It's Bamford who breaks the story that Bloch, a foreign service officer, is under investigation for spying for the Soviets. The story is a big one, and the allegations brought against Bloch are almost certainly true. But in fact, charges never emerge and a crime is never proffered. Thanks to a heads-up from a reliable source, the KGB has a critical head start in scrubbing the Bloch record and warning Bloch himself to clam up and demand a lawyer when FBI investigators come calling. The reliable source, of course, is Bob Hanssen.

As for James Bamford, like everyone else who "knew" Bob Hanssen, he's thrown utterly for a loop when GRAYSUIT's identity finally becomes public.

Bart Borrasca and Hanssen are a less unpredictable pairing, more a matter of likes attracting each other. The two meet in the early 1990s, through the Community Nonproliferation Committee, a joint CIA-FBI group that gathers monthly at a CIA facility in Rosslyn, Virginia, just across the Potomac from DC. Borrasca worked with intercontinental ballistic missiles in the air force before retiring and joining the Agency. He has hands-on experience with their targeting. Hanssen's nuclear-weapons credentials are slim at best, but he always likes to be at the heart of things, listening away.

Like Hanssen, Borrasca has a reputation among his fellow CIA analysts for eccentric, sometimes impulsive behavior. Both are desk jockeys with a passion for espionage tales, for cloak and dagger. But what they really seem to have in common are Hanssen's "insider" stories about the Clintons.

Bill Clinton is still in the middle of his first term when Borrasca lets his CIA superior in on a Hanssen-supplied secret: his FBI buddy is heading up an operation targeting the president himself—hidden cameras and microphones, heavy secret surveillance, the whole works. Hanssen has even intimated he might let Borrasca listen to or, better still, see some of the surveillance. The CIA manager Borrasca confides in sends him to a CIA attorney, who tells him to drop Hanssen cold. Instead, Borrasca begs for a reprieve: "Please don't say anything about this that would ruin my relationship with Hanssen. It's very important to me."[2]

Two years later, still Hanssen's good friend, Borrasca dies of cancer at age forty-nine. But the story about the FBI's bugging the White House lives on. Hanssen tells almost the same tale to his closest friend, Jack Hoschouer, and also variations on the Clinton's evil ways to Bonnie time and again. Hanssen also ransacks FBI electronic case files for information on the First Family, including more than twenty searches for "Hillary Rodham Clinton," "Hillary," "Chelsea," and simply "Clinton."

Hanssen and Jim Bamford are fellow pallbearers at Borrasca's funeral, in September 1996, at the Ivy Hill Cemetery in Alexandria, Virginia, where he now rests under a gravestone shaped appropriately like a bishop's miter because that is yet another link between Bob Hanssen and Bart Borrasca: they are both Opus Dei members, and in the early years of the prelature, the awarding of such miters was a powerful symbol of acceptance within the endless intrigue of the Vatican.

Religion, faith, Opus Dei, Catholicism—they always come up in discussions about what is real and what is not in Bob Hanssen's public life. Jim Bamford says Hanssen couldn't stop talking about religion. He hangs a silver crucifix on the wall above his desk at the State Department. Occasionally, he'll sneak away from Foggy Bottom to join right-to-life rallies on the Mall, in front of the White House, or on Capitol Hill. Opus Dei is never far from his mind.

"He was forever trying to get me to go with him to meetings of Opus Dei," Bamford wrote in his 2001 *New York Times* piece. "After weeks of urging, I finally agreed. At the meeting, Hanssen was in his element. He reveled in that closed society of true believers, like a fraternity brother exchanging a secret handshake. Even today . . . his faith seemed too sincere to me to be a ruse."[3]

The columnist Robert Novak writes his own maybe-this/maybe-that Bob Hanssen piece four months later on July 12, 2001, in the *Washington Post*. Hanssen, he confides, had been the primary source for a 1997 Novak column about a veteran FBI agent who had defied Attorney General Janet Reno and resigned from the Bureau rather than turn over the names of top-secret sources in China to the Justice Department.

"Could Hanssen have felt some genuine concern about the security of US assets in China if they fell into the hands of the attorney general?" Novak wonders. "Could he have experienced a sudden change of heart after disclosing the identity of US assets in Russia? Or was he merely using me to undermine Reno—and his boss, FBI director Louis Freeh, as well? . . . He really may have been living a double life, one as a patriotic, religious American and the other as a spy of the century. That sounds fanciful, but any other explanation fails."[4]

As with Bamford and Novak, so with Jim Ohlson. Hanssen stops a lot of his colleagues and acquaintances cold at the door, but for those who walk through it, he has a knack for making people invest in him. His sincerity, his faith, his patriotism shine through the shortfalls.

"One of the first things he did was to give me the book by the founder of Opus Dei. I'm not Catholic, but I'm a church-attending Protestant, so he knew I took religion seriously, and he made a point of making me aware of Opus Dei and pitching me on this book."[5]

In the same vein, Ohlson's last email exchange with Hanssen, in January 2001, is also tied to faith. George W. Bush's nominee to be attorney general, the former Missouri senator John Ashcroft, is under furious assault by a coalition of liberal groups concerned that Ashcroft's often expressed conservative religious views will hamper his judgment on issues like abortion.

On January 18, Ohlson emails Hanssen to let him know that the *Wall Street Journal* is about to carry an op-ed piece in support of Ashcroft, written by Jim Skillen, head of the Center for Public Justice, where Ohlson has come to roost after retiring from the Bureau.

The article, Ohlson writes, begins: "Do deeply held religious convictions pose a threat to government? May we trust a man like John Ashcroft, whose outlook appears to be saturated by faith, to serve as US Attorney General?"[6] And goes on to answer in the affirmative.

In response, Hanssen emails: "Read *Lord of the World* by Robert Hugh Benson. You are seeing the logical consequences of an idea as he predicted, an idea injected into a healthy society. The book is futuristic fiction from the past. In the end, belief in God is the ultimate 'hate crime.' 'When the Lord comes will there be any faith left in the world?'"[7]

Sounds cut-and-dried, the words of a true believer—a soldier of God, a man who can't stop spreading the Word. And yet in the dozens of communications with his Soviet handlers that are contained in the charging affidavit eventually brought against Bob Hanssen, there are no paeans to Catholicism or Opus Dei, and the word *God* never appears once. Indeed, in the entire 100-page affidavit, the only mention of God is in the concluding sentence of the oath of office Hanssen took upon joining the FBI on January 12, 1976—the oath that ends "So help me God." And Hanssen seems to have had no trouble at all kicking those words under the table.

What's real with Hanssen, and what isn't? What does it mean to be his best friend, for example?

According to David Major, he and Hanssen spent literally hundreds of hours talking together in the office and socialized together out of the office with their wives. By just about all accounts, Major is also Hanssen's godfather within the Bureau hierarchy—a high-ranking protector for a sometimes troublesome employee. If he isn't Hanssen's best friend at the FBI, he is certainly in the top two.

"Did Hanssen ever compromise anything you were working on?" I ask Major.

His answer: "Ha! Oh, God, yes! He compromised *everything* I worked on!" And he goes on to tell this story: "In my office, I had a Russian officer's hat that I was very proud of. I got it in Europe. This guy was a KGB officer I had recruited. He presented it to me as a token of our friendship. Bob came into my office and asked me about the hat, so I told him the whole story. He then went back and told the KGB about the hat and the source behind the hat. Thank you, Bob Hanssen!"[8]

Yet, even today, Major finds it hard to come down too heavily on the man who managed to undermine him professionally at just about every turn. "Bob was testing what the KGB could do," he says with a certain amount of pride. "The KGB knew they were dealing with a pro!"

In the same spirit, he tells the story of his retirement party: "They're big deals at the FBI, these roast-and-toast events. I had about 250 people come to mine at Ft. Myers. The room was packed. I was very honored by that. It's like a wedding. I waited at the door and shook hands with everyone.

"During the party, Bob Hanssen said to my sons, 'You know, your dad is the smartest counterintelligence officer in the FBI.' Now is that a compliment from the worst spy we ever had or is that not a compliment? I was so good, but I couldn't catch your ass!"[9]

Then again, maybe that's the point. Hanssen has to be so good— "uncatchable," as Major once describes him—that the Bureau doesn't look so bad for his stealing so many secrets and upending so many operations over so many years, right under everyone's nose. He has to be so religious that his faith and his espionage exist in different parts of his psyche, and thus there is no reason to doubt the former even once the latter is laid bare for all the world to see. He has to be so good a friend that friendship itself survives all the surrounding deception.

That Jack Hoschouer was Bob Hanssen's best friend is beyond any question. Even after high-school and college-summer days, they stay in constant touch and visit each other as often as they can. Hoschouer is best man at Bob and Bonnie's wedding. He's godfather to *all* the Hanssen children, and when Victor Cherkashin and his principals ask Hanssen to provide the names of possible

American recruits for the KGB, Hanssen puts his best friend's name on the list—to commit a crime that carries the death penalty. Hoschouer believes the KGB took the lead seriously.

"I was the attaché in the American embassy in Bonn," Hoschouer says, "and I became friends with my Soviet counterpart. He was getting ready to rotate back to the Motherland, so we were having lunch, and he said, 'Jack, have you ever wondered why I've never asked you anything of intelligence relevance?'

"And I said, 'Yuri, I understand completely, because we don't want that to get in the way of our friendship.'

"And he said, 'Yeah.'

"I suspect this was Yuri's way of letting me know that he had been given the mission of scoping me out."

But that's in retrospect. Hoschouer won't know about this until months after his best friend's arrest, when a fuller picture of his espionage begins to emerge.

"Being on that list didn't thrill me much," Hoschouer tells me, "but I told Bonnie, and I asked her to pass it on to Bob, that I forgive him for that betrayal of me. As his friend and as a Christian, I feel it's my job to forgive him for that. It's water under the bridge."[10]

With Hanssen, every relationship seems to be ultimately transactional: What's in it for me? Every relationship also seems to teeter on the razor's edge of betrayal. Even what Jack Hoschouer calls Hanssen's damsel-in-distress moments are freighted with extra weight.

Hanssen's efforts to upgrade the moral tone of the FBI clerk staff are met with resistance. But among the clerks in the FBI's Soviet Analytical Unit, he has more than a few fans. Bob takes an interest in their careers. Drawing on his old ham-radio skills, he helps one learn Morse code. For another, he buys a piece of equipment that will help her do the job better—paid for with KGB funds to be sure, but that's not the point here. Yet another clerk is so enamored of Hanssen that she names her son after him. It seems on the surface like unfettered generosity, a big spirit.

Mike Rochford, who watches some of this, says no dice: "He wanted the analysts and clerks trusting him so he could break down compartmentation."[11] Quid pro quo.

Even Hanssen's most celebrated damsel-in-distress turn is larded with caveats.

Hanssen first meets Priscilla Galey at Joanna's, a weary "gentleman's club" on M Street NW, between 18th and 19th Streets—a ten-minute walk from the FBI headquarters on Pennsylvania Avenue. Hanssen is there for his usual lunchtime fare: a hamburger, a Coke, and a little something titillating for the midday hour, in this case, Galey. Priscilla Galey's fare, in turn, consists of arriving onstage in a prim business suit, quickly peeling down to nothing except what the law barely allows, then segueing into a bump-and-grind pole dance.

Priscilla is new to the club, a fresh face (and body) so impressive that Bob sends a $10 tip back to her dressing room, along with his FBI business card and a note so thoughtful that Galey rushes out to thank him.

"He was dressed in a dark suit, not a hair out of place, not a piece of lint, not a wrinkle," she later recalls. "I was a little afraid of him at first."[12]

Hanssen is up-front about his name, if not his exact reason for being at Joanna's. He's there on "official FBI business," he tells the stripper. So far, according to Jack Hoschouer, it's a pretty typical Hanssen moment.

"He had a reputation for going to strip clubs. I went with him a couple times. He'd tip a girl, and she'd come over and sit with us for ten minutes or so. Then he'd get up and go to the men's room, and the girl would say to me, 'Is he really in the FBI?' That made him a cool guy. And that would be it."[13]

This time, though, the story is just beginning. Galey agrees to have lunch with him, and things take off from there. In time, Hanssen will pony up $2,000 so Galey can have her teeth tended to—an entire new upper plate. Not long afterward, he treats her to a sapphire-and-diamond necklace. The two fly together, on separate planes—on his tab, which by then is in effect the Soviets' tab—to Hong Kong when Hanssen has FBI business there and stay for two and a half weeks, in separate hotels. Back in DC that summer of 1991, this time lunching at a Mexican restaurant, he gives her an envelope with ten $100 bills inside, the keys to a used Mercedes valued at $10,000, and an American Express card to use when the Mercedes needs servicing.

When he isn't lunching with Galey or traveling with her or showering her with mole-financed booty, Hanssen looks to her betterment: daytime trips, for example, to the National Gallery of Art only a few blocks from the FBI headquarters, where he tends to focus her attention on religious subjects; also, upscale footwear to replace her stripper stilettos, pronunciation tips, and so on.

Their relationship echoes George Bernard Shaw's *Pygmalion*—with Hanssen as a lugubrious Henry Higgins and Galey as his saucy Eliza Doolittle. In the Hollywood version (or the *My Fair Lady* musical take on the same source), Galey is a beautiful butterfly slowly emerging from her gritty cocoon, albeit with a complicated overlay. Hanssen is playing with the idea of setting her up in an apartment near the Soviet embassy on Wisconsin Avenue—the love nest earlier mentioned, which he can also use for direct burst communications with his spy handlers. (According to Mike Rochford, it was the Soviets who put the kibosh on that idea.)

As for love itself, Galey will later say they never had sex. Hoschouer disputes that version: "Bob told me they had sex one time and it was the worst sex he ever had. He said she was just going through the motions."[14]

Either way, the love/spy nest never comes to fruition, and the affair comes crashing down near the beginning of its second year when Galey returns to her hometown in Ohio and uses the Mercedes-dedicated Amex card for personal expenses—cartons of cigarettes for herself, Easter dresses for her nieces. She thinks Hanssen will understand at least the clothing outlay. He talks frequently about his deep Catholicism, and the dresses are, after all, a religious-holiday expense. Instead, after dumping what he estimates to total about $85,000 on her, Sugar Daddy goes ballistic and stays that way ever thereafter.

Absent Bob's guiding hand, or maybe just freed from his overbearing presence, Galey drifts into crack cocaine and eventually prostitution to help pay for it. She wrecks the Mercedes, sells the sapphire-and-diamond necklace along with a laptop computer her techie boyfriend has also given her, loses the new upper teeth after a nightlong binge, and does a year in jail. Through the whole painful descent, and despite Galey's cries for help, Hanssen refuses to lend a helping hand or even respond to her pleas.

According to Priscilla's mother, Hanssen says that she "had made her bed, and now she had to lay in it . . . [It's] like she never existed."[15]

In the end, it feels a lot more like a story about control—about being the puppet master—than a story about love and rescue. Bob and Bonnie's relationship has a lot of the same threads running through it.

Just as he played control games with the psychiatric patients at Chicago State Hospital, Hanssen likes to play control games with Bonnie, too. Early on in their marriage, he stares silently at his empty coffee cup during breakfast, trying to will Bonnie to get up and refill it—just as his father did. His Northwestern friend Marty Ziegner remembers Bob slowly tipping over a water glass, trying to "train" Bonnie to catch it before the water spills.[16]

According to Ziegner, Bonnie doesn't put up with these little trials for long, but Hanssen is stealthily conditioning her in other ways, as well. Bonnie has a Manichean view of the world. Just as there are Republicans and Democrats, so there are good and evil, in the same relationship. Opus Dei, the conservative wing of the Republican party, evangelicals—they aren't just doing political combat with liberals. They are locked in moral combat, with the soul of the nation at the center of the fight.

Similar to the way he plays Bill Borrasca, Hanssen uses Bonnie's us-and-them worldview to tie her ever tighter to him. From his "insider position" at the FBI, Hanssen is increasingly able to "confirm" her deepest suspicions about the depth of the depravity creeping over America. Why, for example, is Bill Clinton elected president in 1992 despite his obvious support for the evil of abortion? Bob has the answer: Clinton's campaign was financed with gold stolen from the Russians, and he, of course, is in a unique position to know this is so. It's all "Deep State" nonsense a quarter century before Donald Trump popularizes the term, but effective all the same—only her Bobby can keep Bonnie safe from Satan's work in the world.

Also, unknown to Bonnie, she becomes a minor soft-porn star. On multiple occasions, Hanssen posts descriptions of his sex life with Bonnie to an Internet bulletin board dedicated to such matters. One such posting describes "beach time" in the early years of their marriage, along Lake Michigan, only a few blocks from their apartment. Bonnie, he writes, likes to sunbathe in her two-piece on a bluff slightly behind and about eight feet above the beach itself. Hanssen, by his own account, has other things in mind.

"I was always interested . . . to see how low I could actually pull down her suit [bottom], as opposed to just rolling it, and that would vary. It would vary with how hot she got, and I don't mean from the sun. Several times I managed to get it and keep it for long periods down around her mid thighs, completely exposing her little tight bare ass. Now that was quite a sight indeed."[17]

Another posting, more vivid, describes their premarital sex. "I found she enjoyed having sex most when she was topless in my Volkswagen facing me on my lap with her tits bouncing wildly in the passenger side window . . . She didn't seem to want to get caught, but it seemed to be that the risk of being seen aroused her. I gradually saw that such risks were more than a passing fancy for her. They drove her wild. . . .

"Well we were a perfect match in this regard because what turned me on most was the thought of other men seeing her, wanting her, being aroused by her."

These postings—prurient and pornographic—come as shocking news to Bonnie once reporters begin mining Bob's past after his arrest, but followers of Hanssen's Internet soft porn would not have to work very hard to identify this North Side Chicago sex kitten. Bob describes Bonnie by name—first name, at least—in these postings. He also signs all the postings with his own name and occasionally includes nude photos of Bonnie. "Invasion of privacy" hardly begins to describe these postings, but there are worse invasions, far worse, as she will also eventually learn.

In early 1970, Jack Hoschouer is serving as an advisor to a Vietnamese battalion when he opens a four-by-six-inch brown envelope Bob Hanssen has mailed him.

"Inside were photos of Bonnie," he tells me with considerable embarrassment. "She's sitting there, and in every picture she's less and less dressed. I thought, *What is this about?* So I sit down and write Bob a letter: 'Hey, buddy, did you screw up? Send me something you shouldn't have?' And I destroyed those photos. A day or two after that, I get a letter from him: 'Did you get my surprise package?'"[18]

A few months later, Hanssen sends his friend a second surprise. "I was learning to do photography—there was a workshop at the American military base next door—so Bob sent me some negatives to practice on, and you can guess what they were. Here I was, a guy in Vietnam, and a friend sends me some naked pictures of a beautiful woman. What was I going to do? And that continued off and on.

"For some reason, Bob was really interested in my seeing Bonnie nude. One day I was staying with him, and Bonnie was in the shower, and Bob came and grabbed my arm and pulled me through the door—not that there was much to see. It was all steamy.

"I've often thought, *Why did he do this?* One, he was bragging about his beautiful wife. Two, he often referred to me as a hero because I'd gone to Vietnam and commanded an infantry company in combat and all that stuff. Maybe this was a hero's reward or something like that, but it got way out of hand.

"He couldn't have gone to Vietnam. He was 4-F, something about his eyes, and he wouldn't have wanted to at any rate. But in some sense, I think it made him feel less than worthy that he didn't.

"Was Bob getting off on this? I think that's on the money. Was he using me? I think that, too. I would say going all the way back to high school, the rifle in the basement, all that—he would do something, I would try to talk him out of it, and he would drag me along. Mostly it was immaturity and a tendency to want to control."[19]

The story, though, doesn't end there.

Hoschouer remains a frequent visitor at the Hanssens' Virginia house when he is back in the States and is at least an occasional spectator to Bob and Bonnie's nighttime activities when he is staying there. Unknown to his wife as usual, Hanssen gives his friend a pre-sex heads-up so Hoschouer can pull a patio chair up to the bedroom window and watch the fireworks. Later, Hanssen rigs the bedroom with a camera to create a closed-circuit sex theater. Now, Hoschouer can sit in the family den and watch Bob and Bonnie all he wants.

In one of his harder-core porn postings, Hanssen describes intentionally positioning Bonnie so his friend can watch penetration take place. Hoschouer will later say that he never asked to be a voyeur. Instead, he says, Bob insisted. Still, Hoschouer has the choice of watching or not watching, and he seems to have consistently chosen the former.

Once, Hanssen even mentions securing a "date-rape" drug so Hoschouer can participate, as well. That, at least, never happens, but even the contemplation of it says volumes about Hanssen's understanding of his marriage: Bonnie is his to use as he pleases. And maybe his understanding of friendship as well: Jack Hoschouer, his best friend, is also his to use as he pleases.

Before long, he has extended that dominion to the FBI itself. It, too, is his to use as he pleases—an ATM of secrets begging for withdrawals. Both relationships, work and marital, are built on trust, but Hanssen's trust runs only in one direction.

Cephalopods are a group of mollusks distinguished by having their arms attached to their heads—think squid, cuttlefish, and octopuses. But what's really unique about cephalopods is that they can change the color of their skin almost instantly.

The secret to this is chromatophores, tens of thousands of color-changing cells just beneath the surface of the skin that allow cephalopods to become almost indistinguishable from their backdrops or suddenly stand sharply out from them to scare off a predator or startle a would-be meal.

Was Bob Hanssen a human cephalopod? Probably not, at least completely. Norwood Park, where he grew up, was predominantly white and heavily

Republican—this in Mayor Richard Daley's Chicago, when usually only one of fifty alderman laid claim to the GOP. Like many of his fellow FBI agents, Hanssen was most likely a cradle conservative.

But if Hanssen isn't lying through his eyeteeth when he tells Victor Cherkashin that Kim Philby is one of his heroes, it's worth wondering just how long he has been planning his spy career. Long enough, for example, to marry into a family conveniently built around Opus Dei and with FBI connections, too? Long enough to use Opus Dei as an opening handshake of sorts to assure Ohlson, Bamford, Borrasca, and others of his pro-Catholic/anti-Communist bona fides? Long enough to master the arts of affection and love and rage when they were only means to an end?

Does Bob Hanssen not fit in easily with the beer-and-football culture of the FBI because beer and sports talk simply aren't his thing? Or does he not fit in so that, in Mike Rochford's words, he will "not be shown great attention by his superiors and his coworkers"?[20] Is Hanssen more comfortable around the Bureau's analysts and eggheads simply because he is also that way? Or is it because, again in Rochford's words, "he was happy to deepen the wedge between agents and analysts and manipulate that into getting them to break down compartmentation . . . and share with him things they shouldn't have"?[21]

There's really no way to know, but the questions have haunted those who knew him well in the months, even years, after his arrest. Hanssen, Jim Ohlson told me in retrospect, "was real good at faking emotions when, in fact, he had no emotions."[22]

That sounds like protective coloration, but the very best protective coloration Bob Hanssen ever had is the badge he carries everywhere—the badge of an FBI special agent.

PART III

CHAPTER 10

TRUST ME!

Like a jujitsu master, Robert Hanssen uses the FBI's own practices, protocols, and ingrained assumptions against it. A Bureau analysis—named Spiderweb—has determined that Soviet intelligence services do not fill or clear dead-drops on Mondays, and thus the FBI doesn't monitor known or suspected drops on the first day of the work week. Hanssen, though, is at the crossroads of such information. Privy to the Spiderweb analysis, he does the sensible thing: arranges for the vast majority of back-and-forth with his handlers to take place on surveillance-free Mondays.

Similarly, Hanssen risks sending his early communications to Victor Cherkashin through Viktor Degtyar because he has access to an FBI list of Washington-based Soviet intelligence officials whose mail is monitored, and Degtyar, putatively a press secretary for the embassy, is not among them. For all practical purposes, Hanssen has the Bureau doing reconnaissance for him.

Hanssen also takes full advantage of an FBI culture built around trust: in a vetting process and training program that supposedly winnow out those of questionable character, in the sanctity of the oath-takings that elevate trainees to bona fide FBI agents, and in the special agents—the ones who get to handle top secrets, people like Robert Hanssen—who are a rare breed unto themselves.

George Ellard serves as deputy counsel of the commission that investigates the Hanssen case after the damage had been done and a reckoning is at hand. In the FBI, he tells me, "there are two classes of people—special agents and lower life-forms. The Bureau could not fathom that one of its own special agents could betray it."[1]

Trust is the FBI's great strength, its internal bond, and, in the wrong circumstances, its Achilles' heel. To trust absolutely is to expect no evil. Bob Hanssen has a finely tuned nose for weakness, and trust is his first foot in the door. Information technology kicks it wide open.

"Hanssen's espionage was an astounding failure of security," Ellard says, "but it was complicated by the fact that we were just getting into the IT era. The FBI is always late. Hanssen was practically alone there in his knowledge of IT, and he took great advantage of that. He would survey ongoing investigations, for instance. And he would bring in his own equipment. For the first time, the disk was available to place information on. Hanssen didn't have to leave the building with reams of paper. It all goes a long way in explaining why he was able to escape detection."[2]

So does the simple reality that Hanssen is practicing what seems like IT magic in a place that not only desperately needs it but is loaded with secrets—a place where every day for a Soviet mole is Halloween: trick or treat!

"One of the things that is unique about Bob," David Major tells me, "is that he stole only what he had natural access to."[3] But one of the things equally unique about the FBI in Hanssen's spy-saturated era is that he had natural access to so very much. To quote from the Webster Commission report:

> [Hanssen] did not hesitate to walk into Bureau units in which he
> had worked some time before, log on to stand-alone data systems,
> and retrieve, for example, the identities of foreign agents whom
> US intelligence services had compromised, information vital to

American interest and even more immediately vital to those whose identities Hanssen betrayed.[4]

Example: In July 1991, when Hanssen resumes his mole work in earnest after a year's detail to the inspector's staff, he grabs "the first things I could lay my hands on," he says in his cover note to the KGB, and packages it neatly for handlers. In this case, the first things lying around are almost 300 pages of information invaluable to the enemy. Imagine what Hanssen might find if he really worked at it.[5]

At FBI headquarters and the larger field offices, you almost literally cannot turn around without bumping into a secret. Toward the end of the 1990s as Hanssen is nearing retirement, the FBI Mail Services Unit is taking in annually some seven million pieces of mail, 125,000 FedEx packages, and around 700,000 courier deliveries, an estimated 15 percent of which is classified either "secret" (material whose unauthorized disclosure may cause serious damage to national security), "top secret" (material whose unauthorized disclosure could cause "exceptionally grave" damage to national security), or "sensitive compartmented information" (SCI, classified information concerning or derived from intelligence sources, methods, or analytical processes required to be handled within formal access control systems established by the director of Central Intelligence).

Additionally, the FBI receives thirty thousand classified teletypes a month from other government agencies and generates on its own 185,000 internal documents classified secret or higher. If secrets were water, the FBI long ago would have drowned in them.

In Bob Hanssen's FBI, Headquarters and all field offices are deemed secure areas where classified material can be openly stored, travel freely from room to room and floor to floor, be left out during the day, and minimally secured at night. The same thing applies to hard drives that contain secret-and-above materials—no regulation requires that they be secured after working hours.

The hottest secrets, the SCIs, are mostly to be found in SCIFs, or sensitive compartmented information facilities, but here, too, laxness often prevails.

Access might or might not be tightly controlled. Documents are vulnerable as they move in and out of the facilities. A curious agent, or a dedicated snoop, is hard to defend against.

The benefit of all this openness is that special agents with a need-to-know don't have to go through tons of rigamarole to secure access to files pertinent to their work. Such "open storage," though, is open to just about everyone. FBI employees without a need-to-know, for example, have relatively easy access to even top-secret materials. With minimal subterfuge, even non-Bureau contractors working inside FBI facilities can steal a peek at classified documents and perhaps even collect them for removal.

In Hanssen's own words, from one of his post-arrest debriefing sessions: "You could bring documents out of FBI headquarters without . . . ever having a risk of being searched, or looked at, or even concerned about."[6]

Indeed, the only real protection against outside contractors or clerks or rogue agents doing just that is the FBI's own in-house police, and their effectiveness, the Webster Commission finds, is compromised pretty much at every turn.

"FBI uniformed security police, who provide the primary line of defense against unauthorized entry at Headquarters and other facilities are understaffed, insufficiently trained, and ill-equipped to deter improper removal of classified material. The authority of these officers is undercut by providing FBI executives with 'gold badges' that allow them and visitors they escort to bypass normal security and 'executive escorted visitor badges' that allow uncleared visitors repeated escorted access."[7]

In short, come and get it!

The inspector general's team finds that throughout Bob Hanssen's entire FBI career, his access to classified national security information—whether hard copies or disks—is rarely monitored and lightly supervised at best.

It takes Hanssen little time to understand that he can walk out of the FBI's New York field office or its national headquarters in Washington, DC, with copies *and* originals of some of the US government's most sensitive classified material with little or no fear of being stopped or detected. Sometimes he walks out of FBI headquarters with secrets and walks back in with them on the same day. Once, Hanssen carries out of the building a volume containing top-secret and special-access program information about "an extraordinarily important program for use in response to a nuclear attack," photographs it all in the back seat of his car, and hauls the volume back inside.[8] (That's the sanitized language the Webster Commission report uses. The program information in question is almost certainly the one that details evacuation plans for the nation's leaders should the Soviets launch a first-strike attack.)

Other times, Hanssen ferrets out original documents, passes them to his KGB handlers for their closer perusal, gets them back on the next under-the-footbridge exchange, and returns them to Headquarters that has almost no way to know they have gone missing.

Most often, Hanssen does the everyday work of espionage in plain sight for everyone to see. By the KGB's own record-keeping, Hanssen hands over some 6,000 pages of documents to the Soviets between 1985 and 1991. (Think of six five-hundred-sheet packs of copy paper.) Close to half of those are literal pages, before Hanssen began using computer diskettes. According to Mike Rochford, "most of those were copied on the fourth-floor Xerox machine [at Headquarters], which didn't have a counter [or] a pin number on it."[9]

In theory, the October 1995 streamlining of the Bureau's antiquated technology should work to Bob Hanssen's disadvantage. The paper-heavy FBI is about to burst into the Computing Age. Electronic file use can be monitored in ways that paper file use resists. Agents have to log on and the log-ons eventually leave a trail. In practice, the Automated Case Support system, or ACS, makes it almost too easy for Hanssen to do self-surveillance. At the core of the ACS and its most extensive database is the electronic case file (ECF), home to electronic communications and other documents related to ongoing FBI investigations, programs, and issues—the equivalent of a closed FBI intranet. But in reality, neither ACS nor ECF is all that closed.

Earlier in 1995, the New York field office is asked to assess the ACS system before deployment. As part of its review, the field office gives an intern from the Massachusetts Institute of Technology (MIT) ordinary user access and challenges him to find vulnerabilities in the system. Before the afternoon is over, the intern has accessed multiple restricted files. Sure, the intern hails from MIT, cradle of geniuses, but when the system in question is meant to be the information center of one of the pillars of the American intelligence community, shouldn't even a huge MIT brain have to break a sweat?

Not surprisingly, the New York field office and other outposts treat the ACS as an unreliable digital partner, refusing to upload highly sensitive case information for fear of compromise. At the Bureau's Engineering Research Facility, a program manager operating a top-secret/SCI program will not upload into ACS even sanitized versions of his unit's reports, as he later tells Webster Commission investigators.

For Bob Hanssen, though, the ACS and ECF are gifts from above. The 2001 charging affidavit in Hanssen's case lists seventy-nine separate examples of his personal and persistent trolling that pop up in an ECF audit of his usage from late July 1997 to late January 2001, a month before his arrest—roughly one search every sixteen days. Search terms include his name with and without middle initial, his street address (9414 Talisman), "FISA and cell phone" (to see if a tap had been authorized on his own cell),[10] "CCTV" (to see if he had been captured by any surveillance cameras), and the names of specific dead-drop sites. The most common search term is "Dead-Drop" itself coupled with all sorts of qualifiers ("and Virginia," "and KGB," "and Russia" as well as specific date ranges).

Like all ACS users, Hanssen has an identification number and unique password that could be used to audit his searches, but no one bothers to do so even when the mole hunt is in high gear and the FBI and CIA are desperate to crack the case. Little wonder the inspector general's analysis concludes that "the FBI lacked the ability to know what it knew"[11]—even after it has put in place a state-of-the-art system to help it do just that.

Or to quote again from Hanssen's post-arrest debriefings: "Any clerk in the Bureau could come up with stuff on that [ACS] system. It was pathetic . . . It's criminal what's laid out. What I did is criminal, but it's criminal negligence . . . what they've done on that system."[12]

By the very nature of their positioning within opposing intelligence organizations, moles like Bob Hanssen are hard to spot, according to Dave Szady. "It doesn't matter what country you are looking at. It's all the same because the intelligence organizations the moles are spying for are protecting their sources, while the sources are hiding themselves within the environment where they're working."[13]

That's a lot of layers of the onion to peel back. Nor is it easy or even possible to identify moles or would-be moles from external factors. Again, according to Szady, "We did a lot of looking into what makes a spy a spy. We had psychiatrists, psychologists, analysts, everybody in on this, and we had all the spies that were in custody interviewed. And we tried to come up, okay, how can we profile somebody who's going to be a spy?

"At the end of the day, the conclusion was: we can't. They're all different, and we all react differently to the problems that often cause spies to sell out to the opposition. Whether they're financial, emotional, psychological, whatever they are, some people handle the problems and move on. Others say, 'This is easy. I can take this information and make money. I need money and I won't be caught.' Still others say, 'I hate these people I work with,' or 'I should have been promoted and I wasn't,' or 'I'm a better spy than those idiots will ever know.'

"The fact is, you can't profile, and that's why it used to break me up when everybody said, 'Oh, you should have known it was Hanssen.' That's total nonsense. No, we shouldn't have known. We couldn't have known."[14]

Maybe or maybe not. A few people, some very close to Hanssen, will claim in the aftermath to have had glimmers along the way. But a culture built on trust and arrogant about it—especially compared to its longtime rival across the Potomac River in Langley, Virginia—would seem to be particularly susceptible to what the Greek tragedians called *hubris*, the sin of overwhelming pride. And Bob Hanssen fits in there snug as a bug in a rug.

"Here's something the FBI learned from the CIA," Mike Rochford tells me. "The CIA had been historically penetrated, and the Rick Ames case forced it into a new era of tighter compartmentalization on the most sensitive cases. They chose to continue doing their jobs of recruiting assets but operating below the radar of the enemy.

"How do you do that? You make the assumption that your organization is always penetrated, and you superimpose the strictest of compartmentalization standards whereby you shut down rumor mills and casually sharing knowledge of compartmented cases. Informal access to knowledge of sensitive recruitment cases is shut down as best you can.

"The FBI had not historically been penetrated enough for us to adopt this kind of strict compartmentation. So we tended to be sharing things with friends and fellow agents over drinks and in car pools, and we created informal, casual, almost conversational access to sensitive cases through trusting another person just because they were fellow agents.

"Guys like Hanssen took advantage of that openness. It was a harsh lesson."[15]

One telling example of the way the CIA and FBI differ in their application of the trust principle is that during his nearly twenty-five-year career with the Bureau, Hanssen is never once required to submit to a polygraph test despite, according to the IG report, "his extraordinarily broad access to extremely sensitive human and technical intelligence information from across the intelligence community."[16]

If Hanssen were a CIA officer, polygraphing would be a regular part of his life, and almost certainly an intrusion if not a full brake on his spying. The CIA begins using the polygraph as a screening tool for new recruits not long after World War II, shortly after it is organized out of the Office of Strategic Services, and eventually expands the practice to include contractors and the validation of operational assets. By the 1990s, people with the most sensitive access—CIA officers akin in rank and experience to Hanssen—are being polygraphed every five years.

But Hanssen is an FBI agent, not a CIA officer, and that world is far different. The Bureau doesn't implement a polygraph program until 1978, three decades after the CIA, and then only for interrogating suspects in criminal cases. In the mid-1980s, the practice is extended to agents in sensitive positions (again, Hanssen for example) but enforcement is scattered at best and never applied to the one person in the Bureau who has the most to hide. After Aldrich Ames's arrest in 1994, the FBI's Intelligence Branch advocates a random polygraph program, which is rejected by FBI senior management. But lie-detector testing is finally instituted for new recruits, eighteen years after Hanssen joins the Bureau and thirteen years after he first starts subverting its mission.

Furthermore, Hanssen is never asked to complete a detailed financial disclosure form during his entire FBI career, a request routinely made of officers in other agencies involved in intelligence-related work. Splashy living tips the CIA to Rick Ames, but a thorough examination of his financial records is what predicates investigating him. Currency transaction records show three large outlays—cash expenditures for a house, a car, and major home renovations. Investigators also employ rarely used national security letters available to intelligence agencies for just this purpose, to gain access to Ames's bank account, credit card transactions, and loans. Following Ames's arrest in 1994, the CIA even creates a special branch to focus on personnel considered potential security risks because of financial anomalies.

The FBI has the same basic tool kit available to its investigators, but they never bring them to bear on Hanssen, and thus never know about his ever-growing passbook savings account, which is in his own name, in a bank around the corner from Headquarters. Hanssen's managers and coworkers might wonder how he manages to send all five children through private schools and eventually on to college on a special agent's salary, but in the absence of obvious frivolous extravagances, they either buy into his vague stories about being a sharp investor and family inheritances or, just as likely, they don't much care.

Many of Bob Hanssen's colleagues want to think about him as little as possible, and the FBI as a whole seems to do just that beginning in early 1995, once he is assigned to be the Bureau's State Department liaison. During Hanssen's six years in that post, he has no supervisor, files no reports, and receives no performance reviews. True, he is subjected to his first background investigation in 1996—two decades into his FBI career—but that is a sham all too typical of the Bureau's perfunctory personnel investigations generally. To quote from the IG report:

> The system in place for background reinvestigations discouraged thoroughness. The principal investigators were not given access to the necessary source materials, such as the employee's personnel file, security file, and credit reports, and they primarily interviewed references supplied by the employee.
>
> They did not interview the employee. Moreover, the principal investigators merely collected information; they were not required to provide analysis or to make investigative recommendations. As a result, information developed through background reinvestigations received little analysis.[17]

The reality is much uglier than that. The special investigators who do these background checks are mostly retired FBI agents working on contract, and they are required to use a format developed during the J. Edgar Hoover years known by the acronym CARLABFAD after the nine topics to be covered in the investigative report: the subject's character, associates, responsibility, loyalty, ability, bias and prejudice, financial responsibility, alcohol use, and drug use.

The rote format predictably encourages rote questioning. Investigators will sometimes simply ask an agent if a fellow agent was "CARLABFAD" and get it all over with in one answer. (Given that most interviewees had been recommended by the subject being investigated, odds of acing the CARLABFAD test are high.) Not surprisingly, such rote questioning also often leads to autopilot reports dictated to one of four FBI typing centers around the country, submitted to case managers for review, and then buried in another file added to the mountain of files within the FBI that no one will ever look at again, except maybe after the fact—if someone is arrested for espionage, for example.

Hanssen's 1996 background check does have its moments. One supervisor tells the investigator that Hanssen is in the "doghouse" with an assistant director about an issue related to a foreign intelligence service. A coworker says he's a "maverick" with his "own ideas on things" who doesn't always "toe the line" with management. Another reference describes Hanssen as "intense" with a "mixed reputation," and another supervisor calls him "unusual."[18] One interviewee notes that he is a friend of a Soviet defector, and the defector is, in fact, an interesting person: Victor Sheymov, a one-time Russian spy who has successfully resettled in northern Virginia and founded Invicta, a firm that provides encryption services to the government and private enterprise. But it is all words to the wind. No follow-up is done on any part of it.

Nor is there follow-up on any interviewee references to Hanssen's financial situation. Two people tell the investigator that Hanssen's children attended college on academic scholarships, a third says Bonnie is from a wealthy family that assists with such costs, and a fourth hints that Hanssen has money troubles. More words to the wind, but also a reflection of the dismally low profile security generally has at the FBI, just as Bob Hanssen is itching to get back in the spy game once more. Between 1994 and 2000, the number of personnel assigned to the Security Countermeasures Branch actually declines by 18 percent, according to the Webster Commission. As of August 2001, a half year after Hanssen's arrest, six-tenths of one percent of the total FBI staff is devoted to security.

Of all the FBI's Hanssen-related failures cited in the IG report, polygraphing is probably the most controversial. Longtime agents, those who arrived in the Bureau before entry-level polygraphing, tend not to favor them. Jim Ohlson, who retires as head of security in the Counterintelligence Division—with responsibility for granting clearances—tells me that excessive polygraphing and other forms of intrusive monitoring creates an "organization filled with cookie-cutter people who don't have any creativity."

Polygraphing "is a quick reaction that makes everybody feel good. But in the end, you're eroding trust and not even knowing it."[19]

Lie detectors are also far from 100 percent reliable. In fact, they are basically higher-tech voodoo, according to the American Academy of Sciences. For the most part, results are inadmissible in courts unless all parties involved in the proceedings waive objections.[20]

Dave Szady adds that polygraphing isn't all that successful at the CIA either, despite (or maybe because of) its broad use. "When I first went to the CIA [as head of the joint FBI-CIA Counterintelligence Group], the Counterintelligence Evaluation Branch was responsible for investigating failed polygraphs and trying to clear them up before they are referred to the FBI. When I went over there, we had three hundred of these cases. Three hundred!

"George Tenet asked me about why such a high number, and I said, 'We don't have three hundred spies; we have three hundred people having problems passing the polygraph. Probably none of them are spies.'

"You have CIA officers who have been in the organization for years and involved in all types of operations around the world—giving and taking information, maybe illegally, given the countries that they are in—and they're trying to pass these polygraphs, and for some reason, they are failing them. Then they're investigated, and their careers go on hold even though the only evidence is a failed polygraph.

"I remember someone telling me, 'Well, you know, there's about 5 percent of the people taking the polygraph who have false reactions, or we can never know whether they are lying or telling the truth.'

"You have to look at it and say, 'It's a tool. It's only as good as the person giving it.' A lot of times, the CIA officers would run into a young polygrapher who wouldn't have any idea what these officers have been through over the years."

All granted. Still, the intelligence community knows by the late 1980s that a mole in one of its component parts is sending American assets within the Soviet intelligence services to the slaughterhouse. The intelligence community can deduce from the assets lost that the mole somehow has access to a broad array of highly classified information and thus sits atop or near one of those crossroads that every multiparty information network creates.

How many people fit that description? Hundreds surely, maybe more, but within the FBI component of the intelligence community, Bob Hanssen fits it very well. He has bragged about his broad access in his second communication with the KGB's Victor Cherkashin: "Please recognize for our long-term interests that there are a limited number of persons with this array of clearances. As a collection they point to me."[21]

And yet no one ever "flutters" Bob Hanssen, to borrow a term popular with spy novelists. Who knows what they might have found? Indeed, if the story Eric O'Neill is told by a trusted FBI source is accurate, the Bureau does almost precisely the opposite.

"He told me that Bureau asked Hanssen to put together a list of people who potentially could be GRAYSUIT. Hanssen, he said, put together a great list, and all of them pointed way far away from Hanssen himself. Then he had a huge amount of fun watching the FBI chase its tail all across the country."[22]

The only thing that might keep Hanssen from committing espionage once he is inside the henhouse and armed with his special-agent badge is a personal sense of honor, but if he has one, it isn't to the FBI or to the nation he professes to love or to the values of the church he seems to hold so dear.

While Hanssen is the reason for and focus of the 2003 IG report, its authors can't help but note that the weaknesses within the Bureau's internal processes that Hanssen exploits—the FBI's inability to account for some of its most sensitive documents, its failure to limit access to those documents to those with a need-to-know, and the ironbound trust culture that underlies all this—have been a subject of long-standing concern. With Hanssen, though, those weaknesses are a two-edged sword: they make it easier for him to commit his mole work, and they make the mole harder to find once its existence becomes unignorable.

According to the IG report: "This deficiency is significant with respect to both deterrence and detection, because the FBI's inability to account for its most sensitive documents makes an access-based investigation for an FBI mole extremely difficult to pursue. The starting point for any such investigation is a list of those employees who had access to a compromised operation; at the FBI, that determination is often impossible to make."[23]

Bottom line: Bob Hanssen may or may not be a perfect spy, but he has found a near-perfect environment to pursue his treason.

CHAPTER 11

PUFFS OF SMOKE

I t's 5:00 A.M. on the morning of August 23, 1988, when Clyde Lee Conrad Jr. is rousted from his bed in Bad Kreuznach, West Germany, and charged with multiple counts of high treason and espionage on behalf of the Hungarian and Czechoslovakian intelligence services, who themselves have been feeding Conrad's espionage product to the Soviets.

Almost simultaneously, all around the world, FBI and military intelligence agents fan out to interview any and all known associates of Conrad, especially during his time as custodian of often top-secret and higher documents at the 8th Infantry Division headquarters at Bad Kreuznach.

Joe Navarro is one of those called to action, paired up with army intelligence agent Al Eways, to interview former Conrad associate Roderick Ramsay, then living just outside Tampa, Florida. In all, it should be a routine morning. Conrad has lots of former associates, and agents conduct these "informational" interviews all the time. But the first time Al Eways mentions Clyde Lee Conrad by name, Navarro notes something potentially interesting: the steady contrail of smoke from Ramsay's almost omnipresent cigarette wavers just a bit, a slight tic of the hand.

Navarro waits until Ramsay seems at ease again, then introduces Conrad's name himself, with the same result: the smoke trail takes another brief, sharp turn. A third repetition of the same small phenomenon convinces Navarro that Ramsay bears further investigation.

Four years later, and two years after Conrad begins serving a life sentence, Navarro is finally able to prove beyond a reasonable doubt that Rod Ramsay had been an integral part of the spy ring, and in August 1992, a Florida court sentences him to thirty-six years in prison.

The point being twofold: First, Robert Philip Hanssen isn't the only American spy during the 1980s and 1990s to endanger life on this planet. Among the treasures Conrad bestows on the Soviets are American nuclear launch codes. And second, such spies do sometimes, maybe even often, get caught and are brought to justice, but in the absence of a source within the enemy's intelligence network, reeling them in requires attention to detail. The FBI, in effect, serves as Hanssen's own force multiplier. It doesn't seem to notice a thing, or, just as often, it chooses not to see what is in front of its own eyes or finds a pretense to excuse it away.

Ray Mislock, then serving as chief of the FBI's Eurasian Section including Russia, gets the shock of his life one day in 1993 when Bob Hanssen walks into his office at FBI headquarters, hands him a sheet of paper, and says, "You didn't believe me that the system was insecure."

"It was an exact copy of a document I had just written on my computer," Mislock will later recall. "I think it was a memo I was writing to the director. The memo was sensitive, and classified."[1]

Mislock is understandably enraged, but not at Hanssen. Instead he goes charging into the office of Harry "Skip" Brandon, who bears responsibility for computer security in the Intelligence Branch. "We had a very animated conversation," as Mislock tells it. "I was really ripshit." From there, still ripped, he storms off to the counterespionage wing, where he spends the next half hour disconnecting all the computers from the local area network.

Finally, Mislock and Brandon end up in Bob Hanssen's office, where Hanssen happily and proudly shows them exactly how he has hacked Mislock's memo. Soon enough, the vulnerability is fixed, Hanssen's reputation as the go-to guy for all things computing is further burnished, and what Mike Rochford terms a "puff of smoke"—a little inkling of the future—disappears into the mists of the J. Edgar Hoover Building.

Only in retrospect will Mislock dwell on how he has been played. Hanssen, Mislock speculates, "went in to look and see if there was anything to indicate he was being watched. He had to come up with a story to explain why he was in the system in case there was some tracking software he didn't know about. So he came forward and was the person who pointed to the vulnerability."[2]

Indeed, there is such software. Every keystroke on FBI computers is recoverable . . . if anyone goes searching for them.

Another puff of smoke: At just about the same time, not many doors away in what has become the nerve center of Major Case 43—soon to be the Aldrich Ames case—Jim Holt is sitting at his computer writing an eyes-only note to the assistant director about the squad's findings to date, unaware that down the hallway in the Analytical Group, Bob Hanssen has hacked into his computer, too. This time, the only reason anyone knows about the incursion is because another analyst sees Holt's note printing out with Hanssen looking on. Mike Rochford remembers the aftermath.

"'You can't do that,' this guy told Hanssen. 'That's not right. What are you doing?'

"And Bob says, 'I'm just trying to show how vulnerable the Bureau is. It's a new computer system, and I'm going to fix it.' And this guy says, 'You better go tell the section chief you've done this, or I will,' so Bob goes and reports it to I. C. Smith."[3]

Except by I. C. Smith's own testimony, Hanssen never reports the hack to him. Nor does anyone ever follow up with Smith to see if Hanssen has. "I would think a responsible person would have ensured that occurred," Smith says. If anyone did try to do so, the record has long since dried up, and the damage to Hanssen himself is minimal to nonexistent.[4]

Mike Rochford remembers a discussion about whether to fire Hanssen in the wake of this second hack and that the discussion went nowhere. "They figured, well, he's just a broken-wing employee who went beyond the scope of what he was assigned to do. He took more initiative than anyone was comfortable with."[5] Which sounds a great deal like the rationale David Major offers up when I ask him about the hacks.

"A lot of people made a big deal about Mislock's hacked computer," Major says, "but there's a story behind it. When I came back from the White House in 1987, we didn't have an intranet at our Headquarters, so we couldn't communicate with each other. People didn't want to have it, and there was great resistance from management, but finally the computer unit gets it set up. And Bob looks at it and says, 'This system is not secure. It's a bad system.'

"We say back to him, 'Bob, it's not your job. They'll get it done.' But he keeps saying, 'No, it's a bad system. The people working on it are not capable of doing it.'

"So he goes into his computer and immediately hacks into Ray Mislock's computer, prints out the report, and brings it to Ray's office. He wasn't hacking in to get intelligence. He was trying to make the Bureau better, which was one of the dichotomies of Bob Hanssen. He was trying to show us we needed to do something different."[6]

Or maybe Hanssen was trying to prove he's the smartest person on either side of Pennsylvania Avenue, and also—as Ray Mislock suggests retrospectively—covering his backside just in case.

Literally, when Hanssen is performing this hacking wizardry, he is no longer a spy, or, more accurately, he's a retired spy. Hanssen has been lying low ever since the USSR collapsed in 1991, waiting to see what, if any, secrets might bubble out of Moscow's Lubyanka Square, the epicenter of the vast Soviet intelligence network. By 1993, though, post-Soviet Russia appears to be settling down, the old itch is on Hanssen, and his internal surveillance of FBI files seems to convince him that the coast is clear.

That same employer-supplied surveillance has also left Hanssen somewhat mystified. Over his previous years of spying, he has handed the Russians a virtually complete roster of all double agents the FBI and US military services are running, often as joint operations. The resolution of such matters is predictable: imprisonment, maybe torture and a grisly death as with TOPHAT. But the record clearly shows that a number of the joint operations he has ratted out continue unimpeded. Why?

Unable to control his curiosity or maybe offended that his spy product is being discounted or just missing the rush of it all and seeing the bills piling up after more than a year on the sidelines, Hanssen decides to get back in the action—and all but offers himself up for arrest, or might well have done so in a more technologically competent organization.

The problem is the spy politics of the new Russia. The natural organization for Hanssen to approach would be the SVR, successor to the KGB, for which he had spied so successfully for about fifteen years. The SVR, though, has become almost a liaison operation with the FBI as Boris Yeltsin's new Russian government tries to play nice with the US intelligence community. That isn't the case with the GRU, the military intelligence wing that Hanssen had first spied for back in 1981, and thus it's the GRU that Hanssen chooses to approach. And there's the problem.

Don Sullivan, then with the FBI's GRU unit and a friend of Hanssen's from their time together in the New York field office, explains, "After the Soviet Union collapsed, the GRU just kept marching on—very aggressive. The theory was the Yeltsin government didn't know what the GRU was up to, so we figured if we started kicking out some of their officers who were doing bad things, that would bring GRU to the attention of the Yeltsin people, then hopefully they would tell the GRU to stand down and this irritant to our relations would be removed. So we were being very aggressive ourselves in terms of catching their officers in the act—dead-drops, things like that—and kicking them out."[7]

And right in the middle of that process is when Hanssen searches the FBI computer system for the address of any Washington-based GRU agent who happens to live elsewhere than in the Soviet compound and comes upon a Mr. Belyayev, living in an apartment building in Bethesda, Maryland, just north of the DC line. That's where he approaches Belyayev, in the underground garage of the building, and introduces himself as Ramon Garcia, "a disaffected FBI agent," and offers to resume his spying.

To prove his bona fides, Hanssen has brought along a package of documents including meeting summaries of all open Russian double-agent cases that he has only recently purloined from his old haunt at the Soviet Analytical Unit, but the meeting doesn't go as planned. Thinking he is being set up, Belyayev tells Hanssen to get lost, and the Russian embassy soon thereafter files an official protest with the US State Department, which refers the matter to the FBI—Hanssen having conveniently identified himself as coming from there—where it lands on Don Sullivan's desk.

"It's not often a spy agency takes a volunteer and turns them over to the host country," Sullivan says. "It's very rare, but we were kicking the shit out of them and had them scared to death. So they did give him up, but not with a lot of detail. When we went asking for more information, the GRU had second thoughts about turning him in and pretty much shut up and wouldn't tell us anything else."[8] Such as, for example, that the would-be spy is several inches over six feet tall, dresses like a mortician, has a ghoulish manner, and speaks in a low, almost whispering voice.

"At that point, there was an espionage investigation opened, but there wasn't a lot to go on," Sullivan says. "I got a request from the WFO [Washington field office] to do a search of the house computer system to see who might have looked up this particular GRU officer's address. So I go to the computer people and say, 'This is what we're trying to do. Can you help?' And they say, 'No, we can't go into the system. We don't have that capacity.'

"The inspector general's report would later say we blew a chance to catch Hanssen at that point. No, we didn't. The problem was we were using yesterday's technology tomorrow, the way the FBI always did."

Whatever the reasons, as in the great tradition of Robert Hanssen leads and other puffs of smoke, this one goes nowhere, too. Robert Hanssen is a devastating spy—there's no question about that—and he's made all the more devastating by the two-decades-plus that the FBI mostly ignores him in its ranks and papers over his peculiarities. But is Hanssen the master spy he aspires to be and almost certainly thinks he is?

The 2003 report by the Justice Department inspector general that probes deeply into the Hanssen case pulls no punches in its assessment of his espionage talents: "Although Hanssen escaped detection for more than 20 years, this was not because he was a 'master spy.' While Hanssen took some important steps to maintain his security—such as refusing to reveal his identity to his Russian handlers—and used his knowledge of the FBI's counterintelligence practices and poor internal security to his advantage, much of Hanssen's conduct when committing espionage was reckless."[9]

The inspector general's report goes on to specify that recklessness. Some items have already been mentioned: Hanssen's almost incomprehensible suggestion that the KGB try to recruit his best friend for capital crimes; his ill-considered 1993 garage approach to the Russians in which he revealed he was an FBI agent; his wanton abuse of the FBI's in-house ACS system and its electronic case files.

Other items in the report describe Hanssen's learning curve in the early days of his espionage. Unable to rein in his techie impulses, Hanssen rigs up an FBI camera to cover the drop site he uses for exchanges during his early dalliance with the GRU. Still, getting back in the game in 1986, he uses an FBI telephone line and answering machine for communications with the KGB.

Rookie errors, one might say—anyone could make them—but the inspector general's broad conclusion must have been equally devastating to Hanssen's own ego and to that of the super-proud, super-American institution that employed him: "In sum, Hanssen escaped detection not because he was extraordinarily clever and crafty, but because of long-standing systemic problems in the FBI's counterintelligence program and a deeply flawed FBI internal security program."[10]

What's really devastating, though, is the analysis that follows. Here's how it begins:

In our review, we observed serious deficiencies in nearly every aspect of the FBI's internal security program, from personnel security, to computer security, document security, and security training and compliance. These deficiencies led to the absence of effective deterrence to espionage at the FBI and undermined the FBI's ability to detect an FBI mole. Moreover, the absence of deterrence played a significant role in Hanssen's decision to commit espionage. As he explained during debriefings: "If I had thought that the risk of detection was very great, I would never have done it." Hanssen also exploited many of these weaknesses—particularly in document and computer security—to pass sensitive information to the KGB.[11]

Which brings us back to Mike Rochford's puffs of smoke once again. They are, in fact, manyfold and widely varied.

In 1985, Rochford is detailed to work with Vitaly Yurchenko, the high-ranking KGB officer who has defected to the United States and immediately fingers two American intelligence officers—Ronald Pelton and Edward Lee Howard—then working for the Soviets. Soon thereafter, in November 1985, Yurchenko redefects back to Russia (accompanied by Valery Martynov, on his last flight as a free man), leaving in doubt perhaps forever who exactly he has been working for and to what ends. Either way, Bob Hanssen, who resumes contact with the Soviets that September, has an outsized interest in the case that he makes little effort to hide.

As he often does, Hanssen tries to insert himself into the process, hanging around the office of Ed Worthington, who is responsible for distributing transcripts of the debriefings with Yurchenko to the major field offices, and repeatedly offering his services as a courier to speed the transcripts between Washington, DC, and New York. Finally, Worthington has had enough, according to Mike Rochford.

"He tells Hanssen, 'No, you're not doing that. I'm going to put it in the mail. Now, get the hell out of my office.' So Ed goes down to take a pee, and as he's walking back, he sees Hanssen copying the Yurchenko transcript on the Xerox machine. He puts his finger in his face and says, 'What the hell! Don't you know what *no* means?' And he grabs the documents and puts them back on his desk.

"Now that's culpability. That's something that should be reported. But there was no mechanism within the Bureau at that time to report anomalous activities of a security nature. There was never even a security division until after Hanssen. Ed did all the right things afterward. He told the right people, but it never went anywhere. Another little puff of smoke."[12] Which, if reported and amassed, might have added up to a large column of smoke or at least the sort of broken contrail Joe Navarro took notice of, but it never was and never did.

Another example, this one from Hanssen's brother-in-law Mark Wauck from the late 1980s when Mark is detailed to the New York field office and Bob is back in Washington with the Soviet Analytical Unit.

"We were preparing to bring a Russian source out of New York. Bob was totally in the loop because the Analytical Unit down in Washington was getting copies of all the incoming telexes. He called me at home one night—unusual, we weren't really on chit-chat terms at all—and started talking about our plans in New York. I was shocked because we had all been drilled that there was no such thing as a secure call except on our own dedicated lines between New York and DC. The Russians monitored all phone calls between the two cities. After he was arrested, I came to assume that Bob was trying to use me to tip the Russians, knowing they would be listening in. I refused to discuss it with him and specifically rebuked him on the phone, but he just brushed it off, saying those security concerns were grossly exaggerated.

"I told my supervisor about it, but he just dropped it. This is how Bob skated by. He's a space cadet. He's so goofy. He does these things without thinking. It couldn't be because he's a traitor. In retrospect, of course, I should have raised holy hell, but even then, would anything have been done?"

Probably not, as evidenced by a few more puff-of-smoke moments.

★

By 1995, when Bob Hanssen is detailed to the State Department as the FBI's foreign mission liaison, there's no denying that the US intelligence community has been deeply penetrated. Rick Ames has already fallen. Harold Nicholson and Earl Pitts—CIA and FBI, respectively—will follow while Hanssen is still settling into his new job. Both agencies are awash in compromised agents and operations. One might think that antennae would be waving in both directions, but in this world, Hanssen is like antimatter, ever present yet undetectable by the normal tools even when, as in this case, he's caught in the act trying to hack into the new ECF/ACS computer system back in Headquarters.

"When he was at the Office of Foreign Missions, Bob had access to the new computer system we had set up, but he was limited in what he could read," David Major says. "He could get to the administrative side of my files, for example, but couldn't get to the heart of the file—the investigation. That was password-protected. So he took some password-busting software, added it to his computer, and got it all glitched up. Jim Ohlson, then director of security and a good friend of Bob, called him and said, 'What are you doing?' Bob said, 'I'm isolated here. I was just trying to do a better job,' and Ohlson says, 'Well, don't do that again.'

"Bob didn't know they had a system set up when he tried to enter a new program to bypass it, and he screwed it up. Management knew about that. That could have been a clue."[13] But to repeat an old refrain, it's just another puff of smoke—here one minute, gone the next.

Roughly simultaneously, when Hanssen's fellow FBI spy Earl Pitts is being debriefed as part of his plea-bargain agreement, he's asked if he knows of any other Bureau agents working for the Russians. No, he answers, not with certainty, but then says he has heard that Bob Hanssen hacked into an FBI computer. By then, though, Hanssen's proclivity for hacking is old news. What are you going to do? The guy's a genius. And impatient. And maybe has a screw or two loose. And, besides, he's a colossal pain to deal with.

Just for good measure, in this same general time frame—late 1994, not long before he is detailed to the State Department—Hanssen inquires about a position at the recently established National Counterintelligence Center, a joint FBI-CIA undertaking headquartered on the CIA campus at Langley, Virginia. The application is apparently approved, and Hanssen gets all the right blessings to insert himself right in the dead center of Secret City. But there's one problem he hasn't anticipated. Because the Center is plugged into the CIA computer system, employees there have to play by Agency rules, beginning with an initial polygraph and with regularly scheduled testing thereafter. No thanks, Hanssen says, and takes the polygraph-free State Department job instead.

(That story, by the way, comes from a 2010 email sent by the man who would ultimately be accused of Hanssen's crimes: Brian Kelley.)

And then there's the biggest puff of smoke of them all—the kind that suggests a raging fire just below the horizon. This isn't noticed, either. Or it's noticed and dies aborning. Or maybe just no one important enough really cares. You be the judge.

CHAPTER 12

"DO YOU THINK BOB COULD BE A KGB AGENT?"

It's late August 1990, and Bob Hanssen has a money problem: way too much of it. In February 1991, he receives $40,000 in cash from the KGB. In May, he receives another $35,000, and the spigot is still wide open. In just a few weeks, on September 3, he'll pocket an additional $40,000. Hanssen is awash in cash. The locked strongbox he keeps under his and Bonnie's bed is already straining the hinges with $100 bills. Where is he going to put it all?

To help alleviate the problem, Bob puts Bonnie on a no-credit-card diet. She has become a spendthrift, he tells her. Time for him to clamp down. From now on, when Bonnie buys the family groceries at Giant, she'll pay with $100 bills—unaware that the bills have been hand-counted out of the safe by the KGB's counterintelligence chief in the nation's capital.

He drags his mother, Vivian, into a more naked money-laundering operation, borrowing "clean" money from her for larger expenses, then paying her back with the KGB's dirty money. Does Vivian know she's being used this way? Probably not. But as with being Bob's wife, so being his mother involves a good measure of looking the other way. Vivian might have learned about primitive money laundering when her husband, Howard, came home from the track loaded with cash.

Bob is also making regular deposits into his passbook savings account at a bank only a few blocks from the FBI headquarters, but there's a problem here, too. The Bank Secrecy Act passed in the early 1970s is aimed mostly at organized crime—money laundering, forgery, tax evasion, and so on—but it poses challenges for a freelance spy as well, especially one compensated as Hanssen is in hard cash (and most are). The act mandates the filing of a suspicious activity report, or SAR, for cash deposits or withdrawals of $10,000 or more, in both savings and checking accounts. It further allows any teller who suspects unusual cash transactions to file a SAR on his or her own initiative regardless of the sum.

Legitimate businesses that deal mostly in cash—small retailers, for example—are excluded if they register with their bank, and not all tellers are alert all the time to SAR requirements. Still, the retired bank CEO I consulted on the matter, Dixon Whitworth, has no doubt what would have ensued if Hanssen tried to hide his KGB earnings en masse in a neighborhood bank: "A deposit of 150 $100 bills would guarantee a SAR report by any bank," he assures me. "So would twenty-five $100 bills deposited several days in a row."[1] Stowing his money a few thousand dollars at a time in his savings account is about the only option open to Hanssen other than burying his money in the backyard or cramming those wads of $100 bills into a succession of safety deposit boxes.

Bob Hanssen, in short, is in what might be called a "success trap," especially when his successes are mounting one on top of the other and the money is rolling in. Inevitably, there are going to be moments when the inflow exceeds the capacity to secretly conceal it, and that's what happens in late August 1990, at what proves to be a very inconvenient time.

Mark Wauck is many things: Bonnie Hanssen's brother; a good Catholic (almost a family calling); a lawyer by training and a religious scholar by avocation, with a well-received translation of the New Testament to his credit;

and, of course, an FBI agent. It's mostly in this last capacity that Mark; his wife, Mary Ellen; and their children visit Washington, DC, in August 1990.

The trip is a twofer. Mark is taking part in a two-week conference sponsored by the State Department on the Soviet Union and Eastern Europe, but this is also a long-overdue chance for a family reunion. Mark and Mary Ellen haven't seen Bob and Bonnie since the Hanssens moved back to Vienna, Virginia, in 1987, after their second tour of duty in New York. And Bob and Bonnie are only part of the draw. Mark's sister Jeanne Beglis, a child psychiatrist, and her husband, George, a building contractor and architect, live just up the block from the Hanssens on Talisman Drive. Jeanne, in fact, was the one who found the house for Bonnie and Bob, and George designed and oversaw its remodeling. The Waucks are a tight clan, welded together by faith, conservative politics, and, in this instance, proximity.

"The trip," Mark says, "was really a big deal, because it had been so long since we had last seen one another, and the cousins would be seeing each other pretty much for the first time. We stayed at a hotel in Rosslyn, Virginia [where the conference was being held]. I would go to class during the day, then take the Metro out to Vienna, where Mary Ellen and the kids usually spent the day with their sisters-in-law and cousins, respectively. Bonnie and Bob seemed to be doing well, but there was certainly nothing ostentatious about the way they lived, at least not to my eyes."

Subsequent events, though, will open those eyes a bit wider. "When we returned to Chicago," Mark continues, "Mary Ellen took me aside and told me of a conversation she had had with Jeanne. Jeanne was not in sympathy with Bonnie's devotion to Opus Dei, but she and Bonnie were always the best of friends. Jeanne had told Mary Ellen one day—and Mary Ellen's impression was that this was only a day or two earlier—that Bonnie had quite literally run up the street to Jeanne's house all in a lather.

"Bonnie had just discovered $5,000 in cash in Bob's sock drawer, or some other drawer, and had no idea where he would have gotten it. Jeanne also told Mary Ellen that Bob had lately been buying Bonnie what Jeanne considered to be expensive jewelry. Jeanne's exact words were to the effect that the jewelry was definitely not costume jewelry. Mary Ellen told me that Jeanne had seemed very troubled and thought Bob had some source of money that no one knew about."[2]

(Bonnie, it should be noted, would claim after Bob's arrest to have no memory of this event, but it is indelibly inked in her brother's mind.)

Maybe Bonnie's concern is sparked by Bob's previous side deal with the Soviets, but if so, she doesn't pass that on to Jeanne. And thus Jeanne doesn't add that little kicker when she tells the story to Mary Ellen or when she also relates the same information to Mark's older brother, Greg, a postal inspector in Philadelphia. But there seems to be an unspoken understanding within the Wauck family that Bob Hanssen is capable of almost anything.

"Within a day after we got back," Mark says, "my older brother called. 'Did you hear what Jeanne said?' he asked. So we discussed that, and he said to me, 'Do you think he could be a KGB agent?' It was the kind of thing we could imagine Bob doing."[3]

That conversation and the unexplained cash that sparks it dovetails—maybe *collides* is a better word—with Mark's lingering concern about another matter. In May 1985, Bonnie had called to congratulate Mark after he had been accepted at the CIA's Polish language school at Monterey, California.

"'Isn't that great!'" Mark remembers her saying. "'Bob says we may retire in Poland!' I was immediately disturbed by the idea that a high Bureau official deeply involved in counterintelligence would even entertain such views at the height of the Cold War, and I exclaimed: 'Bonnie, that's crazy!' On the other hand, I was also leery of Bonnie's well-known propensity for exaggeration and wrote her outburst off to hyperbolic admiration for the supposed religiosity of the Polish people and for Pope John Paul II, the first pope of Polish ethnicity."[4]

A third factor also enters in. Mark is stationed in Chicago, far from the details of the mole hunt now gathering steam on Pennsylvania Avenue, but the tom-toms beat as steadily at the FBI as they do in other large bureaucratic organizations, and a dim awareness of the mole hunt, while still shrouded in mystery, has begun seeping into the field offices as well as Headquarters.

Finally, Wauck says, in consultation with Mary Ellen, he decides to take his concerns to someone higher up the food chain, and here a whole new realm of concerns comes into play. "I knew that my suspicions could not be freely expressed. The enormity of the implications and the sensitivity of an investigation of a high Bureau official for espionage, as well as the incalculable harm that could be done to Bob and my relations with my family if my suspicions proved to be unfounded, convinced me that my actions would have to be more than ordinarily discrete. I couldn't risk my suspicions becoming the subject of Bureau gossip, as had the mole hunt."

Other complications factored in, as well. Mark Wauck was in Chicago. The mole hunt, if it even existed, was bound to be Headquarters-based. "After considering the alternatives," he continues, "I decided to inform a person who was not my supervisor, for several reasons. I selected a supervisor who had recently come to Chicago from FBI headquarters, who had worked Soviet matters there, and who was now in charge of Soviet matters in Chicago. If Bob was going to do espionage, I knew he would do it only with Russia, not Bulgaria or someplace like that [considering his previous work in the Soviet counterintelligence division at the New York field office]. He would want to deal with the top, so I chose someone in the Russian program."

And not only in the Russian program but also an agent well connected within the Bureau hierarchy and one he had worked with on Soviet matters in New York, even carpooled with. "These factors were important to me for two reasons. First, it meant that this supervisor knew me personally and would know my reputation, which has always been that of an intelligent, serious, and hardworking agent. In addition, it meant that the supervisor would also know Hanssen. This meant that the supervisor would know that the information was coming from a reliable source (myself) and would also be familiar with Hanssen's reputation as an unusual personality. Thus, two hurdles would be removed from the start, or so I thought."[5]

The supervisor Mark Wauck chooses to divulge his concerns to is Jim Lyle, and the "or so I thought" at the end of the last paragraph becomes important to the story.

The following account of the meeting that subsequently took place between Mark Wauck and Jim Lyle and its aftermath is stitched together from several lengthy interviews with Wauck plus numerous supporting documents that he later supplies.

"Within days of reaching my decision, I approached Jim Lyle at his office on the eighth floor of the FBI's Chicago field office and asked him to accompany me to a ninth-floor interview room to discuss a matter of great importance. The interview rooms are small and windowless, with only a desk and a couple of chairs. Ordinarily, we would have just closed the door to his office, but I very deliberately chose to inject this bit of melodrama into the proceedings because I wanted to impress on my supervisor the great seriousness of what I had to say.

"Once we were alone in the interview room, free from prying eyes and the possibility of interruption, I disclosed my suspicions and detailed what had aroused my concerns, repeatedly stressing the confluence of the money, Bonnie's mention of retiring to Poland, and my general awareness that a mole hunt was underway."

Jim Lyle, Wauck says, was under-impressed.

"I certainly didn't expect him to unquestionably accept everything I said, but I was somewhat surprised at his persistent skepticism. At some point, he asked me a direct question to the following effect: 'Do you understand the implications of what you're saying?'

"I replied affirmatively, specifically, and quite deliberately, using the word *espionage* for its shock value and to leave no doubt of my seriousness. I said I was aware that I was suggesting Robert Philip Hanssen should be investigated for espionage. My position wasn't that I knew Bob to be definitely engaged in espionage but that, based on the known facts, it was a reasonable conclusion in the circumstances, and there were no factors that I knew of that would dispel the suspicion."

According to Wauck, the meeting ends amicably, with Lyle agreeing to carry the matter forward. "Under the circumstances, I felt confident this meant he would bring it to the attention of Bureau authorities. I simply could not imagine that any Bureau employee could fail to pass suspicions of such a grave nature on to higher responsible officials . . . I never learned any further information that I thought was relevant. I made no follow-up inquiries, partly because Bob made a number of comments that, probably mistakenly, led me to believe that he had been confronted in some way, perhaps even polygraphed, but also because, in any event, I had no idea where I should direct such queries. As the years went on, I assumed Bob had been cleared and my suspicions had, fortunately, been unfounded. I still believed that I had had no other choice but to report my suspicions but was understandably happy that nothing had come of them."[6]

Jim Lyle's account of the same events—also stitched together from a lengthy interview—is so diametrically opposed to Mark Wauck's version that the two don't seem to exist on the same planet, but of course they do.

There are two things to clear up at the outset, Lyle tells me. First, "I was Wauck's supervisor when we had this conversation, not some outside supervisor he turned to. Mark had been working in the Polish squad, but he had filed a complaint against that supervisor, and besides, the Polish program was floundering generally, given that the Warsaw Pact nations were falling apart. With all that going on, Mark expressed a preference to come to my Russia squad, and I took him on as a favor to my boss, Wags [aka Mike Waguespack]."

Second, "I've never been in an interview room with Mark Wauck. Our conversation, if you can even call it that, took place in a very specific spot of the squad area in the Chicago field office. Where we were is important because that could have occurred only in 1992—we moved to that area in February or March of that—not in late 1990 or early 1991 as Mark contends."[7]

According to Lyle, the encounter in question began almost as obliquely as it could. He had stopped by the squad area to see the agent who sat next to Wauck, by a window. Finding his desk empty, Lyle left him a "see-me" note.

"I was turning to go away," he says, "when Mark said, 'Could I run something by you, to get your opinion?' And I said 'Sure.' So Mark started saying something about how he had learned through family—his wife, as I recall, who heard it from Bonnie's sister—that Bob's wife had found some cash in one of Bob's dresser drawers, and she didn't know where it came from. I seem to recall he said $3,000. But again, this was secondhand knowledge from Mark—hearsay.

"I said, 'Well, she's married to the guy. Why doesn't she ask him? Did she?' And Mark shrugged his shoulders and said, 'I don't know.' So I said, 'Is there a problem with that? A lot of people might have cash in a drawer for some reason or another.'

"Keep in mind that I knew nothing about a mole hunt at this point. I knew nothing about source compromises in Washington. I didn't know any of that, and this just came up: I'd heard secondhand that Bob's wife found some cash in a drawer and didn't know why it's there. I don't even recall his telling me there's a problem.

"The only other thing I remember his bringing up was that Bonnie had concerns about Bob's having a relationship with a Russian defector [Victor Sheymov, previously mentioned]. They had apparently been talking about going into business together after Bob retired or something along those lines.

"Well, Bob Hanssen was head of the Soviet Analytical Unit at Headquarters. A lot of those analyst guys talk with and have relationships with Russian defectors. The mere fact that Bob had a relationship with a defector, not an onboard KGB officer, didn't strike me as unusual.

"I recall ending it by saying, 'If Bonnie's got a problem, why doesn't she talk to Bob about it?' And I don't recall Mark illuminating anything else for me. If anyone says that I said I was going to launch an investigation, that's fiction. I came away from that thinking only, *What was that all about?*

"I'm a literal guy. Maybe not the brightest bulb in the box, but not the dullest or dumbest, either. If Mark had told me that he and his family had concerns that Bob was living beyond his means and might be involved in espionage with the Russians, I would have had him explain that to me. And if he told me about a mole hunt in Washington, I would have said, 'Come on, we're going to see the ASAC [assistant special agent in charge]' because if there is such as issue, we won't be looking at that in Chicago.

"But he never came to me to report anything. He struck up a conversation with me while I was standing beside his desk. He asked me for an opinion, and I said I don't have an opinion."[8]

Stylistically, Mark Wauck and Jim Lyle are very different people. Wauck is more openly cerebral, an academic who somehow washed up in the old Beer, Guts, and Glory FBI. Lyle is amused by memories of Mark wandering around the New York field office in his stocking feet—just like, well, an academic.

Lyle, Wauck says, plays the "Aw, shucks, I'm just a dumb hillbilly" card a little too often. He has a fondness for reducing complex subjects down to quotes from George Patton, as memorably played by George C. Scott in the 1970 biopic *Patton*.

Inevitably, too, the deep rift in memories between the two has led to some harsh words. Jim Lyle speculates that the new and improved version of their 1992 conversation that Wauck fed to investigators after Hanssen's arrest is his "get out of jail free" card: *See, you can't blame my brother-in-law on me. I did everything I could to bring this to the Bureau's attention.*

Lyle does remember hearing about a related 1990 conversation, but not one in which he took part. "One of the IG report investigators interviewed an agent who said that Mark asked them once in the squad area, 'I've got a hypothetical for you. What would you do if you had information about somebody . . .' and went on to lay out a scenario similar to the one he told me but with no names attached."[9]

Lyle also wonders if Bob Hanssen curtailed his spying in late 1991 not because the Soviet Union was collapsing but because Wauck family members, consciously or not, tipped Bob to their concerns.

For his part, Mark Wauck believes Jim Lyle must have at least stated his concerns about his brother-in-law somewhere upward in the thick FBI hierarchy. "What's the first rule of a bureaucracy?" he says. "CYA! Cover your ass. Lyle must have sent it up the chain at least as far as his boss, Wags."[10] Where it went from there, though, is anyone's guess. Maybe nowhere. Wauck speculates that the reason both Lyle and Wags depart the FBI just about the time the post-arrest inspector general's report comes out is all the evidence needed that the IG has sided with his version of events. The dates on that, though, don't quite match up.

Whoever is right and to what degree, though, is not the real issue. The real issue is that the FBI not only has little capacity to recognize these internal puffs of smoke but also has little interest at either the macro- or the microlevel in pursuing them once they do arise—and little capacity to do so as well.

CHAPTER 13

SUMO WRESTLING

If Mark Wauck's mistrust of his own brother-in-law is just an odd blip on the radar screen, then maybe ultimately nobody is to blame. Not everyone loves their in-laws. Families have issues. Even big clues sometimes get overlooked in the crush of events. But this is more than run-of-the-mill mistrust in an institution built on its opposite premise. Mark Wauck himself describes the telephone call from his brother Greg on the day following Bob Hanssen's arrest as follows:

"'Well,' Greg says, 'surprised, but not surprised.' He was willing to talk in those terms, and I was willing to listen."[1]

Remember, these are brothers-in-law of the accused, and Mark Wauck is not the exception at the FBI. Yes, lots of people are shocked when Hanssen proves to be the mole—or, more accurately, lots of people are shocked that the mole comes from the Bureau, not out at Langley in the spy-riddled CIA. But years before that moment, a lot of people didn't trust Bob Hanssen much further than they could throw him, while the few who did trust him implicitly seem willing to overlook any evidence that their faith was misplaced.

"I don't know an agent who ever invited Hanssen out for an arrest or trusted him enough to tell him who they were targeting," Mike Rochford says.

After the big stir over Hanssen's hacking of Jim Holt's computer—and after the apparent lack of repercussions for the same—Rochford says, "Those of us who were working on penetration issues in that unit decided that if they're not going to take action against him, let's do a little guerilla warfare. If we see him in the bathroom, if we see him in the hall, we're going to walk the other way. If we see him in our office, we're going to kick his ass out. And we don't tell him anything off-line. Not that we thought he was a spy—we didn't. We just thought he was a little different."[2]

But does anyone check with I. C. Smith to see if Hanssen actually reports his hacking as instructed? No, just as Mark Wauck never checks over the next ten or so years to see if the serious concerns he raised about his brother-in-law ever get beyond Jim Lyle. There's a space somewhere in the middle of the Bureau where all troubling news about Bob Hanssen seems to gather and die a natural death.

I. C. Smith himself tells a similar story from his time as Chinese section chief with the Intelligence Branch. Hanssen was dripping with ambient mistrust, he says, but the defenses against him were all localized.

"When Hanssen was over at the State Department, he was told that he should come to Headquarters for meetings of section chiefs. Well, I frankly wouldn't talk about anything that was sensitive in those meetings because of his presence. I didn't think he was a spy, but there's a time-honored tradition in the intelligence community—'need to know'—and he did not have a need-to-know for a whole lot of things that were discussed in those meetings. We'd go to the meetings, and there would be Hanssen with that dour look on his face, and those black suits, and that arch visage, and I just refused to talk about anything that was sensitive."

In fact, Hanssen did have a need-to-know, but that was his high-paying avocation, not his steady-check vocation.

Yet another senior agent who worked closely with Hanssen on a small team and cannot be named because he is still operational, says the same thing. "We didn't trust Hanssen, not because we thought he was a spy but because he was terribly indiscreet. We were not inclined to give him inside details of what we were doing. He would often talk about our investigations and sources with people who had no need-to-know. There wasn't a level of trust there."[3]

How many "not because we thought he was spy" statements does it take to add up to "maybe he might be a spy"? Apparently a great many.

During Bob Hanssen's nearly a quarter century with the FBI, he does have one meltdown that is all but impossible to ignore. By early 1993, Hanssen has risen high enough through the ranks to become chief of the FBI's National Security Threat List Unit, also within the Intelligence Branch, operating out of the Headquarters building. The title is long and the work certainly important, but the unit is lightly staffed with a few other agents and a small handful of clerical workers, including Kimberly Lichtenberg.

Lichtenberg will later say that Hanssen gives her the creeps—that he likes to brush up against her and lean in to her whenever he gets the chance, that he stares down at her as she sits at her desk, the usual predatory office behaviors. But that isn't the trigger point here, at least not directly.

At 3:30 on the afternoon of February 25, Hanssen summons Lichtenberg and an unnamed typist to his office. There has been unrest among the clerical staff, and Hanssen intends to get to the bottom of it. Lichtenberg says she tells him she knows nothing about the situation, but Hanssen persists. Finally, as the time nears 4:00, the secretary faces a dilemma. Lichtenberg commutes into DC from just south of Baltimore, thirty miles away. If she doesn't leave immediately, she will miss her car pool ride and have no easy way to get home.

"I said, 'I have to leave to catch my van,'" she recalls. "I turned and walked out. I thought the meeting was over. It was a little before four, when I usually leave. I was not being flippant. I was respectful."[4]

Hanssen, though, obviously thinks otherwise. Lichtenberg has almost covered the thirty feet or so between Hanssen's office and her work cubicle, when her boss catches up with her and shouts, "Get back here!" Then he grabs her by the arm, spins her around so hard that she loses her balance and falls to the floor, and begins dragging her back toward his office. Finally, Lichtenberg staggers back on her feet, slugs Hanssen in the chest with her free hand, breaks free, runs to the station chief's office, and races from there to her car pool van.[5]

The incident doesn't go unnoticed within the Intelligence Branch, or unremarked upon. I. C. Smith says the assault on Lichtenberg "should have been reason for dismissal right there, but it wasn't."[6]

"I knew that lady," Mike Rochford adds. "It was terrible what he did, but they didn't report it. The Bureau didn't do the right thing."[7]

Actually, the incident does get reported, but to little avail. Agents interview Lichtenberg at her home the next day, note her bruised arm and cheek, and file a report. A friend who has witnessed the assault also gives a statement to in-house investigators, supporting Lichtenberg's account. But like so many other things about Robert Philip Hanssen, both statements seem to disappear into the weird ether of the FBI. Lichtenberg's effort to file charges with the District of Columbia comes to nothing, either. The DC detective she meets with does a brief follow-up, only to be told by the FBI that the assault is an internal matter. One source close to the action alleges that the FBI further pressures Lichtenberg's friend to change her narrative of the events that afternoon.

Internally, too, there is not a unanimous opinion that this is quite the savage assault it seems, bruises or not.

"Normally," David Major says, "this would have been a firing offense. But this was a he-said/she-said situation. She said, 'I'm outta here,' and she got up and left. What do you do if you're a manager? If you've been well-trained, you let it go. She put you down in front of other people, but you take care of it the next morning. But Bob made a big mistake. Allegedly—*allegedly*—he grabbed her arm and said, 'Where are you going, Kimberly?' and she slipped and fell, and was down on the floor, shouting, 'Stay away from me!'

"I stuck my head out my office door because I heard a commotion, and I saw the two of them on the floor, and then she got up and left. I never saw him dragging her along the floor. Next morning she went to the police, and the inspectors came in and found them both guilty, which is what they do in these circumstances."[8]

Hanssen is suspended five days without pay for his actions, but according to Major, the Lichtenberg incident is "the end of Bob's professional career." With a stain like this on his record, he is never going to get to the golden circle of the senior executive service, never going to get his own division to run, never going to join the suits on the ninth floor. But he is never going to get there in any event. No one (other than David Major probably) thinks that's in the cards for Bob. Apart from the ego rush, Hanssen himself might not even want it. He thrives best in the shadows. The golden circle is way too well-lit.

In effect, then, Hanssen's only real punishment for the assault on Kimberly Lichtenberg is to forfeit a week's pay—no big deal for a guy who until recently has run such a profitable sideline. As for the stain on his record, it's mostly confirmation of what is already common opinion: Bob Hanssen is at best moderately creepy when it comes to women, and definitely not a people person in any event.

And Kimberly Lichtenberg? She's not ready to give up the fight. Eventually she files a civil complaint against Hanssen seeking $1.36 million for "assault and battery, gross negligence . . . and intentional infliction of emotional distress." But here again, the weirdness compounds. In successfully defending its employee, the Justice Department, which oversees the FBI, argues that "defendant Robert P. Hanssen was acting within the scope of his authority as an employee of the United States at the time of such alleged incidents."[9]

In short, in the execution of their duties, FBI special agents are free to wrench secretarial help to the floor and drag them down the hallway. No wonder Bob Hanssen comes to think of himself as untouchable.

Bob Hanssen has one other force multiplier in his quest to become a master spy—or maybe just to burrow deep into the bowels of the Bureau and steal and sell as many of America's secrets as he can: his FBI is an outward-directed organization.

Crime is what animates it—big, splashy crimes; corruption on the industrial scale; buildings blown up; gangsters brought down; cheats exposed in high places; perp walks; public enemies #1. And its mammoth size and budget—almost thirty-five thousand people, nearly $10 billion a year—exists

largely for this purpose. Not surprisingly, many of its post-Hoover-era directors have traditional crime-fighting backgrounds. Robert Mueller and Louis
Freeh were both federal prosecutors. Long before that, Freeh cut his eyeteeth
as an FBI agent tailing New York gangsters into, among other venues, steam
baths. Freeh's two predecessors as full-time director, William Sessions and
William Webster, did time as US district court judges.

Unsurprisingly, too, scoring successes in such operations—bagging public
enemies, bringing down corrupt judges and union bosses, leading the perp
walk—is the best way up for aspiring agents. The 2003 Webster Commission
says as much: "Until the terrorist attacks in September 2001, the FBI focused
on detecting and prosecuting traditional crime. That focus created a culture
that emphasized the priorities and morale of criminal components within the
Bureau, which offered the surest paths for career advancement."[10]

Bob Hanssen doesn't have to work all that hard to fly beneath the radar
in an institution so intent on looking outward for its enemies and rewarding
those who bring them to ground. But the commission goes on to note yet
another way that the cultural emphasis of the Bureau on traditional crime
benefits the man who will become its most famous traitor.

"This culture extolled cooperation and the free flow of information inside
the Bureau, a work ethic wholly at odds with the compartmentation char-
acteristic of intelligence investigations involving highly sensitive, classified
information.

"In a criminal investigation, rules restricting information are perceived
as cumbersome, inefficient, and a bar to success. However, when a criminal
investigation is compromised, usually only a discrete prosecution with a limited set of victims is at risk. In sharp contrast, when an intelligence program is
compromised, as Hanssen's case demonstrates, our country's ability to defend
itself against hostile forces can be put at risk."[11]

Translated, it isn't just sloppy procedures that turn highly classified information within the Bureau into low-hanging fruit for the likes of Hanssen; it's
a cultural bias, almost a cultural imperative, far harder to police and far more
rewarding for those determined to harvest them.

But in the end, the greatest force multiplier Bob Hanssen has at his dis-
posal is the fact that the FBI—one of the world's most honored and famous
investigative bodies—has almost no capacity to investigate itself. More locally,
and more critically, Hanssen's immediate neighborhood within the sprawling
FBI—the Soviet Analytical Unit, where he spends much of his career and
purloins almost all his sell-through to the Soviets and Russians—lacks not
only the capacity to self-investigate but also any incentive to do so, according
to I. C. Smith.

"For years, the Soviet Unit dominated the counterintelligence side. It got
most of the money because it faced most of the threat, not because the KGB
or GRU were better than the intelligence organizations the rest of us were
dealing with—they weren't—but because the Soviet Union posed a greater
retaliatory threat to the United States. There was a kind of superiority complex
over there: *I'm working the big stuff. You guys working China or Bulgaria, you're
the second-teamers.* That was their attitude."[12]

Hanssen got a pass on Kimberly Lichtenberg, Smith says, "because of cro-
nyism within the Soviet Unit." He got a pass on hacking Ray Mislock's and
Jim Holt's computers, because the Soviet Unit found "a denial of the facts"
convenient in such matters. All those puffs of smoke that went to the Bureau's
Middle Earth to die owed their early demise, according to Smith, to the fact
that the Soviet Unit had "become overly bureaucratic. They knew what the
issues were. They knew what it looked like, and they weren't searching for
alternatives."[13]

The Soviet Unit, Smith told me, "became very smug in the way it went
about its business. In my view, they adapted some of the characteristics of
their target, the KGB particularly. They became more a sumo wrestler than
a long-distance runner."[14]

What better place for a mole slip-sliding through the shadows and skirting
the margins to work? To find the master spy it has done so much to help
create, the FBI and its Soviet Unit are first going to have to get out of their
own lumbering way.

PART IV

CHAPTER 14

THE VAULT PEOPLE

It might be Valery Martynov who finally kickstarts the FBI into at least the opening stages of a mole hunt. Double agents come and go, but Martynov, whose FBI code name is PIMENTA, is different—jovial, good company over a drink, a loving father. The agents who work with him also bond with him. Yes, he accepts money for his spying. He's not like TOPHAT in that regard, but he has other reasons for doing what he does.

"PIMENTA was such a nice guy," says Jack Thompson, one of those agents, "and he did it for all the right reasons. His son suffered from ear infections as a young child, but the Russian doctors wouldn't give him the medicine he needed. PIMENTA said he did it to get back at a sick regime. He felt his government had betrayed him.

"When he was ordered by the KGB resident to escort Yurchenko back to Moscow, we were concerned. He could have called us, and we would have picked him and his family up in the middle of the night, anytime, anywhere, but he played it as if it were an honor to be one of the four men chosen."[1]

The KGB, though, is acting on Bob Hanssen's tip, and Martynov is received back in his homeland with the opposite of open arms. The Soviets also go out of their way to make certain his family suffers along with him. His wife and children are summoned back the next day, on the pretense that Martynov has reinjured a knee, and arrive to an unhappy welcome. His wife is interrogated harshly. Martynov's son is allowed to see him only one more time, just before his father is executed by a firing squad.

The only happy side to the entire story comes several years later. So popular is Martynov with his handlers that they eventually prevail upon the FBI to provide funds for resettling his family in the United States—the first time that's ever been done by the Bureau for asset survivors, according to Jack Thompson.

Valery Martynov attaches a face to what by the fall of 1986 has become an undeniable problem. Assets are disappearing. Operations are going haywire. In Mike Rochford's words, "These losses were personal."[2] The FBI responds with the Vault.

"In October 1986, the FBI created the Analyst Group," Thompson explains. "I was detailed to FBI headquarters to be one of the 'Vault People'—that's what everyone called us. It was just a windowless room with poured concrete walls. It wasn't specifically created to be a vault. Just happened that the FBI headquarters was built in such a way that right next to the elevator bank were these poured concrete piers that came together in a trapezoid shape that created the vault. Some clever engineer decided to put a combination lock on it and turn it into a secure space. I was stuck in there with Jim Holt, Art McClendon, Mike Duke, Reed Broce, and Barbara Campbell."

The Vault People are supervised by Tim Caruso. As too rarely happens in the FBI, need-to-know is enforced and the chain of command kept tight. The Vault People report only to Caruso—or Bob Wade or Don Stukey, deputy chief and chief of the Soviet Unit, respectively.

"We were briefed that the Agency and the FBI had suffered a lot of losses throughout the Soviet operations, and we didn't know why," Thompson says. "It could have been poor tradecraft, faulty communication, or human penetration. Our task was to get smart on every Soviet case—every case we had against the Russians, whether it was recruitment, a technical compromise, a double-agent operation in the States that had evaporated—all of them, as well as Agency cases.

"We reviewed each case individually, did an assessment, and wrote a report on each case as to the likely means of compromise if we could. One of the things we quickly realized was that no case was clearly just the FBI, but that in every case that was compromised, the CIA was involved. That suggested to us that if there was a human penetration, it might be in the CIA. During that time, we were also meeting with a CIA analytical team that was doing the same thing we were doing."

The Vault People delivered their report in September 1987 and mostly disbanded, but Thompson remained in the Vault to help put together another report for the Bureau on how to handle recruitment in the future and how to better document the knowledge of recruitment cases and disseminate information so the location of a recruitment would be harder to determine.

"We recommended that a Sensitive Source Unit be created at Headquarters. And they did that. They created a special unit to handle recruitments and defectors and double-agent operations. We also recommended that dissemination of sensitive-source information come out of Headquarters, not out of the field office that was running the case. You don't want the geographic source known to whoever is getting the information.

"We also strongly suggested that a bigot list be maintained by the Sensitive Source Unit, identifying every single person who has official knowledge of a recruitment operation so that if there is a problem in the future it will be easy for investigators to create a population of names of people who knew about the case, because we had a very hard time identifying everyone who had official knowledge of these cases that went down.

"And we further recommended that every field office maintain a list of names of agents and support employees assigned to each recruitment squad and maintain those names into perpetuity, because we had a hard time reconstructing that information, too."[3]

Both reports put a finer face on the challenges the Bureau was facing in protecting its counterintelligence operations and resources, but both also illuminate in the margins broader impediments to moving the investigation forward. Routine violations of the need-to-know principle make it all but impossible to pinpoint who might have access to any secret that goes missing or turns up on the enemy's radar screen. In the end, the Vault People's September 1987 report states that there is no evidence of a Soviet mole in the FBI—without directly adding that there really couldn't be any such evidence, since all evidentiary trails have been obliterated.

Two other internal studies follow over the next four years, both analytical as opposed to investigative. The first, begun in 1987, focuses on historical allegations of foreign penetrations of the FBI. By late 1988, that team has made it halfway through the 1960s. An interim report concludes that two penetrations occurred prior to 1964, but that is about as far as the team ever gets. The following summer of 1989, the whole project is abandoned without ever getting anywhere near the Bob Hanssen era.

The second study is seemingly more relevant. It examines fifty-plus FBI operations—human assets, technical operations, double-agent and recruitment programs—that have been compromised since 1986. This team's final report, rendered November 1988, is blunt about the continuing problems within the Bureau's Soviet operations but concludes that a mole within the CIA is a far more likely explanation than a mole within the FBI itself—even though most of the significant operations the team members studied have been compromised by none other than FBI Special Agent Robert Philip Hanssen.

On November 23, 1987, for example, Hanssen hands over to the KGB a cable-like report about a meeting the previous month with a "valuable source" the KGB Soviet log-in notes identify only as "M," a survey of information provided by the Soviet defector-redefector Vitaly Yurchenko, and a technical document describing COINS-II, the up-to-date version of the Community On-Line Intelligence System.

Two and half months later, on February 8, 1988, Hanssen is back with detailed information on another Soviet defector and his first computer diskette packed with classified documents. Another seven weeks later, on March 28, he sends along his fourth diskette. By then, to judge by the KGB's shorthand entry for the subject matter, he has begun leaking to the Soviets the fruit of all the Vault People's labors. The entry tag reads simply: "The FBI's Double Agent Program."

And so it goes almost unrelentingly. Diskette 5 provides "everything" about a particular KGB officer; further information on KGB defector Victor Sheymov, Hanssen's "friend" and prospective future business partner; and further information on other Soviet FBI recruits. Diskette 6 spills the beans on more FBI recruitment operations.

By 1989, Hanssen's mole work is at such a fever pitch that he has to approve a new KGB-proposed dead-drop site under yet another footbridge, this one in Canterbury Woods Park in Springfield, Virginia.[4] Meanwhile, on the other side of his business model, the money is pouring in: $30,000 on August 7, 1989; $50,000 on August 17 deposited into Hanssen's escrow account at a Moscow bank; $30,000 a month later in return for the document that effectively caves in the tunnel mentioned earlier, the one under the new Soviet embassy in DC.

As the 1990s bloom, both the FBI and CIA seem to finally be getting serious about the many assets lost and operations compromised in the mid-1980s, but at both ends of the intelligence community, the effort has an air of unreality.

A joint special investigation unit (SIU) is formed to delve into the losses and prepare a list of suspects who might have been responsible for them. To bolster the investigative side of the operation, the FBI creates a new squad within the Washington field office (WFO) to jump on leads generated by the SIU and reanalyze the same amalgam of Bureau penetrations that supposedly has been picked apart by the two earlier analytical teams. Reanalysis, though, yields the same old conclusions, and the SIU is slow to supply leads for investigation. By the end of 1992, the WFO squad is basically out of business.

The SIU itself makes greater headway, compiling a list of forty CIA employees who have access to the Soviet operations compromised in 1985–86, and eventually determining (by a vote among team members) that the most likely mole out of the forty is Rick Ames. And, indeed, there is plenty of evidence to point to Ames. But the SIU's final report, issued March 1993, fails to highlight Ames. Nor does it include any similar list of FBI employees with access to the compromised operations and disappeared human assets—a list that would almost certainly include Bob Hanssen. Furthermore, while the final report hints at the possibility of a KGB mole operating inside the FBI, it recommends no meaningful action to determine just where and who that mole might be.

The 2003 report by the Justice Department's Office of the Inspector General is harsh in its criticism of these initial efforts to stem penetrations of the FBI. The efforts, the report says, "suffered from a lack of cooperation with the CIA and from inattention on the part of senior management [of the FBI]. . . . Senior management was almost entirely unaware of the scope and significance of these losses, and throughout the 1980s, the FBI failed to work cooperatively with the CIA to resolve the cause of these losses or to thoroughly investigate whether an FBI mole could be responsible for these setbacks."[5]

Some of those closest to the Hanssen investigation are equally harsh in their evaluations of the inspector general's report.

"I'm not against after-action reports," Dave Szady says. "I think they have to be done. But when you start second-guessing, and you start criticizing, and you're a twenty-four-year-old assistant US attorney out of Vermont, and everything you know about espionage comes from James Bond movies . . ."[6] Szady trails off there, but you get the idea. You can't model real-life spying in a law-school classroom.

David Major says the idea that senior management was disengaged from the scope and significance of the Bureau's losses is equally absurd: "That's the media talking."[7] (The alleged deficiencies of the IG report might be one of the very few things Szady and Major agree on about the Hanssen case.)

But whatever its inefficiencies and missed opportunities, this flurry of attention to the FBI's penetrations does seem to have caught the attention of at least one important person: the penetrator-in-chief.

"I knew Bob Hanssen very well," Jack Thompson says. "I replaced him as acting chief in the Soviet Analytical Unit when he took a squad back in New

York City. But I knew him even before then, when he was assigned to the Washington field office before he went to Headquarters.

"He was always an odd duck—Doctor Death, as people called him, or sometimes Lurch [from *The Addams Family*] since he was quite tall. There was always that crucifix on the wall that you had to stare at when you walked into his office, but you could talk with him back then like any ordinary person.

"Then, after being in the Vault, I went over to the Department of Energy as director of counterintelligence operations and investigations. Part of my responsibility there was to go back to Headquarters every week or two and touch base with all the unit chiefs, to make them aware that DOE had a viable counterintelligence program and could support them in their double-agent operations. Bob was one of those unit chiefs, so I went in to see him periodically, but I noticed that his demeanor toward me had changed.

"Bob knew I had been part of the analyst group that was trying to identify him, and he was never affable when I stopped by. In fact, he used a technique I came to realize was intentional, something probably picked up from the *Seinfeld* show.

"Kramer had this girlfriend who was a very low talker, a mumbler. Because of that, Kramer couldn't sustain the relationship. Well, Hanssen became a mumbler when I was around. He knew I was hard of hearing because of firearm damage to my right ear, so he would mumble, and I couldn't understand what the hell he was saying. He knew if he did that, I would cut short my visits, which I did.

"That was very smart of him. He's an intelligent guy, but he has this personality defect where he has betrayed the trust that close friends and loved ones have placed in him throughout his whole life."[8]

That part about him would never change.

CHAPTER 15

ODD COUPLE

B ob Hanssen and Aldrich Ames are forever tied together in the history of American espionage. Their peak spying years—1985 to 1991—parallel each other. They have the same handler, Victor Cherkashin, and the same sub-rosa employer, the KGB.

Hanssen and Ames equally and eagerly give up American assets to the Soviet intelligence service not only for their cash value but also to protect themselves. (Dead men tell no tales.) Both get caught lying by their wives—Hanssen in the basement writing a letter to the GRU; Ames when his second wife finds his KGB meeting schedule on a flimsy yellow paper tucked into his wallet. And both offer similar excuses for their initial treachery: their spying is a con game, a way to make ends meet.

Both also have almost perfect contempt for their institutional security systems. Commenting on the two, Richard Haver, a CIA counterintelligence officer who helps with the damage assessment after Ames's arrest, first notes Hanssen's disdain, then adds, "Rick Ames felt the same way about that CIA security system: it would never catch him. Some breach from the other side might turn him in, but it would never catch him because he was inside the system."[1]

Of the two, Ames, of course, earns the most money by far, but he has the shorter spy career and compromises fewer vital operations. He is also the first to be caught, by a half dozen years, and with good cause. Ames is almost a caricature of the rapacious mole, grabbing all the goodies he can get. Hanssen is the polar opposite of his fellow, almost conjoined, spy; he holds his appetites close to the vest.

"How do you catch spies?" asks David Major, who befriends both Ames and Hanssen. "You catch them with other spies—with technology, with surveillance, or with penetration, but it's almost always penetration. And Hanssen knew that. If there was a penetration, he would have been in a position to see it."[2]

But Hanssen also knows that the sort of protective coloration he wraps himself in—family man, patriot, Opus Dei—also works in reverse. You can blend into the backdrop or you can stand out like a sore thumb. Rick Ames does the latter, almost with abandon.

Start with what most spies aim for: money. Hanssen has his small extravagances—the used Mercedes for Priscilla Galey, for example; the two-week trip she takes with him to Hong Kong; the occasional grand gesture for his best friend. Jack Hoschouer recalls in particular an uncomfortable moment from the summer of 1990 when Hanssen insists that he accept a $7,500 Rolex watch as a present.

"I said no, but he kept pressing it on me. I tried to give him money, but he wouldn't take it. He said he had bought it for himself, but Bonnie thought it was clunky and ugly and insisted he take it back. So he gave it to me instead. I wore the watch and Bonnie said, 'Oh, you've got a watch just like the one I made Bob take back!'"[3]

Eventually, Hoschouer reasons that Hanssen has probably learned from his policeman father where to get things wholesale and makes peace with the gift. In any event, it's a far cry from a splashy lifestyle. Hanssen drives a Ford, while Bonnie transports the kids is an aging minivan plastered with right-to-life stickers. Bob is a spy, sure, but he's in the game to provide a better middle-class life for his wife and family, a proper moral education for his children, college degrees they can be proud of—the American dream, funded by the KGB.

His fourth letter to Victor Cherkashin, sent November 8, 1985, after he has received his first payment, shows just how aware he is of the money trap:

> As far as the funds are concerned, I have little need or utility for more than the 100,000 [originally asked for]. It merely provides a difficulty since I cannot spend it, store it or invest it easily without tripping "drug money" warning bells.
>
> Perhaps some diamonds as security to my children and some good will so that when the time comes, you will accept my senior services as a guest lecturer. . . .
>
> Eventually I would appreciate an escape plan. (Nothing lasts forever.)[4]

The diamonds, in fact, do come. In 1988, his handlers oblige him with a stone worth around $24,000. Two others follow in short order, for a total value of more than $54,000, but Hanssen soon gets cold feet. Unlike those wads of $100 bills with which the KGB pays him, diamonds present no storage problem. He can stow them in the back of a safe deposit box or easily hide them in his basement or under a potted palm, but to extract anything like the full value out of a diamond requires selling it into a thin market of reputable dealers and therein lies the danger. Rather than risk it, Hanssen returns the first and third diamonds to his handlers and asks for their cash value, which the Russians gladly present to him, appropriately on Christmas Day 1989.

It turns out this is a wise or at least fortunate move on Hanssen's part. The FBI has heard from a defector that a Soviet mole within the American intelligence community is being paid in diamonds and sends a team to investigate, under Mike Rochford's guidance. "We sent a whole squad to New York, visiting Hasidic Jews in the Diamond District on West 47th Street. We showed them pictures of our top twenty suspects [and] asked them if they recognized anyone. One or two of the merchants said they maybe recognized a picture, but as it turned out, none were Hanssen."[5]

Nor could any of them have been Hanssen. The twenty suspect photos shown around the Diamond District were all CIA officers.

If the KGB ever tried to pay Rick Ames in diamonds, odds are he might have turned one of the stones into a pinkie ring.

Once he starts spying, and being paid for his work, Ames can't seem to get enough of the good life. He can't display enough of it, either. Sandy Grimes, a member of the Ames mole-hunt team, details the "tells" that shine a spotlight on Ames and his wife, Rosario.

"[Rick] and I had been friends, acquaintances, for many years, since the early seventies. We were young case officers together, we grew up together, we car-pooled. I had seen what I always called the old Rick. I liked him, and if anybody had ever told me in the 1970s that Rick Ames would be a traitor, would be one of the most famous spies of all time for the opposition, I never would have believed it, never in a million years.

"He was a nice guy. But then, after he came back from Rome [in 1989], . . . he was just a different person, and it wasn't just the . . . capped teeth, it wasn't the clean fingernails, it wasn't the Italian suits and the six-hundred-dollar shoes and the silk men's hose. His posture was different. Rick always had been a slob and slouched and couldn't care less what he looked like, but he stood erect, he sat erect . . . he exuded arrogance."[6]

Hanssen's vices—his infidelity, his attraction to porn, the kinky voyeurism, the way he abuses Bonnie to give his best friend a thrill ride—don't see the light of day until he is in the government's hands, never more to be a free man. Not even Bonnie knew about them until then, only Jack Hoschouer. Rick Ames, by contrast, isn't able to control his vices in the least—especially his addiction to alcohol—or keep them out of the public eye. The record on that front is crystal clear.

Ames's drinking and his tenure with the CIA are both inherited. His father, Carleton, is an alcohol-dependent ex–college professor who starts working in the Agency's Directorate of Operations in 1952 and stays until his retirement in 1967. In 1957, Rick, then a high school sophomore, lands a summer job with his father's employer, marking classified documents for filing. Two more summer CIA jobs follow, and then, in February 1962, he joins his father at the Langley, Virginia, headquarters, initially as a GS-4 clerk-typist while he earns his BA from George Washington University, and then as a rising officer in Operations. He never works for anyone else until 1985 when he applies at the Soviet embassy in downtown Washington, DC, to be a KGB spy.

Meanwhile, Ames's drinking grows apace with his responsibilities. In April 1962, a mere CIA clerk, he's arrested in DC for public intoxication. Speeding and reckless driving charges follow over the next few years—one or both while drunk. At a 1973 Christmas party at Langley, Ames—now assigned to support Agency operations against Soviet officials—has to be helped home by CIA staff. At the next year's Christmas fete, a security officer stumbles across Ames and a female employee in what is politely called "a compromising position."

And so it goes as he ascends through the ranks: a drunken argument with a Cuban official at the US embassy in Mexico City; a traffic accident during that same posting when he is so out of it he doesn't recognize the US embassy officer who comes to bail him out; meetings missed because he is tanked; a briefcase left on a subway when he's on his way to meet a Soviet asset; a CIA-FBI softball game just about the time Ames begins spying for the Soviets when he once again has to be driven home, this time leaving behind on the playing field his Agency badge, cryptic notes, and wallet including alias identification documents.

Hanssen's flaws do not go unnoticed. But Ames's are so much bigger, so much more open—his occasional, though often spectacular, antisocial behavior, the times he has been helped out of this place or that. A routine background check conducted in 1983 describes Ames as "a social drinker who was inclined to become a bit enthusiastic when he overindulged in alcohol," but says that no serious alcohol problem had been detected.[7] David Major argues much the same. "Ames was a binge drinker," he says, "not a fall-down drunk."[8] But at some vanishing point on the horizon, the distinction becomes academic.

This pattern of benign neglect continues almost to the end of Ames's CIA career, under multiple supervisors, including those at the Counternarcotics

Center to which he is assigned in late 1991. As a post-arrest investigation by the Agency's inspector general finds, Ames's immediate bosses "were aware of his occasional problems with alcohol abuse, his proclivity to sleep at his desk, and his unwillingness to handle issues and projects that did not interest him."[9] Most if not all of his superiors know, too, that during a September 1992 meeting with foreign officials, CIA Officer Ames becomes so intoxicated that he spews out a string of inappropriate remarks before passing out at the table.

In time, these free passes accumulate into enablement. Hanssen hacks into his section chief's computer and is lauded for his initiative. Ames fails a polygraph test, talks the polygrapher into believing he passed it, and is admired for his quick wit and shrewd tongue. Both are in their own way "broken-wing" employees; exceptions must be made, except that these exceptions involve open access to America's secrets.

"Having a clearance is not equal to having a driver's license," Mike Rochford argues. "You don't just show up, take a test, and you're done. You have a responsibility to maintain that clearance. You have to look left and right and in the mirror, take responsibility for yourself and your neighbors."[10]

No one wants to take responsibility for either man, especially in the aftermath.

As is also the case with Hanssen, Ames's peculiarities, if they can be called that, more or less assure that he will never ascend to the highest levels of the CIA, but they barely dent the onward march of his career or the clearances that come with it. Indeed, by the time of the softball-game debacle—the summer of either 1984 or 1985—Ames is back at Langley as a counterintelligence branch chief for Soviet operations, with full and complete access to all CIA activities involving Soviet intelligence officers worldwide.

By then, too, his first marriage has fallen apart, and he's soon to marry his second wife, Rosario, a Colombian he met in Mexico City. First, though, Rosario has to submit to a polygraph exam and background check—standard procedure when a CIA officer is marrying a foreign national. The background interviews with five of her friends and associates paint her as someone who comes from "a prominent, wealthy family in Colombia,"[11] but no effort is made to verify these statements and no special concern seems to attach to the fact that Rosario's family was from Medellín, home of the famous drug cartel.

Also by then, Ames—as part of his CIA duties—has been meeting regularly with a Soviet official at the embassy in Washington, DC, under an assumed name, posing as someone with an academic interest in US-Soviet relations, in the hope of eventually recruiting him as a CIA asset. In early 1985, that official returns to Moscow, but not before suggesting that Ames continue the conversation with Sergey Dmitriyevich Chuvakhin, an arms-control specialist with the Soviet Ministry of Foreign Affairs. The switchover is apparently an opportunity not to be ignored.

On April 16, 1985, Ames enters the Soviet embassy and asks for Chuvakhin by name. It's their initial meeting, and this is standard protocol. But before Chuvakhin appears, Ames also leaves an envelope for Victor Cherkashin, offering his services as a mole—half a year before Hanssen mails his own application into the KGB—and baiting his pitch, as Hanssen later would, with the names of Soviet agents who have flipped in favor of American intelligence services.

Decidedly unlike Hanssen, though, Ames makes no effort to hide his identity. Among the bona fides he provides Cherkashin is a page photocopied from a CIA directory, with his own name and position conveniently highlighted in Day-Glo yellow.

Chuvakhin is quickly appointed the KGB's go-between with Ames, and a month later, on May 17, he hands Ames $50,000. Four weeks further on, Ames bundles roughly seven pounds of CIA cable-and-message traffic into plastic bags, carries them openly out of the Headquarters building at Langley, heads into DC for a scheduled lunch date with Chuvakhin, and there delivers to him what one CIA official has called the "largest amount of sensitive documents and critical information . . . that has ever been passed to the KGB in one particular meeting."[12] And thus begins the second most famous American spy career of the closing decades of the 20th century.

In Rome, where Ames is posted the following year, the go-between changes, but the regular lunches continue, ostensibly so Ames can recruit Soviets as

US assets but now in fact for just the opposite purpose—a perfect cover. The regular drinking continues, too. One of Ames's supervisors estimates he is drunk on the job about three times a week, almost steady binge drinking if that's what it is. The only big change are the upgrades as Rick and Rosario settle into a beautiful life, *la bella vita*—better clothes, better wine, better teeth, and two accounts at the Credit Suisse Bank in Zurich, one in Ames's name and one in the name of Rosario's mother.

Simultaneously, the losses for the CIA and the intelligence community generally mount ever higher. Different as they are, Hanssen and Ames collectively are hollowing out America's counterintelligence capacities.

Once the number and depth of those losses become evident as the 1980s draw to a close, Bob Hanssen is sitting high and dry in the Soviet Analytical Unit. He's the computer guy, the systems analyst, the mumbler who dresses in black, marches for Right to Life, sends his kids to Oakcrest—the Opus Dei girls' school, at a discount tuition because Bonnie teaches there—and the Heights, and shepherds his good Catholic family to St. Catherine's every Sunday.

By contrast, Rick Ames should be a sitting duck. He's widely known to have a serious drinking problem. He has ready access to top-secret information about American-asset double agents, including those turning up dead in Lubyanka prison and elsewhere. He meets regularly for lunch, first in Washington, DC, then in Rome, with Soviet officials whom he is supposedly courting to work for the United States but has thus far failed to net a single one.

Even when the Agency's Counterintelligence Division receives, in November 1989, a direct heads-up from a CIA employee—an employee who knows Ames well, is aware of the 1985–86 double-agent compromises and Ames's access to those records, has witnessed with his own eyes Rick and Rosario's newly luxurious lifestyle, and knows that, in fact, there is no great bundle of money from Rosario's family that is funding all this—it sits on its hands.

Maybe more remarkably, even when the joint FBI-CIA special task force, in effect, votes Ames off the island just prior to its March 1993 final report, the implication that Rick Ames is the mole the intelligence community urgently seeks is either so drastically understated or the task force itself is of such low priority in the larger scheme of the CIA that top officials there never bother to bring the possibility to the attention of the FBI, which handles investigation of such matters. Nor is Ames's computer access restricted in the least. In fact, it's substantially expanded in the fall of 1993 when changes in the Agency computer system broaden access to classified information.

What, us worry?

Happily for the CIA, Rick Ames seems determined to do the Agency's job for it. His June 1992 communication with his Russian handlers is unthinkable in Hanssen terms: a naked plea for financial help by a mole unable to curb his appetites and so deep in the money trap that all he can do is keep digging down deeper.

"My most immediate need, as I pointed out in March, is money," Ames writes. "As I have mentioned several times, I do my best to invest a good part of the cash I received, but keep part of it out for ordinary expenses. Now I am faced with the need to cash in investments to meet current needs, a very tight and unpleasant situation! I have had to sell a certificate of deposit in Zurich and some stock here to help make up the gap. Therefore, I will need as much cash delivered in Pipe [document drop site] as you think can be accommodated—it seems to me that it could accommodate up to $100,000."[13]

The cocktail-napkin math is probably accurate: a thousand $100 bills can be crammed inside a space no larger than 4.3 inches high, 6.14 inches wide, and 2.6 inches deep. But the need behind the math is what finally forms the predicate for opening a full-bore investigation of Ames, for the National Security Letters (or subpoena) that soon invade his bank accounts and financial records, and for his February 21, 1994, arrest and guilty plea two months later. Basically, Rick Ames, like a lot of nondescript crooks before him, spends his way into prison—in this case, a lifetime tenancy in a federal lockup in Indiana.

Robert Hanssen will never do that, and never would. The two really are the alpha and omega of moledom. But if Hanssen looks carefully toward the horizon on the day Rick Ames is perp-walked out of his home in Arlington, Virginia, he might see the very first storm clouds gathering.

CHAPTER 16

FIRST BLOOD

The CIA's seeming laissez-faire attitude toward the elephant in its room has no trouble catching the attention of Democratic senator Dennis DeConcini, then head of the Senate Select Committee on Intelligence. DeConcini interviews Ames in jail, he studies the Agency's slipshod, halting efforts to root out its mole, and his committee later catalogues them ruthlessly in its November 1994 report on the Ames case. The CIA has:

- Failed to document and address Ames's alcohol abuse, his extramarital relationships with foreign nationals (including Rosario, while Ames was still married to wife number one), his repeated security violations, and his failure to comply with the Agency's administrative regulations.
- Failed to adequately monitor Ames's meeting with Soviet embassy officials at a time when he had access to extraordinarily sensitive information pertaining to Soviet nationals working clandestinely with the CIA.

- Failed to aggressively investigate with adequate resources cases compromised by Ames until mid-1991, six years after the compromises began.

- Failed to adequately limit Ames's assignments and access to classified information after suspicions about him had been raised.

- And, maybe most outrageous in the eyes of these investigators, the CIA has failed to advise the oversight committees of the losses caused by Ames despite a statutory requirement to inform said committees of "any significant intelligence failure."[1]

It's a devastating list. The CIA and its then-director James Woolsey have basically been accused of everything short of poisoning the family dog. But what really seems to incense Senator DeConcini is the way in which he feels Woolsey tries to deflect blame from the Agency after Ames is in custody. In a *Today* show interview on April 21, 1994, Woolsey says there "absolutely" will be a "fair number of espionage cases" brought against people at multiple government agencies[2]—implying that it isn't just the CIA that has a mole problem, even as he seems to forget that any such "cases" would have to be brought and made by the same FBI his agency has kept largely in the dark on Ames.

"[Woolsey] is under siege," DeConcini tells the *New York Times'* Tim Weiner. "The CIA is under siege from the Ames case."[3]

All in all, a doubly bad move by Woolsey, and one that has to warm the heart of the hibernating supermole within the FBI. I. C. Smith doubts that Hanssen has real-time access to the Ames case since he hasn't been polygraphed into it, but DeConcini's ongoing rage against the CIA assures the spotlight shines bright on Langley, not the Bureau, and presages the sweeping changes that follow.

Early in 1995, "prompted by the most devastating espionage case in our nation's history" and citing specifically the CIA's lapses, the 104th Congress enacts what it calls "the most significant counterintelligence legislation ever passed" in the nation's history. Beginning immediately, all agency heads are required to promptly inform the FBI of any actual or suspected illegal transmittals of classified information to a foreign government. Furthermore, the president—Bill Clinton, in this instance—is required to issue within 180 days new and more rigorous standards for access to classified information.[4]

Not surprisingly, Jim Woolsey is gone less than two months after the Senate Select Intelligence Committee releases its scathing report, and is replaced by John Deutch, a noted chemist turned civil servant, who hits the ground running. On October 31, 1995, Deutch announces sweeping changes in both the practices and the culture of the Agency. Old top managers are swept out of office and new ones installed with an emphasis on counterintelligence and human resources; computer security is prioritized; performance standards and expectations are upgraded. Most dramatically, a new National Counterintelligence Center is established at the CIA—to be headed up by a senior *FBI* officer!

Allen Dulles, who shaped the Agency powerfully as one of its earliest and longest-serving directors, undoubtedly rolls over in his grave at this news. J. Edgar Hoover must cackle in his. Style-wise, the two institutions are oil and water—Ivy League and estate wines at the CIA; state universities and beer for the FBI. For decades, they have also often been bitter rivals for the president's ear, access being status and power in such high circles. If the new Center is on CIA real estate, it presumably belongs to the CIA. But if it is in the hands of a top-tier FBI man—at the time, Ed Curran, a longtime assistant director at the Bureau—isn't the FBI really calling the shots, and doing so from inside its enemy's citadel?

Who conceived this madness? (Bill Clinton, actually, who has had a rough first term with both institutions.) And how can this odd marriage possibly work? The answer to that last question is easy: very well. In fact, by some measures, spectacularly, at both the street level and at the top of the executive food chain.

"They said, 'Okay, you kids are going have to learn how to play nice in the sandbox,'" Mike Sulick, then head of counterintelligence at the Agency, tells me. "And we are two very different cultures. They've got badges and guns, and they do enforcement, whereas we skulk around back alleys and pretend to be other than what we are. We break the laws of other countries for the good of our own country. People don't like to hear that, but that's what we do. And we protect our sources, so that's why we don't want to share anything with anybody."[5]

But now, of course, the 104th Congress said they must.

George Tenet, who takes over as CIA acting director in December 1996, has been keeping a close eye on the fractious intelligence community since his days as a staff member of the Senate Select Committee on Intelligence, beginning in 1985, and has no illusions about the challenges inherent in trying to forge a cooperative investigative relationship between Agency and Bureau.

"Forty years of jockeying for supremacy doesn't exactly make for a dispassionate, holistic, well-informed joint effort to go find these people," he tells me.[6]

Those historic problems, he adds, are further magnified by the Ames case, which Tenet has followed from his most recent post as senior director for intelligence programs at the National Security Council. "When you handle a case as badly as the Agency handled that case, and the Bureau's watching all that, you're going to have trust problems. Ames was a failed officer. He falls down in the street drunk in Rome. And somehow he still ends up in [Soviet Analytical Unit]. Holy shit, how did that happen?"[7]

But Tenet is also by nature a team player, a hands-on schmoozer, and, as Mike Rochford quickly learns, a hard guy to dislike: "We [the FBI] got permission to do a FISA search inside the CIA headquarters. I briefed Tenet, of course, that day—told him we were going in at eleven o'clock at night. We got your guys meeting us at the door, and I'm bringing special flash-and-steal guys.

"'Okay,' he says. 'You're going to let me know?' And I say, 'I'm going to let Mr. Freeh know, and he'll give you a call.'

"So we're leaving the Agency at 1:30 in the morning, waiting for an elevator, when the director's elevator opens up. It's Tenet. He's in a jacket, and he's chewing his cigar. He says, 'Roch, how'd we do? You're going to call your boss and he'll call his boss and he'll call Freeh, and he'll call me, but that'll be twelve hours from now. I can act very surprised. I'm a great actor. So why don't you tell me now if we're just fine?'

"I say, 'Mr. Tenet—'

"'Call me George.'

"'George,' I say, 'you're just fine.'

"It took leaders like him personally involved in the relationship from the top down to make sure the Agency and Bureau worked seamlessly together. The Agency let me look at files and everything else because they realized the importance of solving these cases. If we didn't solve them, we couldn't build a new class of assets."[8]

It also takes relentless work at the street level to begin ridding the US intelligence community of its moles, and Rochford himself gets a lot of credit for that.

"In 1994, just after the arrest and conviction of Rick Ames, I'm finishing up my work at Headquarters when I'm asked by Bear Bryant [head of the Washington field office] and Steve Dillard to put in for a desk at WFO and form a new squad to look at multiple allegations of penetrations of the intelligence community that are not attributable to Ames. . . . I stole some of the best talent from WFO in order to staff my squad.

"I'd say, 'Hey, I want this man, that woman,' and after I talked to them for about five minutes, they would get this funny call to come take a polygraph. If they passed the polygraph, the next thing they knew is that their desk would be empty and their supervisor doesn't see them anymore. They're assigned to me."[9]

In short order, Rochford's mole-hunt team has grown to include fifteen to eighteen FBI special agents plus three to four Bureau analysts working with a team of five to seven CIA investigator analysts pulled from the Agency's Counterespionage Center. The official launch date is November 17, 1994. The expectation is that the spy squad might need a full year to complete its work. The squad is still operational and in the thick of the hunt more than six years later when Rochford turns it over to Debra Evans Smith.

"Our thinking on the mole hunt was that every day we delayed finding the mole could mean that our sources were going to die," Rochford tells me. "My workday averaged twelve or more hours daily. So, yes, there was a whole lot of stress. I felt like a fireman running from one fire to the next."[10]

This new push to get to the core of the penetrations that are shredding America's intelligence capacity is operational less than a year when it rolls up another CIA-officer-turned-Russian-spy, Harold James Nicholson, on charges of spying for the SVR, beginning two and a half years earlier. The arrest is a textbook joint operation, and by the previous standards of both principals in the new organization, it goes lightning fast.

During the course of a routine polygraph, a CIA examiner notes that Nicholson is trying to game the test by taking deep breaths when faced with a control question—one like "Have you had unauthorized contact with a foreign intelligence service?" as opposed to "Is your name Harold James Nicholson?"

That red flag becomes more meaningful when Gwen Fuller, part of Mike Rochford's new squad out of the WFO, sees Nicholson's name popping out of a chart she's been creating.

"There were so many unsubs [subjects of an investigation whose identity has not been determined] that we split our squad. The other one took Nicholson's case, but I noticed that he had traveled to certain locations during critical times when Russians had also traveled there. So I put it on a chart—people of interest, places of interest, times—and he just stood out. I left this on a piece of paper for his case agent, and thirty minutes later, he goes to Mike Rochford and says, 'This is very exciting. You have to look at this.'"[11]

Exciting it was, and more. Soon thereafter, a Russian mole informs the CIA that his intelligence service is working overtime to gather information on Chechen rebels. Nicholson, it turns out, has been showing up in odd places at CIA headquarters asking about Chechnya and then making up stories to explain why.

As with Rick Ames, the mounting evidence dovetails with what is already known by those who have worked in any proximity to Nicholson: he's not a particularly reliable guy. Jack Thompson, who was part of a special FBI unit put together in the spring of 1995 to carry the investigation forward, tells me: "Nicholson really knew how to play people. He played up the role of being a single parent, a model dad. He'd tell his colleagues, 'Oh, I'm taking Star [his daughter] to Great Falls this weekend for horseback riding,' but he almost never did. His kids were latchkey children. He would regularly stay in his office reading reports until ten thirty at night. Then he'd call home, ask the kids what they wanted to eat, and drop by McDonald's to pick up dinner on the way home. Their mother was an aging hippie, living in a cave in Oregon. She'd abandoned the children many years before."[12]

Soon, the FBI is all over Nicholson's case. Agents are on his tail when he flies to the Far East as part of his duties. They're watching in Singapore when he meets with an unauthorized Russian national. Not long afterward, back in Washington, DC, they are sneaking peeks when he makes a large cash deposit that doesn't appear to come from any legal source of income. That, in turn, is enough for the CIA to transfer Nicholson to a nothing job with limited access to information to Russian matters, and Chechnya in particular. From there, it is only a matter of time before FBI agents arrest Nicholson on November 16, 1996, at Dulles International Airport as he waits to board a flight to Zurich, carrying with him a computer disk bearing classified information lifted from CIA files, and only seven more months before he is sentenced to twenty years for betraying his country. A joint operation doesn't get much smoother than that, but Nicholson isn't through with his betrayals.

"While Nicholson's in prison," Thompson says, "he recruits his oldest son to get in touch with the Russians in Mexico City, and the son passes some information to the Russians and comes back with $47,000. Nicholson got an additional eight years tagged on to his twenty for that, and the son was put on probation for five years.

"What kind of a father does that? Nicholson is unbelievable. He was a very duplicitous person, but you have to be duplicitous to have that kind of career."[13]

The next mole to be unearthed, counterintelligence agent Earl Edwin Pitts, belongs to the FBI, and is far more closely an echo of Robert Hanssen. In 1987,

Pitts, then with the Bureau's New York field office, as Hanssen is when his spying begins, offers his services to the KGB via a letter to Rollan Dzhikiya, Communist Party chief at the Soviet (later Russian) Mission to the United Nations in New York, who quickly passes him on to the KGB's Aleksandr Karpov at a get-together at the New York Public Library's main branch at Fifth Avenue and 42nd Street in midtown Manhattan.

Like Hanssen, Pitts also has much to offer, including, in the words of the charging affidavit: "recruitment operations involving Russian intelligence officers, double-agent operations, operations targeting Russian intelligence officers, true identities of human assets, operations against Russian illegals, true identities of defector sources, surveillance schedules of known meet sites, internal policies, documents, and procedures concerning surveillance of Russian intelligence officers, and the identification, targeting, and reporting on known and suspected KGB intelligence officers in the New York area"[14]—not to mention, again like Hanssen, ever-ascending clearances that eventually give him access to the crown jewels stored in SCIFs.

Five years later, Pitts and Hanssen are both involuntarily retired by the collapse of the Soviet Union, but here the road forks. Hanssen, unknown to his handlers by name, face, rank, or serial number, has nearly a decade of freedom ahead of him, while Pitts, open about his identity from day one, is flipped back to the FBI in 1995 by the same Rollan Dzhikiya, who has remained in the United States and is hoping for a green card so he can attain permanent resident status. A sixteen-month false-flag operation ensues, until December 1996, when Pitts, like Nicholson and Ames, is rolled up, pleads guilty to high crimes against the United States, and is sent away for many years: twenty-seven in his case, to be exact.

Bottom line: The FBI and CIA have a lot to be proud of. Cooperation works. United they stand; divided they fall. And the fruits of their labor and rewards for faithful toil are behind bars—or soon headed there—for all the world to see. Nicholson has sold the identities of every US intelligence officer covertly stationed in Russia. Pitts has turned over a computerized list of all Soviet officials thought to be operating in the United States, including the intelligence agencies they are known or suspected to be operating on behalf of. They are a definitive pair of bad apples. Add in Rick Ames, and the three have definitely spoiled the barrel. No doubt about it, a big hole in the intelligence community security net has been closed. But there's a problem: a bigger hole remains still.

America's new bumper crop of imprisoned moles is doing plenty of singing—Rick Ames to avoid execution and get a lighter sentence for his wife, Rosario; Nicholson and Pitts to get a few more years in the sunshine once their sentences have been served. But the more they are debriefed, the more the questions begin to overwhelm the answers.

Ames, for example, has the blood of executed Russians all over his hands, but who is corroborating the names he sells to the KGB? For good reason, the KGB rarely pulls the trigger on one identification alone. That would make a disinformation campaign too easy and potentially too costly.

Then there is Felix Bloch, a US Foreign Service officer and one of the more bizarre espionage tales of modern times.

Whether Bloch begins working for the Soviets for money or because he is being blackmailed remains an open question. Nor has it ever been firmly established that Bloch was a spy at all. By the late 1980s, though, he is forking over as much as $10,000 annually to a Viennese prostitute who specializes in sadomasochism, and he is keeping further suspect company in the person of an Austrian-based KGB asset named Reino Gikman. The combination inevitably arouses suspicion.

After an FBI wiretap catches Bloch and Gikman talking on the phone on April 27, 1989, the Bureau opens a classified investigation. By then, Bloch has been reassigned back to the State Department in Washington, DC, but he is still traveling regularly to Europe, where the FBI observes him meeting with Gikman in Paris on May 14 and in Brussels two weeks later. With that, the Bureau is ready to drop the hammer on Bloch. But instead, the case slowly evaporates.

Within two weeks, Gikman has disappeared behind the Iron Curtain. On June 22, Bloch gets an early morning call at home from one "Ferdinand

Paul," who says he is calling on behalf of Pierre, as Bloch knows Gikman. Pierre, he says, "cannot see you in the near future [because] he is sick [and] a contagious disease is suspected." The caller then closes the conversation with: "I am worried about you. You have to take care of yourself."[15]

The FBI, which has listened to the call, interviews Bloch later that day, and again on June 23, but Bloch denies that he has engaged in espionage and declines to answer any further questions, and the Bureau can never muster sufficient evidence to press charges or bring Bloch to trial.

We know now that FBI special agent and then head of the Soviet Analytical Unit Bob Hanssen is the one who tips the KGB to the Bloch investigation—on May 22, eight days after Bloch's May 14 Paris meeting with Gikman. Hanssen also may be the one who plays the role of Ferdinand Paul in the June 22 call warning Bloch to "take care of yourself," but that remains a speculation.

We also know from what appears to be Hanssen's very last written communication with the Russians—in mid-November 2000—exactly how he feels about Bloch and the Bureau's handling of what should have been, to his mind, a clean takedown:

> Bloch was such a schnook. . . . I almost hated protecting him, but then he was your friend, and there was your illegal [Gikman] I wanted to protect. If our guy sent to Paris had balls or brains, both would have been dead meat. Fortunately for you he had neither. He was your good luck of the draw. He was the kind who progressed by always checking with those above and tying them to his mistakes. The French said, "Should we take them down?" He went all wet. He'd never made a decision before, why start then. It was that close. His kindred spirits promoted him. Things are the same the world over, eh?[16]

All that is certain as the mole-heads start to roll in the US intelligence community in the mid-1990s is that Rick Ames's movements don't pair up with Bloch, and Nicholson and Pitts are outside that orbit.

As for Bloch, the "schnook" Hanssen almost hated protecting, he quickly loses his State Department job, but the only jail time he will ever serve comes in January 1993—a single night in the Chapel Hill, North Carolina, lockup for stealing $109 worth of cigarettes while working as a bagger at a Harris Teeter grocery store.

Earl Pitts is in some ways the biggest mystery of the lot. During his five years as a spy, beginning in 1987, he has earned in excess of $224,000 from the KGB and later SVR—a lot of money—and yet Pitts's debriefing suggests he has been asked to do very little to earn it. The requests made of him are mostly patty-cake work. Why aren't the Russians bleeding him dry? Is it possible Pitts is, at least in part, a smoke screen, a way of hiding a more deeply embedded, far more valuable asset?

The more these questions hover and multiply, the more apparent it becomes that National Counterintelligence Center's work, while admirable to date, is far from done. Rooting out Ames, Nicholson, and Pitts has helped clear out the underbrush, but something big and dangerous is still lurking in those woods.

CHAPTER 17

AND THE WINNER IS . . .

W e knew now without a doubt that there exists a penetration that the KGB considered to be worse than Ames," Mike Rochford says. "We knew some things were compromised and not attributable to Ames or to Pitts. And this was difficult for agents in the field not to have a person to investigate, not to have a name. It's disturbing and frustrating.

"We worked with a very talented group of analysts and investigators and case officers at the Agency. They were absolutely brilliant. I had the analysts build up a matrix of compromised cases and operations, and we numbered these cases and operations and said, 'Who had placement and access to these things?'" [1]

Gwen Fuller is one of the principal matrix builders. She explains to me how the process works: "The matrix was simply names down one side of the paper, cases across the top, and then the dates when particular people got access to a case. Then you would have to decide, *Okay, how many had access?* Next we would gradually start opening investigations—preliminary or full, depending on how well they matched. We had well over a hundred, maybe up to one hundred fifty names in the very early stages. [Rochford remembers the starting number was closer to 240 names.]

"The investigations took a lot of time. In fact, it was a very long process generally. I took trips to New York to review their files. Sometimes we would get new information, and we had to keep factoring that into the matrix.

"We interviewed many different people as well—people in the FBI, the CIA. We had them sign NDAs [nondisclosure agreements], and we wanted them to have been polygraphed. Typically, we weren't interviewing the subject, but we might interview someone who was peripheral. We knew these weren't the persons we were looking for, but they had worked on a certain component of a case that had been compromised. We might ask them, 'What do you remember about that case? What happened? Why did it go south? And who had access to the case?' Access wouldn't necessarily show in the file. You had to have someone who was there and could tell you all the atmospherics of what was going on. We interviewed a lot of people, and it's amazing that people didn't leak that.

"People would rise or fall on the matrix depending on whether their access to a compromised case was direct or indirect. Some people might have access to two cases. That would push their profile higher. If we had information that the Russians were meeting someone in a certain place at a certain time, and the person we were looking at could be ruled out of having been there at that time, that might lower their importance on the matrix."[2]

Other measures join the mix: security files, psychological profiles rendered by a three-person behavioral panel, medical and financial records to see if the unsubs have particular vulnerability on those fronts. Inevitably, too, the matrix is weighted toward what Mike Rochford considers its three critical elements.

"First, the person seemed to have worked in the Counterintelligence Division of the CIA, which makes us believe it was probably an Agency person. We looked into the Soviet-European Division of the Agency, too, because that was a logical place for some of these operations and cases that went south.

"Second, this person probably had access to and probably helped the Bureau on the Felix Bloch case.

"Third, was this person able to give the KGB specific information that helped them rebuild their Line KR [counterintelligence operation] like the new Counterintelligence Division the CIA had set up?

"Taking everything into account, we would sit around and actually vote as a group on culpability potential for these folks who were on our list. First, we culled it down to about fifty, then thirty-four, then a key seventeen persons."[3]

And finally to one. He was intimately familiar with the Felix Bloch case. He had access to virtually all the cable traffic and classified secrets that were thought to have been passed to the KGB and its successor organization over the past decade and more. He was so smart that he was able to operate under the nose of his supervisors without being detected. He lived practically adjacent to Nottoway Park in Vienna, Virginia, where Soviet and Russian operatives had been seen to hover. And his name was . . . Brian Kelley.

Robert Hanssen was never on the matrix.

Louie Freeh says that he and George Tenet were sitting with their respective national security and espionage chiefs at one of their regularly scheduled meetings when he first learned the mole was CIA, not FBI.

"'Too bad,' I recall saying to Tenet. 'Three strikes and you're out.' I said it half as a joke, but of course it was my strike, not his. I just didn't know it yet."[4]

The various federal agencies and news organizations that do postmortems on Bob Hanssen's espionage will end up faulting this part of the case from virtually every possible direction. On the subject of Brian Kelley, the 2003 inspector general's report on the Hanssen case initially strikes an understanding tone.

"Given the information it had at the time, the FBI's initial selection of this CIA employee as the lead suspect was understandable," the report states. "Although an extensive investigation of this CIA suspect failed to yield any conclusive evidence of espionage, the FBI became convinced that he was a KGB mole. This was due in part to the suspect's ambiguous and sometimes suspicious behavior and in part to a belief that this individual had emerged as the lead suspect as the result of an objective and scientific process."[5]

That's about as nice as the report gets, though.

"The FBI should have seriously questioned its conclusion that the CIA suspect was a KGB spy and considered opening different lines of investigation. The squad responsible for the case, however, was so committed to the belief that the CIA suspect was a mole that it lost a measure of objectivity and failed to give adequate consideration to other possibilities. In addition, while FBI management pressed for the investigation to be completed, it did not question the factual premises underlying it."[6]

Similarly, in a 2003 *60 Minutes* segment on Brian Kelley—titled "The Wrong Man"—host Lesley Stahl all but accuses the FBI of gross incompetence. "The FBI had some of the right clues, but when they connected the dots, they came up with the wrong picture."

"This was a poorly run investigation, where the conclusion was foregone from the beginning," Kelley's lawyer, John Moustakas, tells Stahl. "What this Bureau doesn't do well is it doesn't account for its own blind spot. It has a huge blind spot insofar that it just can't conceive of the fact that an FBI agent could be crooked."[7]

George Ellard, who served as deputy counsel for the inspector general's investigation, agrees: "The FBI was blinded by institutional bias. It never suspected that one of its own would do something like this . . . They were looking outward."[8] Having framed the hunt thus, the squad searches until it finds a CIA officer who fits its definition. And having found the officer who fits the definition, they reinterpret his work history and the results of the various screening procedures the squad uses to cull its list to fit both the suspect and the crime.

Kelley does have a clear connection to the Felix Bloch case—there was no doubt about that. He was given a special award by the director of the CIA for painstakingly connecting Bloch to Reino Gikman, Bloch's assumed Soviet handler. Hardly the work of a spy, one might think—unless, of course, it's all the more reason to suspect that a mole is exactly what Brian Kelley is.

"The FBI came to think that the KGB had given up on Bloch because he was older and nearing retirement," George Ellard says. "By allowing Brian to reveal Bloch, Brian's status would grow within the Agency," and he will become an even more useful spy deep within the intelligence community's bowels.[9]

As Stahl says on *60 Minutes*, "It's like trying to fit Cinderella's slipper on the ugly sister's foot."[10]

Similar criticism comes from within the Bureau's own four walls. FBI counterintelligence agent Thomas Kimmel says that when he tried to do independent research into why so little has been asked of Earl Pitts by his Soviet handlers, he was stonewalled by senior managers. "I think they were almost in a lose-lose situation. If there was a spy in the FBI, that was an admission that we were flawed."[11]

Not surprisingly, the principal targets of this withering criticism beg to disagree. Dave Szady is "volunteered" by the Justice Department to represent the FBI in the *60 Minutes* episode, and he fights back on air.

"That's total exaggeration and totally a misrepresentation," Szady says when Stahl suggests that the Bureau was unwilling to look within its own house for the mole. "And actually, it's an insult to the FBI and to me. The information, the leads, the cases we were losing pointed toward the CIA. Every time we went and looked at the FBI, we were redirected back to the CIA."[12]

Gwen Fuller says much the same: "I don't know of anyone on the two squads who worked this case who felt that this couldn't be an FBI person. They were honest, they were hardworking, and they wanted to get the right person. . . . We had leads, and we were true to the leads. Dot connecting at this stage is very difficult. It's not like a bank robbery case. Espionage cases are among the most difficult to resolve."[13]

Jim Lyle, who initially comes to the case more obliquely as the counter-intelligence unit chief back in Headquarters, agrees: "People say the Bureau never wants to look inside the Bureau. Well, the Bureau will do that if it has to. We never shied away from that. But you've got to look at where the signals are pointing, and from my vantage point, there was multiple sourcing on some of the points, and it was fairly consistent about Kelley. . . .

"The central key point was the Felix Bloch case. They determined Ames couldn't have compromised that, and that's where Kelley comes in. He was the CIA case officer for the Bloch case, so that puts him square in the center— the top three or four suspects without considering anything else. But when they looked at the other main compromised operations and asked themselves if Kelley could account for this and this and this, the answer was always maybe yes or could have.

"A lot of the cases overlapped with the FBI, but Kelley had a lot of interacting with the FBI. A lot of the information the spy turned over to the Russians also impacted FBI operations out of New York, but Kelley had a connection up there, too, so you couldn't say he was clear and free on that front, either. So Kelley stayed in the mix until he was the last man standing."

The breadth of the penetrations and the jurisdictional distinction between the Bureau and the Agency also weigh the scales toward the CIA and help shine the flashlight on Kelley, according to an FBI agent heavily involved in the mole hunt who has to remain anonymous.

"The Agency has worldwide responsibilities. If we have to do anything overseas, we would have to cooperate with them. That means they know all of our overseas operations, but we don't know all of theirs. The compromises were so extreme that we concluded it had to be one of theirs."[14]

And how about Mike Rochford, on whose shoulder most of the blame for Brian Kelley gets laid?

"Analysts have to be free to really look at a case hard," he tells me. "And you can't punish agents for investigating the wrong guy like Kelley. Don't forget, in the Atlanta bombing, even Louie Freeh had the wrong guy. They were going after that poor son-of-a-bitch Jewell.[15]

"There needs to be oversight. Hard questions need to be asked. But I was never so riddled as I was after the Hanssen case by the inspector general's report. They hounded me for going after Kelley. And those questions were totally appropriate and should have been asked. But the unfortunate thing for Brian Kelley is that his access mirrored that of Bob Hanssen."[16]

And that mirroring came at a very bad time in the modern history of American espionage. "We were pressing," Mike Rochford admits, "and we were kind of desperate because we were still losing cases and operations . . . and we were wrong. At the end of the day, none of the people we considered had culpability."[17]

But for Brian Kelley and his family, that "end of the day" will be a long and painful time coming.

PART V

PART V

CHAPTER 18

WHAC-A-MOLE

Patricia McCarthy knows crooks and crime. She has been a lawyer most of her adult life, and a prosecuting attorney for part of that time. There's little in life that can surprise her. But she gets the surprise of her life shortly after meeting Brian Kelley for the first time in November 1999. Both are divorced, and both are immediately attracted to each other.

McCarthy, who will become Kelley's wife before the whole ordeal is over, tells me: "Can you imagine meeting him and both of us discovering there was something special between us, and afterward, he's got to sit me down and tell me that he's under investigation for being the biggest spy of the 20th century?

"He probably expected me to walk. He said, 'You know, you have a law practice. I don't know what's going to happen, but they'll probably follow you,' and they probably did for a couple weeks. But I believed him. I knew this man wasn't capable of this.

"Not that I'm an expert at sizing people up in five minutes, but lawyers sometimes have to do that, and I knew this wasn't him. He was so respectful of and in awe of his Catholic religion. He always said the way he got through this was the three Fs—faith, family, and friends.

"This is a case where they followed this man for four years, twenty-four hours a day, seven days a week, and found nothing.

"I try to be ethical and fair about this. I think there was probably information that led them to Brian. The matrix said, well, this is who it is. I don't have all that information, but there must have been something that led them down that path. But I know for a fact that they decided it was him, then looked for everything that could support that. That's exactly what they did, rather than the other way around—the way where you look at the facts first. They tried to force a square peg into a round hole."[1]

Simply put: with Brian Kelley, the FBI will not take no for answer.

The spring 1998 lie-detector test, for example. Unknown to him, Kelley has been under intense joint FBI-CIA scrutiny for months. With FISA's approval, his house and garage are bugged and searched, and his telephone tapped. A special Bureau surveillance team—agents disguised as joggers, hard hats, mothers strolling their babies, and the like—is waiting for him when he travels to New York and Niagara Falls on Agency business. In Panama, where he has previously served and is now returning, again on CIA business, he is observed "brushing against" someone who may be connected to Russian intelligence or someone Kelley had earlier recruited for the CIA, or maybe both or neither. The moment is logged but not pursued.

Meanwhile, as that spring hurries toward summer, back in the WFO, the mole hunters are concocting their first sting-like operation. Kelley is deeply experienced in double agents, defectors, and the like, so it's only natural he should be detailed to a Bureau-based team trying to evaluate a new, highly placed, top-secret Soviet defector. There's only one hitch though: to be read into the operation, Kelley first has to be polygraphed by the FBI. Well, there's another hitch, too: the polygrapher, Kendall Shull, is in on the game and knows what the outcome is expected to be.

"By then," Shull tells me, "they've tried all these other things. They had surveillance. They had cameras. They had microphones in his house—everything, and they couldn't catch him. They're getting nothing, so the game plan was to put him in access to such highly classified information—and it's the real stuff, not fake information—that he will have to recontact the Soviets, and when he does, they'll catch him."[2]

Shull will later go on to become chief of polygraph for the FBI. However, at the time, he says he's chosen for this job not necessarily because he's the Bureau's best polygrapher but because he's the only person there with a master's degree in polygraph, and perhaps because so many people at the Bureau think of lie-detector testing as more black arts than science: "They wanted the most educated person in the Bureau; they wanted that behind my name as the results moved forward."[3]

On June 12, 1998, Shull and Kelley meet in a mostly bare, white-walled room with a single window shaded by a venetian blind, at a satellite FBI office in Tysons Corner, Virginia, not far off the I-495 beltway. The session is scheduled for 10:00 A.M., but Kelley arrives early and the test gets underway at 9:50, with the two of them facing each other across a desk. Shull's first questions are designed to put Kelley at ease and to determine if he is suitable for testing.

In this opening part of the exam, Shull also previews all the questions to be asked once the actual polygraph begins. Among those questions are the three Shull has been specifically instructed to include—questions clearly relevant to the mole hunt:

- Have you ever communicated secretly with a representative of a non-US intelligence service?
- Have you ever illegally provided any sensitive information to a non-US intelligence service?
- Have you ever received any illegal gift or money from a representative of a non-US intelligence service?

Once the preliminaries are over, the setup changes. Kelley shifts to a formal polygraph chair. He leaves his shirt on, but one tube is wrapped around his chest and another around his stomach. The tubes, Shull says, measure respiration. A blood-pressure cuff goes around one arm to measure heart rate and blood volume, and finger plates are attached to two fingers of the opposite hand to monitor sweat gland activity. Wires from all these components then lead to a box on the desktop that contains the polygraph software.

By the time the formal test begins, Kelley's chair has been turned so he sits facing away from Shull, staring at a blank wall and the window darkened by blinds. Shull monitors Kelley's replies on a computer-generated chart that looks much like an EKG readout, with special attention to the three key questions.

"We look for the most significant reactions or changes in physiology at each question," he explains, "and give those reactions a plus or minus depending on the severity of the reaction. A minimum of three charts get collected with a one-minute break between the charts. For any one question, after the charts have been taken, a total of minus three indicates deception; plus three or more is considered no deception," Shull tells me.[4]

All of which sounds very intimidating for Brian Kelley—examinees frequently refer to the polygraph chair as the "electric chair"—and very scientific in its outcomes; but in this instance, Ken Shull has already been told what the outcome will be and how to deliver the news to Kelley.

"They said, 'Listen Ken, we know he's going to fail this test because he is the spy, but we want you to tell him that he passed, so I did. And he leaves, and then I look at his charts, and he didn't fail the poly. He passed.

"I'll be honest with you. When I saw that he passed, I said, 'Oh, shit!' It was the best thing for him but the worst thing possible for me because I knew they weren't going to believe it.

"I have an option. Polygraph testing can be very subjective. You have to score the charts—give it a mathematical score—but a certain amount of interpretation goes into deciding whether something is a plus or a minus. I'm thinking, I know this guy's a spy and he should fail this test, so I better give this a minus or at least put that into my considerations. I'm also thinking, dang it, he beat me. He beat my test. So I go back and score everything again, do it fresh, and he's still passing.

"When that's done, I call back to Headquarters. I think maybe the director was in the office. I know Mike Rochford was there, and probably Dave Szady, and maybe one or two others. And, of course, everyone was waiting for the results of the polygraph test. I said, 'I'm sorry, but he passed the test.'

"And they said, 'Yeah, that's what you told him, right.'

"I said, 'I told him that, but he really did pass.'

"'No, he didn't.'

"'Yes, he did. He passed the test.'

"So then they started criticizing my poly. There was a video feed set up. They'd been watching it. They said, 'He was obviously practicing mental countermeasures. He looked to us like he was counting the slats on the window blinds. That's why he didn't react to the relevant questions,'" they tell Shull.[5]

The viewers back at Headquarters also can't help noticing that Shull and Kelley seem very chummy in the pretest portion of the examination—and commenting on the fact in their post-test analysis.

"You always try before the test gets underway to build rapport and trust with the people that you're polying," Shull explains, "and Brian and I did get along well, so much so that he made the comment that he'd like to get together afterward on a social basis. I believe he invited me to his house to do something. We just hit it off, and of course everybody criticized that, as well. 'He's just trying to get in your good graces,' they said, 'because he wants you to pass him on this test.' There was even some thought at the time that I would go undercover with Kelley and try to get to know him even more because they were still convinced he was the spy.

"Trust me, I was the only person in the Bureau at that time who thought he wasn't the spy because I believed my charts, and the charts said he wasn't."[6]

Shull even went so far as to run his test results by other polygraphers in the FBI—without identifying the subject or the reason for the test—and they all agreed with him, but to no avail.

"In the end, basically, they threw the poly out," says Shull.[7]

The mole hunters also ignore the results of another sting operation, this one more a classic false-flag operation that goes down in November 1998, the same year as the polygraph.

"I got a knock on my door" at his home in Vienna, Virginia, Kelley tells Lesley Stahl on the 2003 *60 Minutes* segment. "I opened it and there was a gentleman outside, and he said, 'I come from your friends, and we're concerned. Meet us tomorrow night at the Vienna Metro. A person will approach you. We have a passport for you, and we'll get you out of the country.'"[8]

Subtle, this is not. The "gentleman outside" speaks in a heavy foreign accent, at least Eastern European, but most likely further east still. This is far from a scene crafted by John le Carré—aka David Cornwell, who learned his tradecraft with the British MI5—or Charles McCarry, the great American spy novelist who trained at the CIA. In their works, Kelley would have to puzzle through infinite layers of possibility before he reacted. In this real-world encounter, the choice is simple. If he's who the matrix seems to say he is, this is the moment for Brian Kelley to take his mysterious visitor up on the offer and bolt for the border. Instead, Kelley reports the encounter the next morning to Dave Szady, who by now sits atop of the combined FBI-CIA counterintelligence effort.

All of which, according to Kelley's eventual lawyer John Moustakas, is taken as even further proof of his guilt. "Instead of saying, 'Wow, this guy passed a polygraph; maybe he's actually innocent,' they used that as evidence of his guilt. They said, 'He's the ice man. He's the perfect spy. He can beat the polygraph.'"

Ditto for the false-flag operation. "You can imagine their chagrin, thinking, 'Oh, my God, we tried this brilliant ruse and it failed.' And immediately, what do they do, spinmeisters that they are? They say, 'Oh, my God, he's perfect. He's a brilliant spy. He knew it was a ruse, and he uncovered the ruse!'"[9]

And they don't stop there. The longer the investigation drags out, the more a fresh "truth" about the Felix Bloch case takes root—the one George Ellard notes earlier. They believe the praise heaped on Kelley for his extraordinary work as the Bloch case officer—maybe even especially the medal George Tenet presents him for meritorious service—is just what the KGB has been counting on. The Soviets had tired of Bloch. They gave him up to enhance

Kelley's status within the US intelligence community—and thus make him an even more valuable mole—and then gave Bloch a heads-up so he could go silent in the aftermath. Brilliant!

In short, damned if Brian Kelley does; damned if he doesn't. Or so it seems. And damned if they are going to let Kelley get away with it. By now there's almost too much momentum built up and too great an investment in the process to call off the investigation even if they wanted to.

Mike Rochford is the one making the FISA applications in the Kelley case and overseeing ongoing quality control, and the job seems almost endless as the investigation churns through the spring and summer.

"For each FISA application," Rochford says, "I'd go to the operational unit, to the section chief, to the deputy assistant director, the assistant director, the general counsel, the special counsel to the director, and the director. Then I'd go over to the OIPR [Office of Intelligence Policy and Review].[10] They reviewed and signed off on it; then it went up the deputy attorney general. Every application we did went through that process.

"Besides that, I personally briefed the director of the FBI and his deputy and the head of the Soviet Analytical Unit, along with the DCI [Director of Central Intelligence], George Tenet, and his DDO [deputy director of operations] and assistant DDO.[11] I'd also meet weekly with the team of senior analysts at the Agency to include the head of the Counterintelligence Division; the head of the Counterespionage Center, who was always a Bureau guy; and four or five CIA analysts. I would bring along my analysts and my case agents, and we would vote within that group on the most culpable person within the matrix. And we would do this weekly to make sure we were still onboard and still believed Kelley was our primary suspect.

"One or two people might say, well, maybe we should think about this or that, but guess what—the vote was unanimous in that group. Unanimous!

"It wasn't just that we got angry and emotional as the case went along. We included the Agency in our group at the working level and at the senior level, and we voted, and presented that to the FISA judge, and the judge saw enough progress to continue the process.

"This case wasn't as clear the day before Bob Hanssen's arrest as it was the day after the arrest."[12]

But Rochford's determination to see Brian Kelley do a perp walk as Mole of the Century does seem crystal clear, and to Kelley it also seems very personal.

Michelle Van Cleave, who headed up US counterintelligence under George W. Bush, notes as much in her October 2012 Brian Kelley Memorial Lecture at the Institute of World Politics: "Email missives from Brian were legendary among his colleagues and friends. In preparation for tonight, I was looking back through some of mine, and I found a reference to 'Mike Rochford who plays Inspector Javert to my Jean Valjean.' You will recall the Les Misérables parable about honor and redemption, in which Javert was relentless in his pursuit of the former convict Valjean. He could not believe that a thief could change his ways and become a man of honor; he could not believe that he had spent his life pursing a virtuous man."

Van Cleave then goes on to quote from the author of Les Misérables, Victor Hugo: "Probity, sincerity, candor, conviction, the sense of duty are things which may become hideous when wrongly directed; but which, even when hideous, remain grand: their majesty, the majesty peculiar to the human conscience, clings to them in the midst of horror; they are virtues which have one vice—error."[13]

There's a hierarchy to these investigations: work records, financials, psychological profiles, friends and colleagues sworn to secrecy or made to sign NDAs.

Kathleen Hunt, who knows Kelley well from her two decades as an Agency undercover officer, is one of the latter. In hindsight, she realizes that the investigators were working from a spotty but fairly accurate profile of the mole. They knew about the diamonds that Mike Rochford will soon investigate. Somehow they picked up a vibe that the man they were chasing has a soft spot for online porn and strip joints, although maybe that's just a spillover from Felix Bloch's edgy sexual tastes. The problem was, those elements described an actual mole not actually named Brian Kelley.

"They were asking about Brian's knowledge of diamonds," Hunt says. "Did he ever talk about diamonds? Whether he was engaged in Internet pornography. Did he go to strip clubs? Did he ever take me to a strip club? It was outrageous."[14]

There's also an investigative line in these kinds of cases that gets crossed with considerable peril. FISA—secret wiretaps, and so on—is a powerful tool, but it can no longer be used once an investigation goes public and the subject has direct knowledge that he or she is under scrutiny. Hip-deep in futile efforts and frustrating encounters, the mole-hunt team finally decides to invoke the nuclear option.

"The Bureau runs thousands of investigations every year to determine if people are guilty or not," Gwen Fuller explains. "If we find out we can't charge them, then we close the case quietly, and the person never knows he or she was the subject of an investigation. That's as it should be, and that's how it was here. Other people on the matrix were close enough to be the subject of full investigations. . . . But in these kinds of processes, there's a lot of pressure to make progress, and you're never going to know more if you don't become more aggressive, if you don't dive deeper. It's the way things work in law enforcement.

"We still didn't know who it was, but we had done everything we could do, and we did not have enough to even try to prosecute Kelley. We conducted a logical investigation. We checked all the boxes. We did everything we could to determine if he was the guy, and we could not definitely say he was, so the decision was made at some level to interview him—a confrontational interview—and in that way it became public."[15]

Leap ahead to August 18, 1999. Brian Kelley—or GRAYDECEIVER, as the FBI now refers to him—is summoned from his office to a small, nondescript conference room in the Counterintelligence Division at CIA headquarters. Waiting for him are FBI special agents and veteran mole hunters Rudy Guerin and Doug Gregory. Five years earlier, Guerin was in on the arrest of Aldrich Ames. Gregory is widely acknowledged to be one of the Bureau's top investigators; humor is not his long suit.

Who knows what Brian Kelley expects when he opens the door, but it doesn't take long for Guerin and Gregory to disabuse him of any friendly notions and cut to the chase.

"They said, 'We know who you are. We know what you've been. We even know the KGB code name they use for you: KARAT'"[16]—a throwback to Hanssen's interest in being paid occasionally in diamonds.

The only reason Kelley hasn't already been arrested, they say, is George Tenet. The DCI has instructed them to give him one last chance to come clean This is that chance. One thing they don't have to add: that Congress, in the wake of the Ames case, has reclassified espionage as a capital crime. Guerin and Gregory are accusing Kelley of actions that carry the death penalty. That hangs over the proceedings like a dark cloud.

It's not long into the interview when the two interrogators play their trump card. Here's how Kelley describes the moment: "The senior bureau agent [Guerin] jumped up, opened up his briefcase, and slammed a piece of paper in front of me, and he said, 'Explain this!' And I looked at it, and it took me a moment to realize what it was. It was my jogging map stamped SECRET."[17]

Right church. Wrong pew. The map, discovered during a FISA break-in at Brian Kelley's home, is a hand-drawn sketch of nearby Nottoway Park, and Nottoway Park is central to the case the team is trying to crack: the mole has been using the park since 1985 as his go-to site for dead-drops, and FBI surveillance teams assigned to Kelley have noted multiple drive-bys by known Soviet agents. But in this case, two plus two doesn't equal four. Kelley does use the park regularly, for morning runs, and the map they have discovered plots his favorite jogging routes, not any espionage hidey-holes.

Once again, the FBI team has labored hard and comes up with a goose egg. But never mind. After the interview concludes, they turn Kelley over to CIA security personnel who take his badge and walk him out of the building. A year and a half will pass before he's allowed back in. That same day, August 18, 1999, Kelley's daughter, Erin, who also works for the CIA, is "badged" herself and placed, as her father is, on paid administrative leave.

Just about the same time, Rudy Guerin and Doug Gregory are sharing their post-interrogation observations with Mike Rochford.

"Doug never believed it was Kelley, and he was right," Rochford remembers. "Rudy was probably more cautious, but once he saw Kelley, he said, 'Mike, I don't think it's him.' I was surprised, but I said, 'We got to continue the operation.'"[18]

In fact, Operation GRAYDECEIVER is just getting to its ugliest stage.

"Not long after the interview, the WFO people came over to Headquarters with a proposal for a massive physical search on Kelley's residence, a destructive search," Jim Lyle recalls. "The way FISA works, the field offices don't go to the Justice Department. Headquarters goes, so they have to ask us to go to OIPR and get that whole process going, and I say, 'No, I'm not doing that.'

"Not much time passes before I get a call from the ASAC [assistant special agent in charge] over at WFO, and he says, 'I hear you're not going to support us,' and I said, 'That's right. The case is on overt status now. FISA doesn't apply anymore. Secondly, how many times have you been in that house, and what did you find that provides probable cause to get a Fourth Amendment search warrant right now? The answer is zero. You've got no probable cause to even go into that house right now, let alone destroy it. I'm not going to DOJ for that.'"[19]

Score one for Brian Kelley—his domicile isn't going to be reduced to splinters in the search for hidden clues, at least not yet. Meanwhile, though, his family has come under full-bore assault from Mike Rochford's SIU, and the gloves are off.

"My mom [Brian Kelley's ex-wife] was first," says Brian Kelley's son, Barry. "She got questioned by the FBI, and it was pretty grueling. After that, everything happened fairly quickly. It wasn't like one person got questioned by the FBI and then it was several weeks before the next one.

"After my mom, they went to both of Dad's sisters and their husbands with the threat that they were going to go to Dad's mom if they didn't tell them everything they knew. She was in an assisted living center in Connecticut.

That probably would have put her in her grave right there on the spot. There were a lot of threats being made.

"They got my brother down in Kentucky. They pulled him out of his office into the lobby and started questioning him right then and there. This was the day after his daughter was born, so he thought at first it was a prank.

"My sister, of course, was badged and locked out of the Agency just after my dad. They made a lot of threats to her, too—what would happen if she tipped us off that this investigation was underway. The whole thing was heart-wrenching for her. Think about that. Not that everybody at the CIA knew her—it's a big place—but just the thought of people saying, 'Did you hear about Erin Kelley getting walked out?' At the Agency, you don't get walked out because you're a good person. Rumors are spread. From a reputation standpoint, you have that hanging over your head.

"I travel quite a bit for work, and back then, I was bouncing around New York—White Plains, Long Island, the City. They were chasing me all over the place, trying to figure out where I was going. They finally caught me in New York City.

"I got a phone call, and they said, 'We need to talk to you.' I said, 'That's fine. I'm flying home this afternoon, so I'll see you in the morning,' They said, 'No, we need to talk to you right now.' And I said, 'I got to go to the airport,' so they actually picked me up from the office where I was when they called and drove me to LaGuardia, which is not the shortest trip on a weekday afternoon, and along the way they told me that Dad was a spy and a traitor to his country—maybe the worst spy in American history.

"I kept telling them, 'Based on everything you're saying to me, on all these things, that's not my Dad. No way, you got the wrong guy. There are two reasons why people would betray their country. It's because they got burned in the past or it's money. Neither one of those profiles fits my dad. You're talking about a decorated US Air Force officer. He wouldn't betray his country. He wouldn't.'

"At one point, I said, 'Is the arrest imminent? Am I going to walk out in the morning and see it on the front page of the *Washington Post*?' And they said, 'Yes.' The flight down to DC is a short one, but it felt like ten hours."[20]

On the ground at Reagan National Airport, Barry Kelley calls his dad, and Brian Kelley agrees to come over to Barry's house.

"I met him in the driveway, and it was a pretty long, emotional hug. This is the guy you grow up thinking is the king, and now his kids are being told he's the biggest traitor in US history ever, a mastermind, always one step ahead of us.

"And for the next couple years, we're going to get up every morning and go down the driveway to get the *Post*, wondering, *Is today the day? Is this it?*"

Thankfully that day never comes, I remind Barry.

"Yes," he replies, "but which is worse—having it done and over with, or waking up every day wondering if this is the day?"[21]

Patricia Kelley is never questioned by the FBI. She and Brian didn't marry until near the end of his purgatory, but she gets the last word on these investigative interviews of the Kelley family: "That was like a Mario Puzo movie. You can see it being made. It's all these simultaneous scenes—interviewing Brian's sisters, their husbands, the children. Then they threaten to go to his mother. It was vile. It would have killed her, and they got nothing from that. *Nothing.* Brian told me about the interviews several weeks after we started dating, and I said, 'That's a shakedown.' As a prosecutor, if you don't have anything, you go in with both barrels blasting."[22]

The one who has it worst in all this, of course, is the principal player: Brian Kelley himself. Kelley, however, dies in September 2011, at age sixty-eight, so his widow, Patricia, has to speak for him.

"Brian would tell you he was bewildered. He was in a state of emotional shock. For eighteen months this man lived under the threat of CNN and NBC showing up on his front steps because he had been indicted for the biggest espionage trial of the 20th century.

"He would sit at his computer and look out the window, and one time, these men in blue and gold jackets—FBI colors—started walking up the sidewalk, and he just panicked. It turned out to be the lawn people.

"He was on administrative leave, but he had to call in every single morning, Monday through Friday. How humiliating for a man who was a patriot, a national treasure. He was like the pied piper of counterintelligence. He loved what he did, and he did it well. And this was his reward.

"Brian would always tell me, 'It's just this world. In counterintelligence, this can happen to anyone. But I didn't go this route for my family to be subjected to this."[23]

Eventually, inertia overcomes the Brian Kelley case, and it enters into a kind of suspended animation—neither resolved nor abandoned. Jim Lyle, then with the FBI's Soviet Analytical Unit, describes its status: "By the spring of 2000, the WFO can't go any further with the investigation of Kelley. They've done everything they can possibly do. Pretty much every FISA technique known to exist at that time has been used. So the day comes when the big report from the WFO on GRAYDECEIVER arrives, and I'm the first guy to get it.

"I told my supervisor, who was coordinating this, 'I'm closing my door. I don't want anyone talking to me unless they are section chief or above because I'm going to read this word for word.' And I sat there and went through the whole thing. When I finished, I gave it to my supervisor to read and he gave it to the next person up the line to read because the report has to go through the whole chain to decide if it's going to be sent over to John Dion at the Department of Justice for possible prosecution of Brian Kelley."[24]

This is the beginning of May. By the beginning of June, Lyle has moved out to Langley to take over as the new head of the Counterintelligence Espionage Group—the CEG, established after the Ames case and always headed up by the FBI. Above him on the pecking order is Steve Kappes, head of the Counterintelligence Division, the umbrella organization that includes CEG. And above Kappes is Jim Pavitt, deputy director of operations for the CIA, only two tiers removed from George Tenet.

"My very first day as the new head of CEG," Lyle tells me, "Steve Kappes came down and said, 'Have you met Jim Pavitt?' And I said, 'No, not really.' So he said, 'Come on, I'll introduce you to him,' And away we went to the Headquarters building, to the seventh floor, and into Pavitt's office.

"Pavitt is a real live wire, a mile-a-minute guy. He motioned us over to his little conference table, and my rear end hadn't even hit the seat before he was putting a finger in my chest. 'I got just one question for you,' he said. 'Is Brian Kelley the guy?'

"I just told him the truth. I said, 'Jim, I don't know. He may be GRAYDE-CEIVER, but he may not be GRAYDECEIVER. I read that report cover to back, and it is all circumstantial. It's strongly circumstantial, but there's no proof in there at all that I saw. I'm not talking about proof you can base a prosecution on. There's just nothing there that proves to me he's GRAYDECEIVER.'

"I said, 'I think we're not going to know the answer until we get new reporting.' Then I told him that I had approved an operation to do that—a promising operation that may or may not produce anything."[25]

Its name was Operation PENNYWISE, and in the end it produced everything that was needed and much, much more. But Brian Kelley would remain in limbo for another nine months.

CHAPTER 19

HE'S BACK!

That a mole hunt is underway at all is supposed to be knowledge held within a small community of analysts and investigators, but that intention has long ago flown out the window. That the hunters have now settled on a particular CIA officer is supposed to be more tightly held. And that the CIA officer has a name and rank, in theory, is available only to those within the inner circle of the hunt. As ever, though, "theory" stops at "actual's" door.

Bob Hanssen learns about the hunt and the CIA officer in the spring of 1999, while routinely (for him) trolling unnoticed through the FBI's ACS system. According to the inspector general's report on his case, "Although the FBI did not intend for documents related to this highly sensitive investigation to be uploaded into the ACS system—because of widespread concerns about the system's security—many such documents were uploaded due to failures in training, simple human error, and insufficient concern about maintaining operational security."[1] With the Bureau, the more things change, the more they seem to stay the same, and the more advantage Bob Hanssen takes of the situation.

Exactly one day after learning the hunt suspect is a CIA officer, Hanssen learns his name: Brian Kelley.

Hanssen, Barry Kelley says, "monitored the investigation of my dad the entire time. He was one step ahead of the FBI."[2]

"Entire time" might stretch it. Barry's father got on that unsub list early, but once Hanssen knows, he has no intention of letting a golden opportunity slip through his hands.

"I was told he was shocked to learn that the FBI believed I was a master spy," Brian Kelley writes in his 2008 review of *Breach*, a movie about the Hanssen case. "Ironically, he downloaded relevant investigative reports on me from the ACS and included them as part of his initial communication with the SVR when he alerted them that 'Ramon Garcia' was back in the game. For more than a year and a half, Hanssen passed copies of the FBI's investigative reports on me to the SVR via his customary dead-drops. He would later claim that he was trying to 'save' me."[3]

How Bob Hanssen might have "saved" Kelley is lost to history, and perhaps to reason, but Hanssen is also determined to use Brian Kelley to save himself, on multiple levels.

On the surface, it's déjà vu all over again. Money woes have piled up once more in the Hanssen household. Even though Bob is near the top of the FBI pay scale, he and Bonnie have car loans and bank loans to cover, mounting credit card debt, the endless tuitions for their children. Bob has also run through the $94,000 he borrowed from his mother in the mid-1990s and repaid with KGB money that is no longer arriving. Approached once more by her son, Vivian Hanssen this time delivers bad news: the well is dry, and she has no more to lend.

There's also, maybe as always with Hanssen, the boredom factor. The FBI has stashed him at the State Department in what amounts to a sinecure. Workload is minimal, expectations light. The upside are the long lunches in the State Department cafeteria, sometimes with luminaries like Jim Bamford, sometimes with admiring old friends from the Bureau. But one thing Hanssen's lifetime hero James Bond never does is linger over a cafeteria lunch, especially without a martini (shaken, not stirred) at his elbow, stone crabs on the plate, his gizmo-heavy Aston Martin at the ready in valet parking, and breathtaking action only a few scenes away.

One of Hanssen's new State Department friends, Ron Mlotek, chief legal counsel for the Office of Foreign Missions, gets a taste of this secret-agent alter ego when Hanssen pops open the trunk of his car to reveal a Bureau machine gun he had checked out, a nine-millimeter pistol, and a stash of ammo wrapped in waterproof bags.

"I could drive my car into the Potomac River and come out shooting," he tells Mlotek.[4] Ian Fleming would be envious.

Getting back into the spy game, Hanssen will later tell his debriefers, has the usual financial component. He's rolled a big chunk of his credit card debt into a home mortgage during several refinancings and is now losing money monthly based on his FBI salary. But he also says that reentering espionage feeds the "excitement" and "stimulation" he craves, the self-image he has been paying homage to for nearly half a century, and maybe the literal sexual kick of having his colleagues virtually watching as he sells the Bureau, the Agency, and his country down the river.

That fall of 1999, just about the time Mike Rochford's interrogators are dropping the kitchen sink on Brian Kelley, harassing his children and other family members, and threatening to question his mother in her assisted living center, Hanssen uses an encrypted message on a computer disk to reconnect with the KGB, still officially known as the SVR but returned to its old hard-nose ways in Vladimir Putin's Russia. Ramon Garcia is back in town, he tells them, and will be open for business as soon as he receives a down payment of $50,000.

Although he doesn't mention it specifically in his opening sally, Hanssen is also as usual well-positioned to deliver the goods. Among the responsibilities in his essentially unmonitored liaison job is conveying highly classified documents between the State Department and FBI headquarters. Now he will be paid by both sides to walk documents out of the building.

As earnest of his good intentions, Hanssen tells them about Kelley, in case they want to extract their agent or warn him as they did with Felix Bloch. It's hard to know Hanssen's full intention here, but he surely knows that Kelley is under twenty-four-hour blanket surveillance and any attempt by the Russians to contact him will cement the case against him and give Hanssen an open field to play on.

In any event, the SVR is quick to respond, and in glowing tones:

> Dear friend, welcome!
>
> It's good to know you are here . . . We express our sincere joy on the occasion of resumption of contact with you. We firmly guarantee you for a necessary financial help. Note, please, that since our last contact a sum set aside for you has risen and presents now about 800,000 dollars. This time you will find in a package 50,000 dollars. Now it is up to you to give a secure explanation of it.
>
> As to communication plan, we may have need of some time to work out a secure and reliable one. This is why we suggest to carry on the 13th of November at the same drop which you have proposed in your letter We shall be ready to retrieve your package from DD since 20:00 to 21:00 hours on the 12th of November after we would read your signal (a vertical mark of white adhesive tape of 6–8 cm length) on the post closest to Wolf Trap Creek of the "Foxstone Park" sign. We shall fill our package in and make up our signal (a horizontal mark of white adhesive tape).
>
> After you clear the drop, don't forget to remove our tape that will mean for us—exchange is over.[5]

The SVR communication goes on in the usual fashion of such a business, proposing a new place to put a signal in case of emergency (a utility pole at the intersection of Whitehaven Parkway and Foxhall Road in Northwest DC), establishing the color coding of tacks to be placed in the pole (white thumbtack for pickups to be made at the old dead-drop site in Foxstone Park, yellow thumbtack for "a threatening situation of any kind"). Ever helpful, Hanssen's restored handlers inform him that colored-thumbtack sets one centimeter in diameter are readily available at any CVS store.

Another dead-drop site is proposed, in the amphitheater of Long Branch Nature Center, also convenient to Hanssen's home in northern Virginia. Packages should be placed under the far left corner of the podium. The housekeeping goes on and on before the letter ends on a broader note:

> We are intending to pass you a permanent communications plan using drops you know as well [as] a new portion of money. For our part we are very interested to get from you any information about possible actions which may threaten us.
>
> Thank you. Good luck to you. Sincerely.

And the note is signed, as before,

> Your friends.

All hunky-dory. Except that it's not.

For starters, the SVR is slow on the uptake. On perhaps as many as three occasions over the next six to seven months—including the November 13 exchange previously agreed to—Hanssen leaves packages for the SVR at dead-drop sites known to both parties. He uses the properly colored thumbtacks with the proper circumferences, and affixes the tape in the right configuration (vertical for a pickup) and the right length. And nothing happens. The Russians don't show up. His tape never gets replaced with the horizontal we-got-your-package, come-get-your-money SVR tape. In each instance, he eventually retrieves the package himself rather than leave it under the footbridge or wherever the site is for accidental discovery by, let's say, teenagers trying to find a quiet spot to neck.

By March 14, 2000, when Hanssen can finally take it no more, his letter to his SVR handlers sounds like that of a jilted lover.

> . . . I have come about as close as I ever want to come to sacrificing myself to help you, and I get silence. . . .
>
> Conclusion: One might propose that I am either insanely brave or quite insane. I'd answer neither. I'd say, insanely loyal. Take your pick. There is insanity in all the answers.
>
> I have, however, come as close to the edge as I can without being truly insane. My security concerns have proven reality-based. I'd say, pin your hopes on "insanely loyal" and go for it. Only I can lose. . . .
>
> . . . I hate uncertainty. So far I have judged the edge correctly. Give me credit for that.
>
> Set the signal at my site any Tuesday evening. I will read your answer. Please, at least say goodbye. It's been a long time my dear friends, a long and lonely time.
>
> Ramon Garcia[6]

One could parse that letter for a long time, and once Hanssen is in custody and the full measure of his actions comes to be laid before experts, it will be the self-pitying element of it, the melancholic tone, the exact meaning of that "edge" that Hanssen claims to have judged correctly to date, "a long and lonely time." The SVR clearly parses it long and hard, too, because Hanssen's next communication to the Russians, on June 8, 2000, sounds far more like his old, emboldened self—a self also greatly mollified by a new infusion of SVR money.

"Thank you for your note. It brought me great joy to see the signal at last. As you implied and I have said, we do need a better form of secure communications—faster."

Techie that he is, Hanssen goes on to propose "without being attached to it" a solution: "One of the commercial products currently available is the Palm VII organizer. I have a Palm III, which is actually a fairly capable computer. The VII version comes with a wireless Internet capability built in. It can allow the rapid transmission of encrypted messages, which if used on an infrequent basis, could be quite effective in preventing confusions if the existence of the accounts could be appropriately hidden as well as the existence of the devices themselves. Such a device might even serve for rapid transmittal of substantial material in digital form."[7]

By way of illustration of the need for faster communication, Hanssen cites the December 8, 1999, arrest and subsequent expulsion of a Russian embassy attaché named Stanislav Gusev. Since his arrival in the United States in March 1999, Gusev has been spotted multiple times in close proximity to the State Department—sitting on a bench, idling in the car, and the like. Assuming Gusev is involved in some kind of electronic eavesdropping operation, the FBI has CIA technicians sweep the building top to bottom before they discover a tiny transmitter embedded in a chair rail in a conference room just down the hallway from the office of Secretary of State Madeleine Albright. Gusev has the remote control for the bug in his possession when FBI agents arrest him. Estimates are that the SVR has listened in on as many as a hundred meetings in that room, of various levels of importance, during the length of the penetration.

"I had knowledge weeks before of the existence of the devices, not the country placing them," writes Hanssen, who is after all stationed at the State Department. "I only found out the gruesome details too late to warn you through available means including the colored stick-pin call. (Which by the way I doubted would work because of your ominous silence.) Very frustrating. This is one reason I say 'you waste me' in the [March 14] note."

Hanssen being Hanssen, he also can't resist delivering a quick minilecture on his native land: "The US can be errantly likened to a powerfully built but retarded child, potentially dangerous, but young, immature and easily manipulated. But don't be fooled by that appearance. It is also one which can turn ingenious quickly, like an idiot savant, once convinced of a goal. The purple-pissing Japanese (to quote General Patton once again) learned this to their dismay."

Finally, Hanssen ends the note on maybe the two topics dearest to him: his own security and money; in particular, a spurned suggestion that the SVR open a Swiss bank account in his name.

"I greatly appreciate your highly professional inclusion of old references to things known to you in messages resulting from the mail interaction to assure me that the channel remains unpirated. This is not lost on me."

(Translation: The old references assure me this is not a false-flag operation, with the FBI playing the part of the SVR in these communications.)

And: "On Swiss money laundering, you and I both know it is possible but not simple. And we do both know that money [in the Moscow bank] is not really 'put away for you' except in some vague accounting sense. Never patronize at this level. It offends me, but then you are easily forgiven. But perhaps I shouldn't tease you. It just gets me in trouble."[8]

Except it sounds much more like a grievance than a tease.

Just as Hanssen's communications with the SVR have become mercurial, so has his day-to-day life—work and otherwise. Jim Bamford continues to find him charming company. Even though Hanssen is more or less exiled at the State Department, old Bureau friends like Don Sullivan consider him a valuable voice of experience.

"In 1996," Sullivan says, "I went to Washington field office as a supervisor of an SVR squad, and Bob over at the Office of Foreign Missions was one of our go-to guys when we had issues that required coordination with the State Department or we had to deal with diplomats. I used to bring Bob over to WFO to give presentations to young agents about how to deal with the State Department. One in September 1999 had thirty-five attendees. He got very good reviews for those events.

"Bob had a unique way of presenting things. 'You're going into a dark room,' he would say. 'The SAC [special agent in charge] is going to turn on the lights for ten seconds, and you are looking for elephants. You're not looking for dust bunnies. You're not looking for cobwebs. You're looking for elephants.' That was his way of saying don't get distracted—go for the big stuff. It was very effective.

"Bob also helped us in a great way in a case where we were trying to get a guy kicked out of the country because he was basically a drunk, and we thought sooner or later he was going to hurt someone. We had documented this and sent it over to State, and when you do something like that, it went through Bob at OFM.

"This was a Russian intelligence officer, and the State Department had an informal policy that when you advised them someone was driving drunk and putting the community at risk, they would gently pass it along to the Russians and ask them to do something about it.

"This time that didn't take care of the problem and the situation was getting worse, so we told the Russians to get him the hell out of here before he kills somebody, and they say, 'Well, how come we never heard about this before?' and in this case Bob is with us. And he steps up and says, 'No, they told you about it, and I told you, too.' And that was enough. The guy was gone. Bob did his job."[9]

Maybe Hanssen proves in this instance that it is possible to work effectively for two diametrically opposed organizations at the same time. But older, even better friends were beginning to see the stress fractures that come from serving two masters simultaneously, especially when one of those forms of service is punishable by death.

Hanssen's behavior has raised plenty of red flags over his FBI career, but the worst of the incidents—his manhandling of Kimberly Lichtenberg—back in 1993 at least had a possible trigger. His father had died down in Florida the day before. With a dad like Howard Hanssen, who knows what forms of rage might be set off by such an incident. (Hanssen's botched approach to the GRU in the Bethesda parking garage happened in the same broad time frame.) However, now, the red flags are flying for no discernible reason.

David Major is Bob Hanssen's godfather at the FBI—a friend, an admirer, highly enough placed to provide cover for Hanssen's odd behaviors and maybe dispel a good many of his puffs of smoke, including the Lichtenberg incident. By the summer of 2000, Major has retired from the Bureau and is running his own company, still in the DC metropolitan area. That's when Hanssen pops in for a visit and leaves Major flabbergasted.

"He just looked awful. He was pale white, and he looked like he had lost a lot of weight. It could have been that he was beaten down by the spying. It could have been the job he had—he didn't like it, and by then, he had been doing it since 1995. Whatever it was, he looked awful." [10]

Jack Hoschouer, Hanssen's bosom buddy from forever ago, sees a more outward sign of disturbance during his last visit before Bob's arrest.

"Bob and I went out to dinner, a Vietnamese restaurant near Alexandria, and as we're driving there *Prairie Home Companion* comes on the radio. I love that show. There was a choir singing the second verse of 'America the Beautiful.' I recognized it instantly. And Bob reached over and turned it off. You could tell he was angry.

"'It's just sacrilegious crap,' he told me. Because this left-wing, suspicious person [Garrison Keillor] had it on his show, it must be bad. I could tell he was under great strain at that point, but I put it down to his religious sensibilities—he thought Keillor was making fun of religion generally. It wasn't the Bob I knew as a kid." [11]

The person who knew Hanssen best—or maybe more accurately spent the most time with him—could also see the cracks forming in the wall, according to Hoschouer.

"Bonnie implied to me strongly that Bob was under really great stress. He was getting very tense, very jumpy. The moment he got out of bed, he would get on his computer and start a search. She said he was obviously under great stress, but she didn't understand why." [12]

One reason might well be paragraph 7 of the "Dear Ramon" response Hanssen receives late in July 2000 to his own communication of early June.

Paragraphs 1 through 6 take care of the niceties. The SVR thanks Hanssen for "striving" to make contact, assures him that the ups and downs back in Russia have not impinged on the spy agency's resources, and guarantees him that its "golden rule [is] to ensure Your personal security in the first place."

Paragraph 7, then, gets down to business:

> We hope that during future exchanges we shall receive Your materials,
> which will deal with the work of IC [the intelligence community], the
> FBI and CIA in the first place, against our representatives and officers.
> We do mean its human, electronic, and technical penetrations in our
> residencies here and in other countries. We are very interested in getting
> objective information on the work of a special group which searches
> "mole" in CIA and FBI. We need this information especially to take
> necessary additional steps to ensure Your personal security. [13]

The communication then ends, eight paragraphs later, with the usual assurances about Hanssen's security and a bit of a blow off on the money front: "We would like to tell you an insignificant number of persons know about you, your information, and our relationship. We assess as very risky to transfer money in Zurich because now it is impossible to hide its origins."

One assumes, however, that Hanssen's attention is still riveted to that earlier paragraph as the letter trails off.

The same themes—security and money—are in play in the letter Hanssen sends the SVR fifteen weeks later, along with a fat packet of materials, which he describes with a museum curator's touch as "somewhat variable in import. Some were selected as being merely instructive rather than urgently important. I think such instructive insights often can be quite as valuable or even more valuable long-term because they are widely applicable rather than narrow. Others are of definite value immediately." [14]

On the money front, he agrees that "Switzerland itself has no real security" but writes that it might be a good place to set up "a corporation I control loaning mortgage money to me . . . It certainly could be done." As for his handlers' persistent desire to meet him out of the country, he refuses to do so for two reasons: first, because "it simply is not practical for me. I must answer too many questions from family, friends, and government plus it is a cardinal sign of a spy"; second, because "it involves revealing my identity.

That insulation has been my best protection against betrayal by someone like me working from whatever motivation."[15]

Hanssen also returns to the theoretical $800,000 on deposit at the Moscow bank and then ties it, perhaps humorously or perhaps not, to the possibility of "retiring" to Russia.

"How do you propose I get this money put away for me when I retire? (Come on, I can joke with you about it. I know money is not really put into an account at MOST Bank, and that you are speaking figuratively of an accounting notation at best to be made real at some uncertain future. We do the same. Want me to lecture in your 101 course in my old age? My college level Russian has sunk low through inattention all these years; I would be a novelty attraction, but I don't think a practical one except in extremis.)"

As almost always, too, in this swan song of his spying career, there have been some communication glitches that have weighed heavily on Hanssen: "For me breaks in communications are most difficult and stressful."

But it's a few sentences scattered through the opening paragraphs that seem best to capture the current state of Bob Hanssen's mind: "Recent changes in U.S. law now attach the death penalty to my help to you as you know, so I do take some risk. On the other hand, I know far better than most what mine-fields are laid and the risks. Generally speaking you overestimate the FBI's capacity to interdict you, but on the other hand, cocksure officers, (those with real guts and not as much knowledge as they think) can, as we say, step in an occasional cow pie. . . .

"Perhaps you occasionally give up on me. Giving up on me is a mistake. I have proven inveterately loyal and willing to take grave risks which even could cause my death, only remaining quiet in times of extreme uncertainty. So far my ship has successfully navigated the slings and arrows of outrageous fortune.

"I ask you to help me survive."[16]

Hanssen's letter is included in the package he delivers to SVR via the Foxstone Park site on November 11, 2000. Less than a week later, the FBI will finally know the name of the mole it has been chasing for what seems like forever.

PART VI

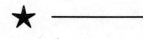

CHAPTER 20

PENNYWISE

Fittingly, the beginning of the end for Robert Philip Hanssen is inspired by maybe the most enigmatic Russian defector ever: Vitaly Yurchenko. He is the KGB officer who came over to the West in November 1985, quickly identified two American intelligence officials then working for the KGB, and, three months later, walked out of the Georgetown, DC, restaurant where he was dining with one of his handlers straight into the Soviet embassy, soon to return to Moscow and receive the Order of the Red Star.

To this day, no one in the US intelligence community knows for certain Yurchenko's motivations or intentions, but his key contribution to Bob Hanssen's takedown is crystal clear. Mike Rochford, who leads the takedown effort, describes how Yurchenko helped launch Operation PENNYWISE.

"The Agency is looking at whether its own flawed operations or the sources themselves have caused the demise of all these assets," Rochford explains, "and the Bureau is looking internally because we've had all these allegations over the years of penetrations.

"The guys in the Vault spent about a year and a half looking at old allegations of FBI agents who might have been working with the Russians that had never been followed up or maybe where an investigation was started but never done thoroughly, and finally suggested that we use an idea Yurchenko had given us—that when you don't have enough sources in the CIA or FBI to deal with these problems, you team together and offer everybody you are interested in recruiting [on the other side] a million dollars. Sooner or later, he said, somebody's going to dance with you, and you'll wind up getting a recruit.

"And we said, 'Hmmm . . . that's pretty cool.' So a group of us that included Gwen Fuller, Jim Milburn, Mike Anderson, and me got together and launched this recruitment effort we called PENNYWISE."[1]

For starters, Rochford's team makes a list of all KGB and GRU officers, either retired or still active, who might be legitimate targets. Then they get every FBI and CIA director beginning in 1992 to sign a letter agreeing to pay $500,000 each if a source they receive proves productive. And then comes the hard part: approaching the targets themselves.

"We'd say, 'Look, we need to know any penetrations in the US intelligence community that you might know about. If you can tell us who your American source is, then you'll get a million dollars—$500,000 from the Bureau, $500,000 from the Agency. And if you know of multiple sources, then you'll get more than a million dollars, right?'

"We don't need you to be a force for us. We just need you to answer a couple questions, and if you help us identify these individuals, we'll give you a pat on the ass and send you away with a lot money.

"In some ways the operation was a little irresponsible. You like to have a recruitment case that lasts for years and win someone's trust over a period of time, but we were still losing assets and operations. So we came up with pamphlets and portfolios for each of our targets, and I would bet that our original list was well over 250 people. We whittled that down as time went along, but I probably pitched thirty or more of these guys myself.

"I ended up going to a lot of places, overseas sometimes, sometimes even in the United States, using one identity or another because we knew they had the equivalent of the NSA [National Security Agency] and were tracking some of us. I chose names of some of my high school buddies for my driver's licenses and passports. And I got to see the world and pitch a lot of poor Russians who didn't know what the hell I was talking about."

PENNYWISE, Rochford says, is yet another valuable wake-up call to both entities involved. "Here you had two agencies, both penetrated and not realizing it, going their own way, then trying to form a partnership when we hadn't worked well together in the past. But we did it anyway because we finally realized that if we didn't form a partnership, we were not going to get anywhere."[2]

The effort even produces some reward. Rick Ames is a walking advertisement for his own espionage, but PENNYWISE helps predicate and close the case on him. Rather than solve the penetrations, though, Ames deepens the mystery: he fails to be in too many places at just the right times to explain the carnage that has swept through both organizations. Ames does, however, help to establish the matrix that has up to this point winnowed the investigation down to one unsub who stubbornly refuses to admit his guilt. And that's where PENNYWISE is focused now—less on discovering a new candidate for spy of the century than on making the breakthrough that will prove Brian Kelley's guilt beyond any shadow of a doubt.

Happily, the first big hit in this final, post-Ames phase of the operation seems to be a big step in the right direction.

The man who would come to be known as Mr. Pym swims into the orbit of Mike Rochford's attention, thanks to an ex-CIA officer named Jack Platt. Through business ties in Russia, Platt has met with Mr. Pym just long enough to learn three things about him: one, his current employer, a Moscow private investigative agency, is hoping to dump him for underperformance; two, he is looking for an American connection to help launch the Russian artifacts business he is hoping to establish; and three, he is a former KGB officer who keeps hinting about dark knowledge.

On the business side, Platt has no interest in what sounds like a nascent smuggling operation. The New Russia, under the ultranationalist Vladimir Putin, is keeping a close eye on even minor national treasures. But when Platt returns to the United States and Mike Rochford tells him about his

make-a-million campaign, Mr. Pym comes to mind, and before long, a PEN-
NYWISE plan is brewing.[3]

A former law enforcement officer with serious credentials in the art world
is temporarily recruited to help lure the Russian to America. Under the
letterhead of the highly respected New York art museum where he is then
employed, the recruit writes Mr. Pym expressing great interest in his artifacts
and invites him to New York to discuss a working relationship, offering him
a per diem for his time.

When Mr. Pym accepts, the FBI books him a room at the boutique
Benjamin Hotel on East 50th Street. The two meet in the Benjamin lobby
in late June 2000, and the Russian shows the recruit the sample pieces he
has brought along, including an exquisite egg adorned with an image of
Christ. Instantly recognizing the few pieces as the real thing, stolen or not,
the recruit hands the Russian an envelope containing his per diem, $1,000
in the aggregate, excuses himself with a promise to meet later, and disappears from this narrative forever.

The next person the Russian encounters as he strides down Fifth Avenue
later that afternoon is Mike Rochford.

"I interdicted him on the streets of New York," Rochford explained in an
October 2013 discussion at the International Spy Museum. "I said, 'Hey,
look. How're you doing?'

"I didn't know him from Adam, and he looked at me like I was goofy and
said, 'Hey, who are you?'

"So I gave him a business card, and he looked at it and said, 'What do
you want?'

"'Well, let's sit down,' I told him. 'Let's just sit down here and have a drink.'

"He said, 'I don't drink with strangers.'

"So I said, 'Well, okay, don't have a drink. I'll sit down and have a beer and
you can have some water.'

"He was playing with my business card and looking at me, and finally he
said, 'Do you have any credentials to validate what this card says?'

"'Yeah, sure. Here you go. More roast beef—that's me.'

"And he said, 'You know what I'm going to do with the business card? I'm going to go to the Russian Mission to the United Nations, give this to the security officer, and I'm going to have him take that to the *New York Times*, and we're going to put it on the front of the *New York Times* that you have ruined my business opportunity as a former Russian diplomat. And you know, your name will be all over the front page of the *New York Times* for being a provocateur.'

"I said, 'You know, probably that's fiction. Probably nobody at the *New York Times* gives a rat's ass about you, but I care about you. You'd be lucky if that thing appears in the *New York Times*' comic strip, but I want to make you the most successful Russian-American businessman in the history of our two countries. This is serious. Only the director of the CIA and the director of the FBI know that I'm here. Nobody else.'

"'How am I going to eat?' he asked. 'My ticket—I have to stay here for a couple weeks.'

"I said, 'I know. Just so happens I'm going to be up here for two weeks. I'll take you to lunch, dinner, breakfast—every day. Let's start with a lobster dinner, on the director of the FBI, tonight. I'll meet you in three or four hours.'

"He said, 'If I show up, I'll come with a security officer from the United Nations. Will you pay for him?'

"I said, 'Sure. No problem.'"[4]

The key to a successful recruitment, Rochford tells me, is "handling someone in the proper moment when he's in a leveraged position."[5] He's not sure he has found that moment with Mr. Pym.

Back in his own hotel, Rochford checks with the technical team in the room next door—the team that has bugged the Russian's hotel room to a fare-thee-well.

"'Was he in touch with the security officer?' I asked them.

"'No, the only call he made was to get the two-ounce bottles for the refrigerator,' they said."

The Russian does show up for dinner—"a little off-balance" but alone. That's a step forward, but the meal doesn't go well.

"He was very aggressive, pretty much told me that 'You can forget it. I'll never cooperate' and 'I should just pack my bags and go home. This is a fool's errand.'"[6] (This is mostly in English even though Rochford is fluent in Russian.)

Back with his team afterward, Rochford is ready to throw in the towel. He's tried enough of these PENNYWISE recruitments by now to know that "When you ask somebody to dance and they don't want to dance, you don't dance. That's it. We're done."

But it's not. Rochford does not catch the next train back to DC, and over the next week-plus, Mr. Pym continues to meet with Rochford despite his reservations, and the conversation begins to shift. First, as they move from meal to meal and drinking hole to drinking hole, Mr. Pym tries to turn the tables, pitching the FBI special agent and assuring him that he can make a lot of money in the former people's paradise. Finally, Rochford says, "We were having Tullamore Dew in some Irish bar—[laughing] we used to call it Tell-Me-More-Dude—and he said, 'I'd like to tell you something,' and he starts telling me about something—the specifics of which I won't go into, but it was very startling. He said, 'I can tell you everything about it, but it's important that we have trust, and that I know that it goes no further except to your director and the director of the Agency.'

"I said, 'Sure, no problem. If we're going to enter into this, then we're going to go up into a hotel room and get off the streets, and we're going to start talking seriously about what we can do for you.' So we go up to a room, and we negotiate what I'll call a contract: what he wanted and what we were willing to provide. He wanted me to sign the contract, but I said, 'No, I'll be your advocate, but the director of the FBI will sign it. It will be Louis Freeh. And it will also be seen by the Agency's director [George Tenet].'

"And then I said, 'You know, we're going to make you the most successful guy in the history of business between our two countries.'"

What the Russian claims to be in possession of in that New York hotel room is either the holy grail of this particular mole hunt or a monster con game. No, he doesn't know the name of the KGB's American agent or where in the intelligence community he is positioned or what he looks like or whether he is seven feet tall in his stocking feet or barely five feet on tiptoes. But he does have, he says, a record of the entire interaction between the mole and the KGB between 1985 and 1991, as well as "some forensic information you might want that I'll put in there too"—a colossal understatement, as things turn out.

The goods, he tells Rochford, were smuggled out of the KGB's First Chief Directorate piecemeal, as insurance against an uncertain future. He personally copied into a notebook the titles of all the documents the mole delivered to the KGB and a brief inventory of each item.

In all, Mr. Pym figures, his package is worth $10 million. Rochford counters with the standard PENNYWISE offer—$1 million—but no one believes that's a realistic figure either, and by now the secure phone lines to Pennsylvania Avenue and Langley are humming nonstop, with calls to and from the mole-hunt team back at WFO that has been in his ear all along and the top brass at both the Bureau and the Agency. In the end, the two agree to a package, including resettlement for the Russian and his family in the United States, that Rochford estimates at about $7 million in aggregate value. And then comes the kicker: by way of down payment, Rochford's new (and maybe only) supersource demands, product entirely unseen, $750,000 in cash up front.

Back in Washington, DC, the FBI agrees to split the estimated $7 million with the CIA but refuses to pony up a penny of the down payment for an ex-KGB officer of uncertain provenance and virtue.

"I don't want to name the guy who didn't want to pay him," Rochford says, "but he was superior to me, and he didn't want to do anything. But at times like this, you can't be shy. You have to believe that what you are doing is right."[7]

Rebuffed by his own organization, Rochford looks next to Langley, in the hope that a spy agency might better understand the risk-reward ratio inherent in the deal he is proposing.

"I was lucky. I had briefed Tenet a number of times, and he liked me, and I had a good relationship with a lot of the Agency people in senior positions, so when they asked me, 'Is this for real?' and I told them, 'Yes, it is,' they made it happen, especially [CIA counterintelligence chief] Mike Sulick. The next morning, [Sulick] sent his agent up on a train with that money in a briefcase, and when [Mr. Pym] saw the money sitting there, that turned everything around. [Sulick] will always be my hero."

The newly recruited source, Rochford says, "wanted to take it all back with him, but I wouldn't let him get on a plane with it. Instead, we found a way to put it in several different banks and make it accessible to him whenever he wanted it, anywhere in the world. The key thing is he knew that it was his."[8]

Before the Russian departs, though, the two men celebrate the deal with a dinner cruise around Manhattan. It's the Fourth of July weekend—Independence Day, 2000—and the fireworks are exploding in the night sky overhead. The opposite side of the contract—goods receivable—is another matter.

The package, Mr. Pym says, has been stashed in his mother's garage for the past five years. The operational plan is for him to retrieve it and pass it, in Moscow, to an undercover CIA officer on August 4, exactly one month from the day the deal is struck. Except the Russian doesn't show up, which does not improve Rochford's standing with the FBI senior executive who didn't want to make the down payment in the first place.

"After my source didn't show up for that first meeting, he said, 'You owe the CIA $750,000.'

"I go, 'Bullshit!'

"He said, 'You got taken, and you talked the CIA into giving you that.'

"I said, 'Stuff happens, quite frankly,' and he shut up and went packing."[9]

Mr. Pym has no particular excuse when Rochford gets back in touch—he just missed it, he says—but by way of atonement he offers up details on the compromise of an American source that he had been personally involved with and that Rochford obliquely has been very involved with, too.

"It was a double-agent case," Rochford tells me, "and believe it or not, it was an agent run by Brian Kelley. I was like, 'Oh, shit!' Here we were almost to the hilt, and we had another case that was tied to him."[10]

ABOVE: Even as a teenager, Bob Hanssen was fascinated by espionage novels and James Bond movies. This 1962 photo was taken his senior year at William Howard Taft High School in Chicago. BELOW: Hanssen's best friend, Jack Hoschouer, on patrol in Vietnam. Hanssen sent him nude photos of his own wife Bonnie while Hoschouer was serving overseas. *Photo courtesy of Jack Hoschouer.*

LEFT: Dmitri Polyakov, code-named TOPHAT, was arguably the most important Russian intelligence asset the United States ever had. In one of his first acts as a mole, Hanssen sold his identity to the Soviets for a reported $30,000.

BELOW: A still from a Soviet intelligence service video of TOPHAT's arrest. Polyakov "knew that if he were caught, he would be sentenced to die," one CIA source says. "He would be taken into the room, asked to kneel down and be shot in the head." His end was actually worse than that.

LEFT: Mark Wauck, Hanssen's brother-in-law and fellow FBI agent, contends that he tried to warn the Bureau that Hanssen might be a spy a full decade before he was caught.

BELOW: Robert Hanssen in happier times. The black suit was almost daily attire, one reason why some of his fellow agents nicknamed him "The Mortician."

ABOVE: Hanssen is at the far right and slightly removed in this 1985 group photo of FBI agents relaxing after a day's seminar in Dallas. Joe Navarro, front row at far left, says, "It was like Bob wanted to participate, but he didn't know how." *Photo courtesy of Jim Ohlson, standing next to Navarro.* BELOW: Brian Kelley and his second wife, lawyer Patricia McCarthy. They had been dating for only a few weeks when Kelley told her he was suspected of being the worst spy in American history. *Photo courtesy of Patricia McCarthy.*

BRIAN JOSEPH
KELLEY
LT COL
US AIR FORCE
VIETNAM
JAN 8 1943
SEP 19 2011
CIA
1984 - 2006
FAITH FAMILY
FRIENDS

ABOVE: Hanssen's favorite drop site for his Russian handlers was under this bridge in Foxstone Park, in Northern Virginia, where Brian Kelley is posing. Kelley lived only a short walk from the site. *Photo courtesy of Patricia McCarthy.*

LEFT: Brian Kelley's tombstone makes no mention of the eighteen months of psychological torture he endured as the lead suspect in the joint FBI-CIA Mole Hunt. His wife says that "Faith, Family, and Friends" sustained him through that ordeal.

ABOVE: Mike Rochford, left, and Dave Szady, right, both played key roles in identifying Brian Kelley as the long-sought mole and in Bob Hanssen's ultimate downfall. *Photo courtesy of Mike Rochford.*

Robert P. Hanssen
Senior Policy Advisor
Office of Foreign Missions

U.S. Department of State
Washington, DC 20520

202-647-5576 TEL
202-736-4391 FAX

ABOVE: In 1995, Hanssen was detailed to the State Department as the FBI's senior representative to the Office of Foreign Missions. Four years later, he resumed spying for the Russians after a nearly eight-year hiatus. BELOW: Bob Hanssen and Don Sullivan in early January 2001, at a luncheon commemorating Hanssen's departure from the Office of Foreign Missions. Hanssen had been summoned back to FBI headquarters to a phony job. In fact, he was under round-the-clock surveillance, including by Sullivan. *Photo courtesy of Don Sullivan.*

ABOVE: February 15, 2001: Three days before Hanssen's take-down, Rich Garcia (white shirt) lured Hanssen (at center) down to the FBI's basement shooting range while Bureau specialists on the upper floors downloaded the mole's Palm Pilot. BELOW: Half an hour before Hanssen's arrest, he pulled into a Northern Virginia strip mall and transferred the drop he was about to make for the Russians from his car trunk to the front seat.

ABOVE: February 18, 2001: Surveillance cameras capture Bob Hanssen emerging from Foxstone Park after making his drop, in his last moments as a free man. BELOW: At nearly 6'3", Hanssen towers over some of his arresting officers on February 18, 2001.

ABOVE: Arrogant to the end: As Hanssen was being led away by fellow FBI agents, he asked, "What took you so long?" BELOW: A quiet Northern Virginia suburb served as the backdrop for the arrest of the most valuable asset Russia has ever had inside the United States intelligence community. Hanssen's chief KGB handler, Victor Cherkashin, once estimated the total value of Hanssen's stolen secrets to be $10 billion.

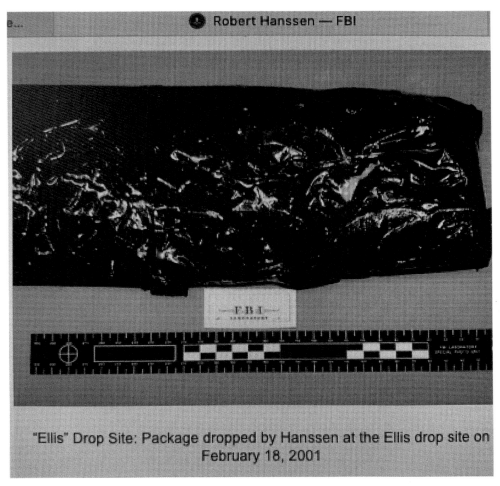

F.B.I
LABORATORY

"Ellis" Drop Site: Package dropped by Hanssen at the Ellis drop site on February 18, 2001

ABOVE: Hanssen's last drop, wrapped in this plastic garbage bag, contained among other secrets the identity of a valuable CIA Russian asset.

ABOVE: After Hanssen's arrest, FBI agents and technicians descended en masse on the Hanssens' Vienna, Virginia, home. Here they are the following morning, carrying away potential evidence for further investigation. BELOW: FBI Director Louis Freeh at a February 20, 2001, press conference, two days after Hanssen's arrest. The Bureau delayed announcing the take-down for 36 hours because Monday, February 19, was President's Day and the FBI wanted maximum news coverage.

To: Michael Rochford
     With Best Wishes

ABOVE: Then Assistant Attorney General Robert Mueller congratulating Mike Rochford post-arrest for Operation PENNYWISE, which produced "Mr. Pym." Mueller once told a roomful of Justice Department attorneys that Rochford's account of recruiting Mr. Pym was "the most fantastic fucking story I've ever heard!"

LEFT (TOP AND BOTTOM): FBI agents are rarely presented medals by the CIA, especially a decoration this treasured, but Director George Tenet made an exception in the case of Mike Rochford. The accompanying citation reads in part: "Michael T. Rochford is hereby awarded the National Intelligence Medal of Achievement in recognition of his meritorious performance for his pivotal role in a highly sensitive joint FBI/CIA operation that resulted in the positive identification of Robert P. Hanssen as an agent of the KGB/SVR. Mr. Rochford recruited a very sensitive Russian agent who was able to provide the information that led to Hanssen's identification and successful prosecution. This recruitment was all the more remarkable in that it was effected in a very short period of time with a very temperamental subject. . . ."

ABOVE LEFT: Bob Hanssen's booking photo. On May 10, 2002, Hanssen was sentenced to fifteen consecutive life sentences without possibility of parole and remanded to the federal maximum-security prison at Florence, Colorado. He spends 23 hours a day in solitary confinement.

TOP, CENTER, AND BOTTOM RIGHT: The U.S. Intelligence Community was broadly and deeply penetrated by the Soviets and later Russians during the 1980s and '90s. Among Hanssen's fellow spies, BEGINNING AT THE TOP: CIA officer Harold James Nicholson, CIA officer Aldrich "Rick" Ames, and FBI special agent Earl Edwin Pitts. Unknown to each other, Hanssen and Ames had the same handler.

ABOVE: After Bob's arrest, Bonnie Hanssen continued teaching at Oakcrest School, the Opus Dei related private academy in Northern Virginia where her daughters were educated. She has never divorced her husband. BELOW: ADX Florence, the federal supermax prison in Florence, Colorado, an address Bob Hanssen shares with Unabomber Ted Kaczynski.

When the source also misses the second meeting date—September 4—the naysayers back at FBI headquarters grow louder, and Mike Rochford's hold on his job grows a little looser. This time the Russian is a little more forthcoming about this botched handoff: he's basically afraid to leave his house. Earlier, back in New York over large quantities of scotch and lobster, Mr. Pym had told Rochford that he had been the middle man on a deal put together by the Irkutsk Mafia, out of Siberia: a million-dollar shipment of caviar that had spoiled at sea before it could reach New York. In the months since, the mafia bosses have been pressing him unsuccessfully for hundreds of thousands of dollars in recompense. Now they are looking for revenge. Not irrationally, Mr. Pym figures he's a primary target of a ruthless killing machine.

Partially mollified, Rochford asks the CIA if they'll give it one more try and they agree—one more only. "If he doesn't show up, we're writing him off," he's told. "No more excuses. Tell him that."[11] So Rochford does.

This time it's a drop-dead date, November 4, and this time the Russian delivers.

"He gives the package to the agent," Rochford says. "She grabs it, makes herself safe, and hugs it all night. Meanwhile, we've been training the people in Moscow Station on federal criminal procedure. I don't think anybody's ever done that before. We show them how a green sheet works: the first name on the sheet is the first person to receive the evidence. That's what the officer who met the Russian source does first thing when she shows up at the Station that next morning with the package: she signs the green sheet. Then the Station pouches it to ship out. Usually, pouches go to the Agency, but we've arranged for this package to come to us. The CIA, after all, is home to the prime suspect in the case.

"The guy who is going to pick it up is from the Washington field office. He says to me, 'Okay, Mike, I'll bring it over to WFO once I have it,' And I say, 'No you won't!' I'm at Headquarters when this is happening, and I'm interacting with Louie Freeh, Tom Piccard, and a couple other guys, and they're telling me, 'Don't bring it to WFO. We don't know where the bad guy is yet. Bring it to Headquarters, and we'll get it right to the laboratory.' So that's what we did." [12]

Mike Rochford's Russian source might be, for the moment, the best-kept secret in the US intelligence community, but the cone of silence is beginning to leak just a bit at the edges. Still, if Brian Kelley has any way to track these rumblings from his homebound exile, he has little reason for celebration. The investigation is still Kelley-centric and will remain that way almost until the nanosecond before it isn't.

"As time goes forward into the fall, I start to hear this guy is going to cooperate," Jim Lyle says of the source. "He has materials he took out of Moscow Center [SVR headquarters in Moscow]. He claims to have a tape. The Bureau and its Soviet Analytical Unit are gearing to accept this stuff we heard.

"When George Tenet asked me about it, I told him I wasn't saying this guy's story wasn't true, but I'm concerned the Russians are diddling with us. I was sure the Russians knew about Kelley being a suspect. That wasn't a big deal—we were in an overt stage by now. But my question is, How did they know? I told Tenet that even if they gave us Kelley, that could be on purpose. Plus, if it wasn't Kelley, if it points to someone else, how can we be sure they're not doing this to protect Kelley?" [13]

Once again, Kelley is damned if he is or damned if he isn't. Or maybe just plain damned. Not long after Jim Lyle lays out the Kelley pros and cons for George Tenet, he gets a call from the Soviet Unit chief at headquarters.

"He said there was a recommendation that Brian Kelley be indicted. I was told it had gotten all the way up to [Attorney General] Janet Reno at Justice—can't remember if it had been approved by her or was just with her. So I called John Dion [chief of the Internal Security Section at the Department of Justice] directly. 'I've got to let George Tenet know if this is accurate,' I told him, and John said it was. So I went to Steve Kappes and told him, and Steve agreed we had to tell the DCI [director of the CIA George Tenet] right away.

"Steve made the call, and they said, 'In twenty minutes, he's going to be coming out of a particular office, and there's a small conference room next door. We've booked it. Be in there. He has ten minutes.'

"So we went over there, and Tenet came bounding in. Bob McNamara [chief legal counsel to the director] was with him. And Tenet said, 'What's this about?' So I said, 'Well, they're getting ready to indict Brian Kelley.'

"'Indict him?' Tenet said. 'And charge him with what?'

"'Espionage?' I said.

"And Tenet looked over at McNamara and said, 'Call Dion.'"[14]

The materials Rochford's source delivered in fulfillment of his contract are of two basic types. First are the file records inventoried in longhand, including the name assigned each document and a description of its contents—most, if not all, of the mole-product handed over to the KGB between 1985 and 1991 from deep within a still unidentified American intelligence-related organization, as many as 6,000 pages of secrets in all. Also included in this first grouping are the letters exchanged between the mole and Victor Cherkashin over the same time frame. This part of the package the FBI gets to work on as soon as the information arrives, on November 5, 2000—or more accurately, translators from the CIA get to work on them. The documents are all in Russian, they're multitudinous, and accuracy is vital to understanding. For the analysts waiting to dive into the treasure trove, the work seems to crawl along at a snail's pace.

"We kept bothering the translators, telling them to hurry it up," Gwen Fuller tells me, "but their supervisor said, 'Hey, ease up,' so we backed off."[15]

While this is going on, the vital forensic information provided by Mr. Pym sits idle in a separate envelope labeled "do not open"—with the understanding that it will remain sealed until Mr. Pym's planned arrival in Washington, DC, on November 15, assuming his ticket is honored in Moscow and he's not rubbed out first by his disappointed Irkutsk Mafia connections. Despite pressure to move ahead, Rochford convinces his colleagues and superiors to honor his source's request, and it's during this "grace period" that Hanssen makes his November 11 data dump to the SVR, one of the largest and most damaging of his career, including the names of CIA, British, and Australian in-place sources.

"Could we have stopped Hanssen's release of that stuff on the eleventh if we had opened the entire package when it arrived?" Rochford wonders aloud. "I'm not sure, but it's an important question because there were some arrests and other things that caused our friendly agencies to stop operations and recall forces."[16]

Mr. Pym does show up on November 15, alive and as planned, and is reunited with his package the same day. Now, the investigation can move on to opening the forensics envelope. Inside are two items. One is a black garbage bag the mole had allegedly used to package a drop for the KGB, which yields two fingerprints that are sent off for analysis. (This garbage bag was packed inside a second garbage bag that weatherproofed the entire delivery. In theory, Hanssen and Mr. Pym are the only people to have ever touched the interior bag.) The other is an audiocassette containing a roughly two-minute snippet of an August 18, 1986, phone conversation between the KGB's Aleksandr Fefelov and a man he knew only as Ramon Garcia. The conversation—it can be found in chapter 5— is cryptic in the extreme, but this is the closest the investigation has ever come to an actual in-hand physical evidence of the mole.

Copies of the tape are made. Men and women at both the Bureau and the Agency who have been cheek by jowl with this hunt for half a decade retire to their offices, turn on their cassette players, listen intently . . . and no one, absolutely no one, can identify to whom the voice might belong. One person, though, to whom it obviously does not belong is Brian Kelley, but even this isn't complete exoneration yet, at least for Mike Rochford: "We know it's not Kelley . . . except if he had a coconspirator."

That at least is one version of these events—the version most frequently told. Jim Milburn, the Soviet analyst who will first identify the mole as Robert Hanssen, recalls events somewhat differently. According to Milburn, the entire package was opened the night it was received and its contents, including the tape of August 1986, were immediately delivered to the FBI lab for evidence and forensic logging and registration.

"Copies of the tape," Milburn says, "were made from the original. In the next few days, agents and analysts involved in the investigation listened to the tape, but none of us could identify it as Hanssen."[17]

By this account, when Hanssen makes his November 11 drop to the SVR, the mole hunters have, in fact, known his voice for almost a week and might have been able to tail Hanssen to the exchange, arrest him on the spot, and prevent a large stash of highly classified documents from falling into Russian hands. But the FBI has thousands upon thousands of employees, and without context, even Hanssen's distinctive whisper gets lost in the rumble.

Finally, on November 16, eleven days after Mr. Pym's package arrives at the Bureau headquarters, the translated documents are ready for review, and here the divergent paths of the story come back together.

Jim Milburn and his fellow analyst Bob King start in on the documents that morning in their squad area at the Washington field office. (Gwen Fuller, the third analyst in the unit, is out of town when the package arrives.) By late that afternoon, just as they are getting ready to leave for the day, Milburn puts the pieces of the document puzzle together and thinks he has the mole at last.

"I wrote Hanssen's name on a pink three-by-five index card. It was the closest article I could grab. In my excitement I spelled his name phonetically: 'Hanson.' Then I palmed it, showed it to King, and told him to meet me in the Vault because the workday was almost over."[18]

Back at Headquarters, the two reconvene behind the Vault's cipher-locked door and compare notes. Milburn has a list of specific correlations between known compromises and Hanssen's communications to Cherkashin to cite. King, recovered by now from his initial disbelief, remembers a reference in one of Hanssen's letters to his handlers of a friend, Jack H., who might be ripe for recruiting. Milburn and King had both worked with Hanssen on an earlier mole-hunt team. On more than one occasion, Hanssen had introduced his best friend, Jack Hoschouer, to them. What are the odds it could be him? What are the odds it could be anyone else?

A copy of the tape of the mole's voice is on file in the Vault—it's a repository for such things. The first time they heard the tape, it had been an exercise in futility, but now they're not listening into a void. When they turn the tape on this time, it sounds like Bob Hanssen is in the room with them. And why shouldn't it? He's a Soviet analyst, too. In one venue or another, they have sat beside him and listened to him for years.

By now, it's going on 8:00 P.M. Milburn and King decide to wait until morning to share the news with the small group of people at the Washington field office who have worked enormously hard on this case for so very long.

"I had a dentist appointment that morning, Friday the seventeenth," Milburn remembers, "so I told Bob King to set up a meeting with Debra Smith, Mike Rochford, and a few others for around 11:00 A.M. That's when I briefed them. I told everyone, 'Look, a lot of people are going to criticize us for not finding the mole earlier and for thinking it was the wrong guy for so long. But the work you did is what culminated in all this, and we've got him now.'"[19]

The sole dissenting voice at the meeting, Milburn says, is the agent who has done so much to produce the evidence that finally brings the mole hunt to a close.

"Mike Rochford kind of blew up at the outset. 'We can't just say it's him. We have to do an investigative matrix and look at other people!' But Bob and I said, 'Mike, it's him. He fits all the connections. And it's his voice.'"[20]

Rochford, it should be noted, recalls that story slightly differently. He first learns Hanssen is the mole that afternoon when King and Milburn brief the Counterintelligence Division back at Headquarters. Either way, the mole team and the support analysts still have a circumstantial case and won't have indisputable forensic evidence—two identified Hanssen fingerprints on the garbage bag—until mid-December. What's more, if they get it wrong again, the mole hunters and the analysts might as well pack their bags and ride off into the night. Their careers at the Bureau will be through, and the Bureau itself will be shamed throughout the intelligence community.

Happily, though, all the work done in the past that yielded the wrong conclusion now speeds them in the right direction. References to Chicago in the correspondence with the KGB line up with Hanssen's biography. The first letter to Cherkashin was sent October 1, 1985, from the Virginia suburbs at a time when Hanssen was assigned to the New York field office, but work records show Hanssen was in the Washington area that day. In fairly short order for such a complicated case, the mole and his spy-product begin to dovetail neatly together—a backdoor reward for the endless hours, days, weeks, months, and years of arriving at this point.

As Gwen Fuller describes it: "The fact that it was such a long-running case worked out in the end. We had done so much work for so many years that we knew a lot. As we started to get new information, we could quickly say, this is credible. And it all started lining up. It's kind of like if you've spent years with a 2,000-piece puzzle and then all of a sudden you get critical pieces in place, and it works out."[21]

By November 20 or perhaps 21, Milburn and King are finally ready to brief Assistant Director Neil Gallagher. Before the day is out, the GRAYDECEIVER operation will be closed down and GRAYDAY opened up.

The CIA is slower to learn that it has been cleared of harboring the mole, but only by a few hours.

"We'd been hearing rumbles out at Langley that the package had arrived at the Bureau," Jim Lyle recalls. "Then I got a call that the Soviet Analytical Unit chief and the deputy chief were coming out to brief a handful of us.

"We were all assembled in the conference room when I thought, *I better go out and make sure they get spaces in the VIP parking lot.* So I walked out the main door, and sure enough, the cars were pulling into the lot. Neil Gallagher was with them, and he went off to brief Tenet.

"Meanwhile, I was walking back toward the building with Tim Bereznay and Sheila Horan [chief of the FBI's Eurasian section and Gallagher's top deputy, respectively] when Tim said to Sheila, 'As a courtesy to Jim, you might want to tell him out here.'

"And so Sheila told me, right outside the main door at Langley, 'It's Bob Hanssen.'

"And I said, 'Bob Hanssen?! Is he still around?'"[22]

Mike Sulick, who took responsibility for the $750,000 blind down payment to Mr. Pym, and Steve Kappes [head of the Counterintelligence Division] find out it's Hanssen only minutes after Lyle.

"We breathed a sigh of relief," Sulick recalls, "because we didn't think we could take the battering from yet another spy. We went up to see George Tenet right away, and he said, 'Make sure people don't gloat about this because this is a loss for everybody, and the shoe could be on the other foot the next time around.'"[23]

Mike Rochford has mixed feelings, too. "I felt good because we had exonerated an innocent guy, and then I felt bad because it's someone inside the FBI, and our ignorance had caused us to look only at the CIA, not the FBI, and it enabled this guy to get away with it for too long."[24]

Rochford, however, doesn't have a big window for introspection. Someone needs to carry this news over to the Justice Department, and the top dogs at the Bureau along with new Attorney General John Ashcroft are heading to Chicago for a conference. Rochford draws the assignment, and by now he's looking ahead instead of behind. Bob Hanssen has been identified. He still has to be arrested and convicted, and practically speaking, that means shutting down any leaks before they can even begin to reach Hanssen's ears, starting with this meeting at the Justice Department.

"All of a sudden," Rochford recalls, "about ten attorneys came into the conference room, plus four or five from OIPR. There were people sitting against the walls. And then the acting deputy attorney general Bob Mueller arrived," who within a year will be the new director of the FBI.

"Mueller sat down and said, 'Mr. Rochford, I understand you have something to brief us on,' and I went, 'Yes, sir, I do, and I respect you and everyone in here, but I'm not going to say another word until you and everybody present signs a nondisclosure agreement and agrees to take a polygraph if this thing gets leaked. If not, I'm getting up and walking out of here.'

"A couple of the attorneys started yelling and saying stuff to Mueller, and Mueller—you know, like a typical marine—stopped them right in the middle and said, 'Give me that form, Mike.' I handed him a pen, too, and he said,

'Okay, I signed it, and anybody who doesn't have the balls to sign it, get the hell out of here. You don't get briefed.'

"And I thought, *holy shit*, but everybody did sign the NDA. So then I told the whole story of how the recruitment went, except I didn't say it was the hardest thing I ever did. And I finished with the last evening [I spent with Mr. Pym]—how we were sitting on some yacht cruising around New York after [he] had agreed to cooperate, and the fireworks were going off on the Fourth of July, and he said to me, 'You're going to make me the richest Russian in American/Russian business history, and I'm going to make you a general. This is going to change history, Mike!' And I said, 'Yeah, sure, that's actually what's coming next.'

"After he hears the story, Mueller said, 'Mike, that's the most fantastic fucking story I've ever heard in my life!'"[25]

CHAPTER 21

BAITING THE TRAP

With espionage cases, euphoria can wear thin in a hurry. As of the end of the third week of November 2000, the FBI finally knows who its mole is and how devastating his treachery has been to the country in general, to the intelligence community and the FBI in particular, and to the specific lives of those he has betrayed, at least three of whom were executed. But all the Bureau has to present as evidence are file names and inventories bought at enormous expense from a shady source and a brief phone conversation so elliptical that a merely competent defense attorney could probably tear it apart.

Plenty of work lies ahead, especially if Hanssen can't be caught in the act of making a drop to the Russians. First, though, there's a previous leading suspect and a once all-but-certain mole to take care of.

"From the moment they identified Hanssen's voice," Mike Rochford explains, "we were running away from the Kelley thing. Within a week, we were having conversations with everybody, and of course one of those conversations was with John Dion at Justice. Randy Bellows had been the lead federal prosecutor on the case, so we got him over here and told him he has to stop the grand jury for Kelley, and Bellows went, 'We're still going to go to grand jury because we've got him on some classified stuff he let out.' And I said, 'No, everything goes away with the predicate of this case.' Anything we found incidentally qualifies for incidental forgiveness—forgiveness they would give a regular employee."[1]

In short, for the first time since he popped up at the top of Rochford's matrix four years earlier, Brian Kelley is finally free of suspicion—but not free of home confinement and certainly not welcomed back to Langley.

"After Hanssen was identified, George Tenet asked me if Kelley should be told," Jim Lyle says, "and I said, 'No, his applecart is where it is. Yeah, it's a bad thing we can't tell him, but it's not going to get any worse for him, and the last thing we want is for the Russians to get wind that we have ID'd who it is."[2]

Tenet buys that argument, but he revisits the matter just a day or two later with Mike Rochford.

"Tenet said, 'How much time do you need?' And I said, 'Well, how much time does anyone need? I mean, it took a year and a half to put Ames away.' He said, 'I can't keep Kelley at home for that long—I'll give you forty days.'

"'How about sixty?'

"'Okay,' he said, 'I'll give you sixty.'

"'But he's your employee,' I told him. 'You can bring him back right now if you want to.'

"And Tenet said, 'No, if we bring him back to the office, word will get around in the community, and your subject will be alerted to rumor and innuendo that Kelley is back inside the building. He's waited this long. We'll take care of him. But you guys promise me you'll get it done in sixty days.'

"'I can't promise,' I told him, 'but we'll do what we can.'"[3]

In fact, it is three months, not two months, and for the first part of that time, several agents keep investigating Kelley unaware he has been exonerated so that even that cessation of activity won't be a tip-off—a zombie case that nonetheless has to be kept on life support.

FISA is among the first stops in the push to bring down Bob Hanssen, which means going through the Justice Department's Office of Intelligence Policy and Review, which, as the OIPR's Jim Baker explains to Mike Rochford, does not exist to make life easy for the FBI. Or as Baker told Rochford: "Mike, my job with OIPR is to protect the American public from the FBI."[4]

"I could have hit him right in the face," Rochford recalls, "but when I thought about it, I realized, hey, you're right. It's just about the facts. OIPR isn't supposed to be a rubber stamp. If I can get it past them, it's going to be easier to get FISA's okay."[5]

But that's not all that easy. After the Rick Ames case, the FISA judges put together a kind of mock court to assess their effectiveness and decided that FISA's oversight had been way too makeshift. To complicate matters further, the Bureau has been to FISA more recently, seeking approval to turn the surveillance dogs loose on Brian Kelley. Do they have the right guy this time or is this the gang that just can't shoot straight? As a hedge against the latter, the FISA judges decide, in Rochford's words, to build the "Chinese Wall" higher for Hanssen. Translation: the Bureau is going to have to work harder to clear the legal hurdles this time around.

With Kelley, though, the FBI had nothing more than a matrix and what proved to be a cockamamie theory about the Felix Bloch case to go on. With Hanssen, the Bureau has tangibles: the two thumbprints, the audiotape, those file names, and the place-and-opportunity timeline that Gwen Fuller and the other analysts are quickly piecing together. With initial FISA approval, the tangibles begin to pile up.

Trying to secretly search and bug Hanssen's house proves a bust. Two of his children are still living there, and Bonnie is mostly a homebody. Instead, the FBI has to settle for buying the house across the street and turning it into a remote listening and monitoring station. Other measures are more productive.

A January 30, 2001, search of Hanssen's Ford Taurus finds a roll of white Johnson & Johnson medical adhesive tape and a box of Crayola colored chalk in the glove compartment and, in the trunk, four cardboard boxes containing six green fabric-covered US government ledger notebooks containing classified information and seven classified documents printed from the FBI's ACS system, including ongoing counterintelligence investigations. Also found: a roll of clear mailing tape and dark-colored garbage bags.

Collectively, it's just about everything Hanssen needs for his sideline business: secrets to sell, packaging materials for the dead-drop site, and tape for the preapproved marking rituals. All that's missing are the colored thumbtacks the SVR has instructed him to use, and those turn up in a second search of the Taurus on February 12.

Still other surveillance yields a steady ongoing array of suspicious behaviors. The evening of December 12, 2000, Hanssen drives four times past the Foxstone Park sign on Creek Crossing, a designated site for signaling his Russian handlers. That same evening, he walks into a store in a shopping center at the same time that a known SVR officer is lingering out front.

Two weeks later, on the night after Christmas, Hanssen is back at Foxstone Park. At a little before 6:00 P.M., he lingers in his car near the sign for ten to fifteen seconds. Three hours later, he parks nearby, walks to the signal site and plays a flashlight over it, and then sweeps the flashlight over some nearby wooden pylons. He then turns, shrugs his shoulders as if in frustration, disgust, or exasperation, and returns to his car.

More late afternoon and evening drive-bys are logged at the same site—on January 9, 23, and 26, and three times on February 5. A week later, on February 12, FBI personnel examine the site in detail and remove a package double-wrapped in black plastic trash bags containing $50,000 in used $100 bills, apparently misplaced by the SVR.

The case against Hanssen, though, remains largely circumstantial. Driving by a suspected crime site is not a crime, and the $50K could just as easily be a drug-deal payment as it could be an espionage purse. As for the classified material in his Ford Taurus, Hanssen has all the clearances necessary for that, and besides, the Headquarters building leaks classified like a sieve.

If Hanssen is going to be taken down with anything like a sure conviction and maximum penalty, it will need to be in person, in the act of espionage, with hopefully the SVR somewhere in proximity to the act. Here the problem is threefold. The first is the bait itself. Investigators already know some of what Hanssen intends to off-load to the SVR on his next drop, and there's no way to seize it back without waving a red flag in the mole's face and botching any real chance they have for catching him in the act.

Jim Lyle is at a CIA Christmas party when one of those documents destined for Moscow comes to light: "I was standing right outside Mike Sulick's office when I saw Tim Bereznay coming along. Tim is not a particularly animated guy, but there was a special scowl on his face—he was a man on a mission. So he got me and said, 'We need to talk to Sulick in private.' The problem was that one of the documents Hanssen was planning to pass to the Russians dealt with an in-place Agency source.

"Next thing I know, George Tenet comes through the door, probably because he'd heard we were all gathered and wanted to know what was going on. I was looking at the actual document while Tim briefed the director, and then all of a sudden I heard Tenet saying, 'Whoa!'"[6]

The other two problems are more or less logistics. As of the moment he is revealed as the mole, Bob Hanssen is four and a half months away from mandatory retirement, and retirees have no secrets to steal and no spy product to sell. Proximity is also an issue. Stashing Hanssen at the Office of Foreign Missions in his waning years at the Bureau seemed like a good idea at the time, but now he's working in Foggy Bottom when he needs to be under constant surveillance. What's more, if he stays at OFM, Secretary of State Madeleine Albright will have to be read into the case and maybe others as well, and no one is anxious to do that at the notoriously leaky State Department. The solution to these latter two challenges is flat-out brilliant.

On December 8, 2000, Tim Bereznay, the chief of the FBI's Eurasian Section, summons Rich Garcia to his office and asks if he has been polygraphed. Garcia is head of the Information Resources Division—what he calls "the overt technical side of the FBI. Basically, I pay the FBI phone bill."[7] Garcia was once an undercover agent working, among other dens of iniquity, the Colombian drug trade. But that was then. Being polyed and read into cases is not an everyday part of his more recent brief. He has no objection, though, and Bereznay continues on.

"Tim said, 'I'm about to ruin your day. We found out who the mole is and it's an FBI agent.' I'm thinking, *Is it my wife [now ex-wife]?* She's an agent, and she's Cuban, and everyone knows she has a temper. Everything is going through my head.

"And then Tim said, 'Have you ever heard of Robert Hanssen?' I said, 'No,' and he said, 'Good, because the powers that be want to bring him into Headquarters from the State Department, where he's currently assigned, and assign him to your shop. They're going to make him part of the senior executive service, and they want you to come up with a position that involves no relevant information that he can pass on to the Russians but that he will feel is significant so he won't take early retirement. They need that time to build up evidence against him in order to charge him with espionage.'

"So they wanted me to create this position and build an office for him across the hall from mine. 'When's he coming over?' I asked. And Tim said, 'Four weeks, the early part of January.' And all I could say was, 'Really?'"[8]

In short order, though, and alerted that Hanssen considers himself a computing guru, Garcia comes up with a beautifully baited plan. "I said, 'Why don't we task Hanssen with setting up a gateway that will allow our information systems to access other systems within the intelligence community—the CIA, the NSA, and so on. We keep talking about doing that, and he'll think he's setting up a system that will allow the Russians to see all information systems within the community. I think he'll be very interested in this project.'"[9]

The powers that be agree, and Garcia sets about the second half of his assignment: to build a two-room office that will be big enough to satisfy Hanssen's ego and that is stuffed top to bottom with listening devices and other monitors. He will need to do this over the Christmas holidays when the Bureau's tradesmen traditionally take their accrued vacation time, and to arrange the work in such a way that everyone who shows up with a hammer or screwdriver won't realize this is far from a normal office.

To get that process started, Garcia reads Bill O'Hanlon, section chief for Headquarters maintenance, into the case, promises him that his workers will all get overtime—"whatever you need"—and asks him to get started immediately. The work entails converting the conference room across the hall into a two-office suite, following a plan that Garcia has already hand drawn.

O'Hanlon takes him literally. The group that was meeting in the conference room that morning had broken for lunch and left their papers on the table. When they return, the conference table is against a far wall, the chairs are stacked on top of the table—along with the participants' papers—and workmen are installing aluminum frames for the new drywall dividers. Toward the end of the afternoon, they've got the drywall screwed into the frame and are ready to tape and spackle the joints when Garcia shuts them down.

The office, he explains to the workmen, is a project for Bill Dies, one of his bosses, and Dies came from IBM and doesn't do things the FBI way. He'll want to have a look at the walls now that the drywall is hung and might want to change their location slightly. So the workmen go off scratching their heads. A few hours later, Garcia's technical team comes in, removes the drywall, fills the walls with electronics, and screws the drywall back in before leaving so that it's ready for taping and spackling in the morning.

Same thing with carpeting the office and cabling it. Bureau electricians install four conduits, each four inches in diameter, but Bill Dies will want to have a look at their exact positioning, too. Overnight the tech guys fill the conduits with a jumble of cables that feed into the telephone office way down the hall on the ninth floor, where the senior executive crowd that Hanssen is about to join roam, and from there to the room on the fifth floor where, as Jim Lyle puts it, "if he even breaks wind, they'll hear it."[10]

And then there's the matter of ultimate verisimilitude. Hanssen is an inveterate and highly invested mainframe snoop, but no one wants him trolling freely through the FBI mainframe now that they know his sideline. Solution: insulate the Bureau's mainframes from him and set up a separate server all his own—one that is a complete copy of the mainframe so Hanssen won't be suspicious of it, but that will give him access only to data up to the day he first uses it; that is, he can't track the ongoing investigation of Robert Philip Hanssen or cherry-pick any new goodies for the SVR.

Garcia tells me, "I had strict orders from the director: 'Richie, I don't want *anything* else going to the Russians.'"[11]

To pull in the necessary programmers to make all this work without reading in their own unit chiefs, Garcia concocts a story that Congress has demanded an audit of the FBI's entire information system. To make sure the administrative staff up and down the hall log off and lock up when they're away from their desks so Hanssen—as he is wont to do—can't wander into empty offices and poke around, Garcia uses his administrative assistant, Barbie, to unwittingly stoke the rumor mill.

"I told her, 'Hey, Barbie, see that office we're building across the hall?' She said, 'Yeah, what's with that?'

"'We're bringing in a real jerk from State, Robert Hanssen. His idea of how to get promoted is to get someone in trouble. If you don't log off when he comes in your office or when you're away from your desk, he's going to use you as a target.' Barbie had been there a long time. She knew how to get rumors out.

"The very next day, I walk into my office a little after noon, and I hear a beep-beep go off, and I look up and see a motion sensor. So when Barbie comes back from lunch, I ask, 'What's with the motion sensor?' and she says, 'Oh, I had it installed. I didn't want that son of a bitch sneaking up on me.' That building was locked down so tight, it was incredible."[12]

Finally, to create this chimera of the proper executive suite, there's the matter of a proper administrative assistant. Eric O'Neill, an investigative specialist assigned to the Washington field office, has already been chosen and read into the case, but this is the federal government, and this case is being compartmentalized to the nines.

"I had to write a justification for the position," Garcia says, "and I needed to post an ad at Headquarters that Eric can apply to. Even then, Human Resources was saying we have to hire qualified candidates in Headquarters, so I had to go back and forth and justify before the career board why it had to be him and no one else. Obviously, I couldn't tell the board why I wanted him."[13]

Don Sullivan, Hanssen's longtime FBI pal going back to New York field office days, has been read into the case at a catastrophic time in his own life: moments after learning his wife has been diagnosed with breast cancer. Sullivan's daily journal for November 27, 2000, captures the moment: "Like being punched in the gut, stabbed in the back, and fucked in the ass all at once. I felt crazy. I wanted to cry, throw things, punch someone. Could have stayed home the last fifteen years."[14]

Sullivan does, in fact, kick a hole in his office wall that afternoon. But after he settles down, Sullivan offers to babysit Hanssen while his former mentor and friend is readying for a final transfer within the FBI.

"They needed someone to go over there and replace Bob at the State Department, and my wife was looking at surgery and chemo and whatnot, so I volunteered to do that because I live in Arlington [just across the Potomac, in Virginia] and being at State was going to put me in a better position to get home if I needed to drive her somewhere. Plus, frankly, I was so damn pissed off at Bob that I wanted a shot at him.

"I was there about a month before he moved to Headquarters, shadowing him as he showed me how to do the job but also undercover because I was reporting back to the investigative team about everything I saw—what equipment he had, that kind of thing. Bob had been almost a hermit over there. Nobody ever went over there and saw his office or what was going on. Now, they were searching the place at night—using FISA warrants to get in there and search his computer and scanner.

"There wasn't much to do. Bob and I had a lot of long lunches in the cafeteria, but there was this one afternoon around five o'clock when we were locking up for the day and the alarm goes off on his PalmPilot. He's looking at it, and his whole demeanor changes. 'I've got to get out of here,' he said, and he gave me the bum's rush. And next thing I know I was standing out in the hallway going, 'Jesus, that was fast.'

"My contact was Kate Alleman. She would stop by my house at night, and we'd sit in her car while I briefed her on the [events of the] day. So I was telling her that night about the alarm going off and how unusual it was, and she said, 'Oh, we were watching. He got his car, tore out into the traffic, and went to look for a drop that the Russians were supposedly going to fill for him.'

"We both kind of laughed about it, and I said, 'Well, we know he's putting alarm reminders on his PalmPilot,' and I think that might have helped them get probable cause to search the PalmPilot, which was in fact how they found out where and when he was going on the day they arrested him." [15]

On Friday, January 12, Sullivan joins Hanssen and a handful of others for an OFM going-away dinner at a nearby Chinese restaurant, and on Monday, January 15, Bob Hanssen officially joins the FBI's senior executive service, or so it seems.

Once Hanssen is installed in Room 9930 at Headquarters, hourly management falls to Eric O'Neill, but the newest member of the senior executive service is nothing if not high maintenance, especially under the circumstances, and Rich Garcia is often the go-to guy when O'Neill is otherwise occupied or the problem is larger than an administrative assistant can handle.

Time and again, for example, Garcia finds himself in Hanssen's office, making small talk while he nudges the TV stand next to him with his hip or a knee, trying to get the camera hidden inside the TV trained back on Hanssen as designed. "I'd be standing there, chatting away, and I'd get a call on my pager, and it would be the monitoring room saying, 'A little more to the left; no, the right. Okay, you're good.' And I'd say, 'Gotta run, Hanssen.'" [16]

Another time Garcia wanders into Hanssen's office to find him gone and one of his own techs hovering over Hanssen's computer, which is lying in pieces on the desktop. "I asked him what he was doing, and he said, 'We got a complaint that it was running slow,' which was no surprise given all the stuff we put in it. So I said, 'Did you replace anything?' And he said, 'Yeah, I took an old card out,' and I said, 'Put it back in—I'm getting him a new computer.'" [17]

Afterward, Garcia realizes this is just going to keep on happening, so he has the computer tech polygraphed, reads him into the case—making him only the fifth person on the entire floor to know Hanssen is a spy—and tells him to sweet-talk the chief occupant of Room 9930 next time he complains.

On another occasion, Garcia is sitting in a meeting when Hanssen complains about having no copying machine. No problem, says one of the uninitiated around the table, and offers his own spare copier, not aware of the thousands of pages of classified material Hanssen has copied over the years for his Soviet patrons.

Garcia intercepts the donor as he's rolling the copier to Hanssen's office; redirects the trolley to the basement, where he removes the hard drive and tosses it in a dumpster; then he goes straight to Louie Freeh's office to report that he has destroyed government property.

Freeh, he says, "chuckled a little bit and said, 'That's all right, Richie. I got you covered.'"

A few days later, Garcia rolls a brand-new, specially ordered copier into Hanssen's office for his use—one that preserves a photographic record of everything that has been copied.

"I swear to God," Garcia tells me, "there were so many electronics in that room you could have fried an egg in there if you wanted to."[18]

There is also an enormous amount of dramatic irony piling up in and around Room 9930, and pretty much wherever Hanssen goes, at least among those who now know him as GRAYDAY. Jim Lyle recalls the morning he drove in from Langley to Headquarters to get a flu shot at Health Services.

"Before I got the shot, I went down to check my mail slot, and there was literally no one there. The deputy director of operations was not there. The two secretaries weren't there. Maybe they'd all gone out for coffee. And I started thinking, *Gee, I hope there's nothing about GRAYDAY lying around here.* So I began snooping around to see, and it was pristine. Then I went over to the safe, pulled out my stuff, and was putting it in my bag when I sensed someone walk in behind me. I turned around, and it was Bob Hanssen.

"I said, 'Hey, Bob, how are you doing?' This is when he was still over at OFM. And he said, 'What brings you down here today?'

"I just said, 'Flu shot.'

"And he started chatting me up about Chicago like he was my long-lost buddy. So I started chatting back, but I'm thinking, *I know who you are, and*

I'm not leaving you alone here. I'll stay as long as I have to. It wasn't long before Mike [Waguespack] came in and I was out of there. Later Mike told me that was the [day] Bob learned that we had created a job for him and were bringing him back to Headquarters."[19]

In the same vein, Rich Garcia remembers Hanssen proudly showing him the Star of Lenin he has brought either from OFM or home to help decorate his office. "He said it's awarded to all the famous Russian spies. I bit my tongue."[20]

Don Sullivan bites his tongue, too, when Hanssen pops back into his old State Department haunt for a visit just as Sullivan is putting together an analysis of KGB awards, based on a briefing of a defector. "I had photos of the Order of the Red Banner, the Red Star, and so on. Bob was very excited to see these photos and was looking them over intensely, and he asked me a lot of questions about the project. I answered them and kept thinking to myself that he probably thought he was going to get such awards some day in Russia."[21]

Sullivan remembers the date of that visit as February 9, 2001, when Bob Hanssen's days as a free man have dwindled down to nine.

Eric O'Neill sees Bob Hanssen from a different perspective. He's less than half Hanssen's age. He has never been an FBI agent—his specialty is foot and vehicular surveillance. And Hanssen is maybe four inches taller than O'Neill—he has a way of looming over people.

Their first exchange is gruff at best. O'Neill reaches out his hand and says, "Bob Hanssen? Hello, I'm—." Hanssen interrupts him with: "You can call me sir or boss."[22]

Idiot, moron, and *dummy* seem to be Hanssen's favorite words in describing most of his colleagues, Rich Garcia across the hall included. O'Neill will soon come to know better than perhaps he wants Hanssen's stands on public morality, homosexuality, Jews, Democratic politicians and policies, and—on the other side of the ledger—prayer, Opus Dei, Catholicism generally, the NRA, and the infallible virtue of OODA, a fighter pilot acronym for observe, orient, decide, and act. The Russian intelligence services are good at it, Hanssen says. The American intel services suck.

And also spies. Hanssen has a lot to say on that subject, as well. The spy, he tells O'Neill, "is always in the worst possible place."[23] Mostly, too, the spy is the worst possible person. Aldrich Ames, for example, "was just a dumb, alcoholic drug addict who barely skated by. . . . He had only disparaging things to say about other spies, too."

The unacknowledged contrast, of course, is the man O'Neill has been assigned to watch practically from dawn to dusk and occasionally beyond.

"I truly believe he wanted to tell somebody about his genius, and we were getting closer and closer. If the investigation had lasted one to two years as some thought it would, he might even have come right out and told me he was a spy"—and maybe even a potential fellow traveler, as the saying goes.

"The FBI came to believe Hanssen was recruiting me to replace him since he was about to retire," O'Neill tells me. Shades of Jack Hoschouer, and, as with Hoschouer, probably meant as an expression of friendship, even affection.

"To Hanssen's mind, this was the greatest thing in world," O'Neill explains. "The awesome secrets, the rush, you get to play James Bond and get paid a ton of money. Who wouldn't love that?"[24]

O'Neill will also learn, as others have before him, that Bob Hanssen can be more than a little creepy. The time, for example, when Hanssen popped out of his inner office as O'Neill was doing a computer search.

"He put his hands on my shoulder and leaned his chest into my back as he bent over to look at my screen," O'Neill says. "I was uncomfortable, but I think it was more intimidation than anything else. He liked having the upper hand."[25]

Like others, too, O'Neill is introduced early to Hanssen's contempt for most things FBI. The ACS system is "complete garbage." "All it would take," O'Neill recalls Hanssen saying, "is one bad bureau person to invalidate the security. ACS works as long as someone is not a spy."[26] True enough, as Hanssen proves.

Another dramatic-irony moment, this one on February 12: Rich Garcia, Jim O'Leary, John Imhoff, Robert Friedman, and Hanssen are on Interstate 95, heading south to Quantico, Virginia, for a morning of shooting at the FBI range there while FBI technicians take apart Hanssen's car in the Headquarters garage for a second time. Garcia is behind the wheel of a black Bureau-owned Tahoe and Hanssen is riding shotgun when Imhoff starts in on John Connolly, a Boston-based FBI agent who has just been arrested on multiple charges, including murder, stemming from his ties to Whitey Bulger and his famous Winter Hill Gang.

"Imhoff said, 'Man, I don't understand how an agent could go bad like that. That's absolutely unacceptable!'" Garcia remembers, "And I was [thinking], *Holy shit, does Hanssen think we're going to arrest him? Is he going to jump out of the car?* O'Leary was sitting right behind him, and he must have been thinking the same thing because I could see him ready to reach over the seat and put a hold on him, but Hanssen didn't have a single change of expression on his face."[27]

By Garcia's lights, the shooting goes well. He goads Hanssen into putting $20 down on who has the better score while neglecting to mention that he was on the Dallas police pistol team when he was a Texas cop.

On the way back, the five men stop for lunch at a restaurant in the far Virginia suburbs of DC.

"I kept getting information on the status of the car," Garcia says, "and they kept saying we need more time. I'd picked this restaurant because it's so remote that there's no Metro anywhere nearby, maybe not even taxi service. We didn't want Hanssen getting antsy and taking off on his own back to Headquarters. We finished lunch, and they needed more time, so I said to O'Leary, 'I think they have really great desserts here,' and we ordered the biggest desserts they had. When we finished those, they still needed more time, so we ordered coffee and then refills. By now, Hanssen was squirming. He really didn't want to be there. So finally we got the all-clear. We got back to the garage and they'd put Hanssen's car exactly where it was, with no way of his knowing it had been compromised. And we dropped Bob off right at his car and thanked him for a nice day.

"The next day, I got a call from Kate [Alleman, who is coordinating all these searches]. 'We've got a pool going on as to who will come up with the best evidence on Hanssen,' she told me. There was a surveillance team monitoring his house, the WFO team, and my team. And Kate said, 'My money is on your guys,' and she was right."[28]

On Thursday, February 15, while Rich Garcia and Jim O'Leary once again distract Hanssen—this time by dragging him to the FBI's in-house shooting range for a chance to win back his lost $20—Eric O'Neill notices that Hanssen has left his PalmPilot behind, almost unthinkable for him, and notifies the Hanssen watch team. In short order, Special Agent Regina Hanson and a few others are in the office, carefully removing the PalmPilot and downloading its contents, then returning it exactly as it had been, or so they hope, leaving O'Neill to sweat out the consequences if they are off by a millimeter or two. Hanssen almost never lets the PalmPilot out of his possession, he pays minute attention to even chairs that have been slightly moved, and O'Neill knows how mercurial he can be.

"Hanssen had a very short temper, and we were learning that he had caused compromises in the mid-1980s that had gotten people killed. He was a very brutal guy. I wasn't afraid he was going to punch me—I'm a second-degree black belt. I was more concerned he was going to shoot me. The FBI's a gun culture. Agents are always supposed to be within reach of their firearms. And what did he have to lose? He knew what was in the Palm."[29]

The sweating, though, is doubly worth it. In addition to learning the exact date and approximate time of Hanssen's next (and final) drop, the techies also download Hanssen's last letter to his Russian handlers:

Dear Friends:

I thank you for your assistance these many years. It seems, however, that my greatest utility to you has come to an end, and it is time to seclude myself from active service.

Since communicating last, and one wonders if because of it, I have been promoted to a higher do-nothing Senior Executive job outside of regular access to information within the counterintelligence program. It is as if I am being isolated. Furthermore, I believe I have detected repeated bursting radio signal emanations from my vehicle. I have not found their source, but as you wisely do, I will leave this alone, for knowledge of their existence is sufficient. Amusing the games children play. In this, however, I strongly suspect you should have concerns for the integrity of your compartment concerning knowledge of my efforts on your behalf. Something has aroused the sleeping tiger. Perhaps you know better than I.

Life is full of its ups and downs.

My hope is that, if you respond to this constant-conditions-of-connection message, you will have provided some sufficient means of re-contact besides it. If not, I will be in contact next year, same time same place. Perhaps the correlation of forces and circumstances then will have improved.

Your friend,

Ramon Garcia[30]

Hanssen includes the letter in the package he leaves for his SVR handlers on February 18. The Russians will never receive it.

The letter, Garcia explains, "links Hanssen, Ramon Garcia, and the Russians, but it's still not an overt act of espionage. Anyone can type a letter, and there's no classified information in it. It wasn't enough.

"We knew the case was getting to the point where they had to make an arrest because they just couldn't keep it going. If Hanssen didn't do the drop that weekend, O'Leary and I were going to arrange for a meeting, including Hanssen, at FBI's research facility at Quantico. We were going to drive him there Tuesday morning, and he was going to be arrested there"—though under far from optimal conditions.[31]

CHAPTER 22

TAKEDOWN

The violation of espionage has no statute of limitations. Anyone who is so stupid or narcissistic to believe they are smart enough to beat it—even someone like Hanssen who never gave up his face to a camera—is wrong. Eventually, the FBI will get a source, and we'll be able to get inside the files of our enemy and pull out enough evidence to get that person in jail. I don't care where you work. Don't spy. It's stupid. You're going to get caught.

—Mike Rochford to Jerri Williams
in an interview on August 2016

The James Bond movies that Robert Hanssen so admires always end in high drama: the chase scene; the swelling music; a lightly clad "Bond girl" perched precariously between life and death in some exotic location; 007 himself daring all for M, England, the damsel in distress, and the little people back home like good old Miss Moneypenny; and finally the closing credits.

Hanssen's end feels more like the inevitable playing out of an over-scripted Greek tragedy set in a monotonous northern Virginia suburb.

Right on cue, the best friend shows up for a final visit that weekend of February 17–18, 2001. Jack Hoschouer is on his way from his home in Germany to see his parents in Arizona. It just makes sense to break the flight in Washington, DC. Hoschouer remembers the visit as unremarkable. Hanssen is more edgy than usual, but even in his calm moments he is often upset about something: left-wing balderdash, the toppings slopped on his McDonald's hamburger, both Clintons, the theory of evolution.

"He thinks that everything now—flower and fauna—was put here just as they are," Hoschouer explains. "I asked him once why whales have hip bones, then, if they were put here as they are. He got real quiet."[1]

As always, Hanssen drives Hoschouer to the airport when his stay is over that afternoon. Dulles International is unusually empty at 4:00 P.M. It's the middle of a three-day weekend, Monday being President's Day. Instead of seeing his best friend to the gate as he sometimes does, Hanssen gives him a present, something to read on the plane: G. K. Chesterton's 1908 novel *The Man Who Was Thursday*.

In the aftermath, much will be made of this "gift." Chesterton is a much-loved figure within the Opus Dei movement. He was Catholic to the core and sometimes mentioned for beatification. The Heights School, alma mater to all Hanssen's sons, even has a Chesterton Hall. Maybe the book is meant as an expression of Hanssen's deep faith. Or maybe it's something more complicated.

The most popular of Chesterton's many novels, *Thursday* is also a tale of supreme deception. Police detective Gabriel Syme is given the name "Thursday" when he infiltrates and becomes one of the seven members—each named for a day of the week—of the High Council of Anarchists. Turns out that not only Syme but all seven are in disguise in one form or another, including Sunday, the head of this council of supposed bomb-throwers.

Was Hanssen trying in his own way to tell Hoschouer that he, himself, was a tale of supreme deception? Or was this nothing more than a case of his sharing a favorite story by a favorite author with his most favorite friend?

Hoschouer favors the latter explanation. "I never had a feeling he was trying to tell me something; he was just giving me a book to read," Hoschouer tells me.[2]

Sometimes a book is just a book, but the timing is hard to ignore.

★

Bonnie is expecting Bob to be back by no later than six o'clock for a family dinner. But Bob has a couple stops to make first and will never get there.

Just on cue, the emotionally overwrought Bonnie begins to panic when Bob hasn't yet appeared as she, her daughter and son-in-law, and their children are getting ready to sit down at the table. She holds dinner for as long as she can, then everyone eats and leaves for home while Bonnie turns her attention to Bob's whereabouts.

His cell phone seems to be turned off and the FBI weekend operator is no help. With mounting hysteria, Bonnie phones her mother in Chicago, tells her to pray for Bob, then calls a friend to ride with her to Dulles. Bob has had some health problems, so maybe he's slumped behind the wheel of his car or lying sick or dying on the parking lot asphalt.

The FBI, of course, has listened to her calls. Now a surveillance team tails her to the airport. In the parking lot, they assure her that Bob is unharmed and lead her to a private room inside the terminal, and there they tell her the truth: her husband of thirty-two years has been arrested for espionage almost three hours earlier, a little before 5:00 P.M. They don't tell her that when Bob is offered the chance to call home and alert Bonnie and their children while in custody, he asks instead for an attorney.

In the aftermath, it's hard not to wonder if Bonnie had a premonition of the evening's horror. Her initial concern seems out of proportion to the length of Bob's absence. Flat tires happen. Maybe Jack's flight has been delayed and Bob is keeping him company. Did something in the days leading up to this moment raise her antennae? Or has the premonition been sitting there latent for twenty years, since she first learned her husband was capable of espionage?

In a weird echo of the Brian Kelley saga, Hanssen's children learn their father is one of the most wanted spies in American history—maybe the most wanted ever—in a brutally stark manner. Seventeen-year-old Greg is at home when their sobbing mother arrives in the company of a small squad of FBI agents. Calls are made as a stunned Greg shows one of the agents the many locations around the house where his father's guns are stashed. The Beglises from across the street are already there when fifteen-year-old Lisa and her boyfriend arrive on the scene, and Lisa breaks down in her Aunt Jeanne's arms.

Ever solicitous of their own, even when their own is the Bureau's worst nightmare, agents book Bonnie and the kids into a local Residence Inn. Their house, after all, has become a crime scene, and armed with search warrants, the FBI is going to do what it has never been able to do previously: search 9414 Talisman Drive from top to bottom.

★

At FBI headquarters, Bureau top brass and agents closely connected to the Hanssen case gather that Sunday in the Division 5 (Counterintelligence Division) operations center that Richie Garcia has put together specifically for this takedown, under the pretense that it's needed for the nonexistent Congressional review and audit—deception upon deception. Among the first to arrive, at around 1:00 P.M., is Neil Gallagher, Louie Freeh's number two. Gallagher's job is to over-worry this, and he has given himself plenty of time. If Hanssen is true to form, and according to basic common sense, he'll wait until dark to make the drop.

As the afternoon goes on, Gallagher gets plenty of company, including Mike Rochford. "I was a Headquarters schmuck as the arrest was going down," Rochford says, meaning out of the action but integral to the outcome.[3]

Jim Lyle is there, as well. "It was essentially a very senior, and fairly small group. As I remember, FBI director Freeh remained in a separate room and was kept apprised there of developments. Tim Bereznay established a secure telephone link with the Washington field office's command post, and it was through that link that WFO kept Headquarters aware of the events, pretty much in real time.

"My role was very limited. Since I was detailed out of the Bureau as the chief of Counterespionage Center at CIA, I was basically there to monitor developments and to securely contact senior CIA leadership, including George Tenet, the chief of the Counterintelligence Division, and the deputy director of operations with pertinent information as things happened during the day.

"As to the atmosphere in the post, there was never any sense of jubilation. It was all very businesslike and matter-of-fact.

"I can't speak for anyone else, but I recall feeling so sorry for Bonnie and the other Hanssen family members as this went down. I could sense how their entire world was going to be upended that afternoon because of Bob's actions, and like all families of FBI personnel, I felt that they were part of the FBI 'family,' also."[4]

The White House reaches Louie Freeh soon after Hanssen's arrest. "President Bush called and asked that I convey his thanks to everyone involved. He'd been in office less than thirty days. It was the first time since I became director that a president had ever thanked the FBI for protecting the country."[5]

Rich Garcia, who has also been watching from a front-row seat as the arrest goes down, returns early Monday morning, President's Day, to lock down Room 9930, then puts a sign on the door that reads: RESTRICTED AREA. DO NOT ENTER. FOR INFORMATION, CONTACT DAD O'LEARY OR SECTION CHIEF GARCIA.

For the next week and longer, he worries that Hanssen has embedded some kind of a Trojan horse in the FBI's network that will allow his SVR handlers to listen in at will. Only later will he think of the room number—9930—as a positive omen: the digits add up to twenty-one, a winning hand in blackjack.

Tuesday morning, Garcia calls Barbie into his office just as Louie Freeh and John Ashcroft are announcing Hanssen's arrest to the TV cameras rolling at Foxstone Park. Bureau brass have delayed this moment for twenty-four hours to give the Russians time to try to recover the package Hanssen has left for them. Maybe just as important, President's Day is also a dead news hole, and they want this played big.

"Barbie looks at the TV," Garcia tells me, "and she says, 'Holy shit!' And I say, 'Now you know what I was protecting you from.'"[6]

Live from Nottoway Park in Vienna, Virginia, Garcia's boss is introducing Robert Hanssen to the world.

"The FBI entrusted him with some of the most sensitive secrets of the United States government," Freeh is saying, "and instead of being humbled by this honor, Hanssen has allegedly abused and betrayed that trust. The crimes alleged are an affront not only to his fellow FBI employees but to the American people, not to mention the pain and suffering he has brought upon his family."[7]

According to Brian Kelley's widow, Patricia McCarthy, the footbridge carefully placed in the background as Freeh and John Ashcroft talk is not the one under which Hanssen made most of his drops.

"They couldn't get even that right," she tells me.[8]

Brian Kelley is among those who don't see the Tuesday morning made-for-TV announcement of Hanssen's arrest. He hears about it from his son, Barry.

"I was driving to work that morning," Barry remembers, "and on the radio there was this announcement that a spy had been captured—'Big spy captured, stay tuned!' So I called my dad. My heart was in my throat, and he doesn't pick up, but finally, thank God, he does. And I say, 'It's over!'

"'What do you mean?' he says.

"'It's over,' I repeat. 'They arrested the spy.'

"And he goes, 'I've got to call you back.'

"It was two days later, and they hadn't told him. Maybe they hadn't gotten around to it, but the person who has accused you should be calling and saying, 'I apologize.'"[9]

And Bob Hanssen? In critical ways, he seems to be on autopilot throughout this closing scene, as if he had no choice but to play out the role that has been written for him. If anything, he appears almost eager to get it over with.

★

In a rational world, Hanssen has choices that Sunday afternoon of his arrest. He clearly senses the sleeping tiger has been aroused—he has written as much, in those words—and clearly knows that the closer he comes to an overt act of espionage, the greater the chance that he will face the death penalty or life in prison, if and when he's caught. What's more, the drop he is about to make is optional. His handlers have urged caution themselves. The drop date and site are to be repeated annually. There's always next year.

Caution also dictates doing the drop after dark when the park is less used, but Hanssen has entered into an irrational zone. Or maybe he is simply closing in on an end he has scripted all along, or to be really mundane, maybe he is just impatient and wants to get home in time for that family dinner. Sometimes the best answers are the simplest. Whatever the reason, it takes Hanssen roughly twenty minutes to cover the fifteen miles from the Dulles terminal to the parking lot at the Pike 7 Plaza strip mall at the intersection of Route 7 and Gosnell Road in Tysons Corner, Virginia.

At 4:21 P.M., still broad daylight, he exits his car, opens the trunk, removes a black plastic trash bag containing an unknown load, carries it back to the front seat, and soon drives away again. Thirteen minutes later, at 4:34 P.M., he arrives at Foxstone Park, only a short drive from his home, places a white adhesive tape signal on the park sign designated for the "Ellis" dead-drop site, and then walks into the park carrying the garbage bag and its contents, including the document that names an in-place and extremely valuable CIA source.

The surrounding woods are dense with FBI agents, but whether Hanssen has any hint of that or not, he continues to the drop site, tapes the package under the same footbridge he has used many times in the past, and then walks back out of the wooded area, in the direction of his car.

A video eerily like the one that records the arrest of Dmitry Polyakov—TOPHAT, Hanssen's first gift to the Soviets—captures his own arrest.

Hanssen is dressed in casual mortuary attire: a dark gray suit and a black shirt. He has a bit of a limp. He looms, bent over slightly at the waist as he emerges from the woods and approaches the camera, with one hand in his pocket. Thirteen seconds into the minute-and-twelve-second video, two heavily armed Bureau agents rush him from the front. In an instant, he's surrounded by three more—all of them with FBI emblazoned across the back of their jackets in big letters, all packing major heat.

"They knew he owned a lot of guns," Mike Rochford tells me. "They wanted to frighten him so he wouldn't do anything stupid."[10]

"Frighten," though, is not an obvious part of this package. Like TOPHAT, Hanssen seems resigned to his fate as the agents spread his legs, pat him down, clear out his pockets, and handcuff his arms behind him.

At forty-eight seconds, the video shifts to a wider view—houses across the street, a neighborhood setting for the drama going down—and then we're back to close-up. Hanssen is turned. He faces the camera, slightly obliquely. Like Polyakov, he is mostly expressionless as he's led away to the usual assortment of waiting FBI vans. Unlike Polyakov, he will not eventually be placed on a slab and slowly tipped into a roaring fire.

The video is mute, but Bob Hanssen is not entirely silent through all this. The honor of arresting the FBI's worst spy in modern memory goes to two WFO-based special agents: Stefan Pluta and Doug Gregory. Pluta is still overseeing the takedown and cuffing when Hanssen throws out a line perfectly balanced between contempt for his employer of a quarter century and a cynicism steeped in gangster movies from the 1930s: "What took you so long?"[11]

A few minutes later, Doug Gregory tells Hanssen, "Bob, this is a sad day for all of us." Hanssen's reply is a direct quote from his own letter to the SVR of less than a week earlier: "Life has its ups and downs"—and exactly the sort of thing James Bond might have said with a wink as Dr. No was preparing to turn him into nuclear waste.[12]

It's hard not to think that Bob Hanssen has been writing this end almost from the beginning.

Camouflaged agents will remain hidden in the woods for several days afterward, hoping an SVR agent will show up to collect Hanssen's last offering, but even a half-baked effort to scout the site would have poisoned that well.

Maybe the takeaway from all this is just what Mike Rochford says: no matter how smart you are, the FBI is always going to get you in the end. But even then, maybe Bob Hanssen gets the last word: if he had just walked away when he could, no one would have known that he is the most damaging American spy since Julius and Ethel Rosenberg.

PART VII

PART VII

CHAPTER 23

COLLATERAL DAMAGE

For Bob Hanssen, the January 21, 2001, presidential inauguration is a breath of much-needed fresh air. At long last, the corrupt Clintons are gone, replaced by a new commander-in-chief who's no stranger to prayer breakfasts and is unapologetically pro-American. Out at the Pentagon, Don Rumsfeld—ex-wrestler, tough to the core—is taking over the Defense Department from Bill Cohen, the former Maine senator who is a Republican in name only.

Russia beware, and Saddam, too! And at Justice, Janet Reno, another Hanssen obsession, is gone and outspoken Christian Conservative John Ashcroft is enthroned as attorney general.

For everything Bob Hanssen claims to be—a gun-loving, abortion-hating, right-wing patriot and devoted man of God—it's a clean sweep. A month later, though, in the aftermath of his arrest, the picture is not quite so rosy. John Ashcroft, who oversees the FBI and whose lawyers will be leading Hanssen's prosecution, and Don Rumsfeld, who has the ear of both George W. Bush and new vice president Dick Cheney, are both pushing for the death penalty for the administration's newly revealed mole.

Hanssen's lawyer, Plato Cacheris, has no illusions about his client. Hanssen has been caught red-handed delivering *three* highly classified documents to a site known to be used by the SVR. This alone is probably good for thirty years behind bars, ten years for each document. If he starts to serve that sentence immediately, he will be eighty-seven years old when he is a free man. But the Bureau's analysts have also used the materials provided by Mike Rochford's source to create a timeline of continuing treachery on Hanssen's part, beginning in 1985. Although it's probably inadmissible, they further know now about Hanssen's first overture to the GRU, back in 1979. Bonnie gave that up within days of Bob's arrest.

The best Cacheris can hope for is a reasonable compromise between execution and innocence: a brokered guilty plea that acknowledges culpability but leverages his client's knowledge of his crimes against the intelligence community's need to know just how thoroughly it has been penetrated and at what cost. Fortunately, Cacheris has a ton of experience in brokering high-profile cases like this.

Now in his early seventies, he's a celebrated Washington institution. Past clients have included Monica Lewinsky, in the Bill Clinton affair; Fawn Hall, Oliver North's secretary, propelled to instant fame by the Iran-Contra affair; and John Mitchell, Richard Nixon's attorney general and ready enabler in the Watergate affair. (The tennis court behind Cacheris's Alexandria, Virginia, townhouse is known to close friends as the John Mitchell Court, in honor of the former attorney general's legal fees.)

Most relevant to this case, Cacheris represented Aldrich Ames only half a decade earlier against similar allegations and with an even larger body count, including some of the same dead attributable to Hanssen: Sergei Motorin, Valery Martynov, and Dmitri Polyakov, for known starters. The difference between then and now, though, is profound. Espionage has once again become a capital crime, as it was in the Cold War days of Julius and Ethel Rosenberg, and the charge in this particular instance has friends in high places.

Death, then, is the pressure point the government prosecution team leans into—death in three senses. The first, of course, is the possible execution of the principal in this drama: Robert Philip Hanssen. The second is the actual and known execution of Valery Martynov, a favorite of the US intelligence community and a man clearly linked by now-recovered documents to Hanssen's 1985 secrets-dump to Victor Cherkashin and the KGB. And the third is the likely life expectancy of the man who will be required to testify against Hanssen if this becomes a capital case and proceeds to trial: Mike Rochford's source, now resettled in the United States with some of his family.

Mike Rochford has a smuggled audiotape of the last tribunal proceedings that sentence Martynov to death, but only the Russian source can testify to personal knowledge of the link—between Hanssen and Martynov—through his former service at the KGB. And there's the dilemma for Rochford.

"I had made an agreement with my source that I would protect him and his identity for the rest of my life. Even today I won't say his name. Those stupid Russians would kill him even now if they knew who and where he was.

"But with the capital case building, I had to go to him and say, 'I need you to testify,' and he said, 'How can you make me do that?' So I pointed out to him that when I recruited him, I made him sign a contract that said he would get a million dollars for every scalp he gave us, but that if we couldn't prove guilt through any other evidence we had, we would use his testimony—first- or secondhand knowledge of this person being a spy—in a court of law. 'It's all in our contract,' I told him, 'and you signed it.'

"I promised him we would work with the prosecutors to protect his identity—*in camera* proceedings[1] and all that—but it's always up to the judge how anyone testifies.

"Well, he immediately just went nuts, starting drinking and stuff. He would have been the most difficult witness because he was so nervous. You know, nobody wants to testify, but this was a special case.

"So we met with Cacheris and Hanssen—told them we're going for the death penalty and my source will be testifying—and Cacheris countered it would all be hearsay. But one of the strange, odd exceptions about a capital punishment trial is that hearsay is admissible as testimony. When we presented this to Cacheris, he turned to his client and said, 'You're going to fry,' and Hanssen said, 'I guess cooperation and taking care of my wife is a good thing.'"[2]

From there, it was mostly a matter of ironing out the details of the plea agreement:

- *How long:* Fifteen consecutive life sentences, as things turn out—that is, forever and a day.
- *Where:* ADX Florence, a federal supermax prison in Florence, Colorado, an address Hanssen shares with, as of this writing, among others, Unabomber Ted Kaczynski and domestic terrorist Terry Nichols, Timothy McVeigh's accomplice in the 1995 Oklahoma City bombing that killed 168 people and injured nearly seven hundred others. (McVeigh was executed in 2001.)
- *Terms of confinement:* Twenty-three hours a day of solitary confinement.

Simultaneously, prosecutors continue to work two new pressure points:

- Hanssen's need to be forthcoming in subsequent debriefing sessions.
- Bonnie's future well-being, the major bait prosecutors have to dangle in front of their mole.

The disposition of the Hanssen case, George Tenet tells me, "was the right thing to do. There was some movement within the administration on the part of Ashcroft and Rumsfeld to push for the death penalty, but we were on the other side of that.

"The predicate of the whole life sentencing, as opposed to death, is that he will be honest with us. He will tell us everything he knows. When you arrest people like this, things become anomalies. Why did this person disappear? Why that person? You need to know if your guy is responsible for those disappearances, because otherwise you're going to be on a bunch of wild goose chases even though you've arrested someone. So the clarity and the speed with which you can do damage assessment basically allows you to shore things up and do things differently going forward."[3]

With Bob Hanssen, though, nothing is ever easy. In all, according to Mike Rochford, Hanssen is debriefed thirty-four times, grilled relentlessly to reveal the complete and sum total of his treason, often hooked up to a polygraph machine. And on the thirty-fourth and final time, he tries to slug the polygrapher—and still ends up failing the test.

"Does anyone ever fully believe these guys?" Tenet asks rhetorically. "But the counterintelligence guys have ways to corroborate things, to lock them down. In the end, our professionals at the FBI and CIA have to come to a judgment: Did we get what we needed?" Clearly, that answer is yes, or close enough to it.

Bonnie Hanssen does a lot more to help herself, and she plays a far more ambiguous role in the saga. With the wives of spies—and it's almost always wives, not husbands—three factors enter into the disposition, according to Rochford: knowledgeability, culpability, and cooperation.

"If Rick Ames's wife, Rosario, had been cooperative with us, even though her culpability was there, she wouldn't have spent sixty months in jail. But she lied; she didn't cooperate."[4]

John Walker and his wife, Barbara, were divorced in 1976, halfway through his eighteen years as a mole. But before and after they parted, Barbara enjoyed the financial fruits of his spying—an estimated $1 million earned in aggregate—and was aware that their son, Michael, had become a minor cog in the spy ring and that Walker had tried to recruit their daughter, as well. Knowledgeability is nonnegotiable in this instance—but Barbara is the one who fingers her ex-husband in a drunken call to the head of the Boston FBI office, after having made several previous attempts where she simply hangs up or is too inebriated to be understood. That act—done for whatever complicated reasons—is enough to insulate her from any prosecution.

And what of Bonnie Hanssen, who for almost twenty years has harbored the knowledge that her husband received tens of thousands of dollars from the Soviets in return for American secrets, and who has been further alarmed in the years since by a large wad of cash lying around the house?

"We talked to Hanssen's wife," Mike Rochford says, "and she was 100% cooperative. She told us everything, and in return we gave her immunity from prosecution and, on recommendation from the attorney general, agreed to give her survivor's benefits from Bob's FBI pension as well, good for about $40,000 a year.

"A lot of people said we tricked the books in not going after her, but her cooperation was important in finding out about that 1979–81 time and figuring out what he had done then."[5]

And, even more important, in keeping Hanssen talking to cement the deal for his wife. In espionage cases like this, Lady Justice is not entirely blind.

Bonnie will continue to teach at Oakcrest, the Opus Dei–related all-girls school her daughters attended. She'll have the Wauck family to fall back on and into and the faith that sustains her. But she will forever be dogged by questions about what she knew and when she knew it, and she remains to this day lawfully wedded to America's worst spy of modern history.

The Hanssen's five children will also get on with their lives. In 2013, a dozen years after her father's arrest and twenty-one years after her own graduation, Susan Hanssen becomes the first Oakcrest alumna tapped to be the school's commencement speaker.

"Knowing what is right and good is not rocket science," Hanssen, then an associate professor of history at the University of Dallas, tells the Oakcrest seniors. "We know what is right. What is right is not the problem—living it is the challenge."[6]

A local news source, insidenova.com, reports on Hanssen's address without noting her infamous parent, but as Susan's uncle Mark Wauck told me, "Father's Day comes around every June for all Bob's children, and their father is in a maximum-security prison in Colorado for the rest of his life."[7]

The collateral damage to those around Bob Hanssen at the FBI or pulled into Hanssen's orbit by his treachery is incalculable, too, beginning with Brian Kelley. The FBI did write Kelley a letter of apology—reluctantly and under considerable pressure from Kelley's lawyer, John Moustakas—but they almost didn't get it to Kelley in time.

"The Bureau doesn't apologize," Jim Lyle explains, "but Neil Gallagher prepared the letter. This was a Thursday. To avoid legal issues, they had to have the letter in Brian's hands by Friday afternoon, and the lawyer was demanding we give it to Kelley personally. So we contacted Steve Kappes at the CIA, and he said, 'You know, that's going to be kind of impossible. He's down in Williamsburg, at "The Farm,"[8] doing a training course.'

"I told Neil, 'Okay, I'm an FBI agent and I'm also chief of the Counterespionage Center at the Agency, I'll drive it there.' So I headed into the Bureau, got the letter, and actually read it. It was a very unusual letter, unlike anything I've ever seen the Bureau do. They didn't go into any great mea culpa—we realize we trashed your name with your family and the Agency, and so on—but they did say, 'You're exonerated.'

"Steve Kappes had called ahead to Brian, and he was waiting for me outside the mess hall when I arrived. We talked for a while, but he didn't open the letter before I headed back."[9]

What Brian Kelley might have made of the letter is lost to time, but what his son, Barry, still makes of it is no secret: "We got a piece of paper that said, 'We're sorry. You're exonerated,' but if you go back to the *60 Minutes* interview, you may change your mind about what *exonerated* means. The agent they interviewed [Dave Szady] never apologized. Freeh never apologized, either. Here are two people who go to church every day, and neither ever apologized.

"Patrick Leahy, the Vermont senator, finally worked it out with Bob Mueller, before Mueller could get confirmed by the Senate [as the new FBI director] that the Bureau would issue an apology. But while an apology on a piece of paper is great, it's nowhere near to closing the gap that was created by accusing him of this and by what he had to go through."

"Was he a changed man after all this?" I asked Barry.

"Oh, Dad was a big believer in his faith," Barry answers. "If he was bitter, he didn't show it. But was he disappointed? Absolutely. If you give your life to the United States of America like he did, in the military and at the Agency, and then have your country turn on you like that, it's horrible."[10]

Brian Kelley does keep busy in the years after his ordeal—with training courses at the CIA and the FBI; and with teaching at the Institute for World Politics, the downtown DC graduate school that focuses on national security issues. He has the satisfaction, too, of seeing his daughter, Erin, welcomed back to the CIA with open arms once the stain on her parentage has been lifted. But there are also bad moments. I. C. Smith is with him one time at the International Spy Conference in Raleigh, North Carolina, when Kelley simply breaks down in front of him, collapses under the weight of what he has endured during his eighteen months as Bob Hanssen's stand-in as worst mole ever.

Kelley also dies relatively young, in September 2011, at age sixty-eight, of a heart attack.

"There's no expert nexus between the investigation and how it affected his body pathologically," his widow, Patricia McCarthy, says, "but I can't imagine the stress he was under. He died in the middle of his sleep. We both went to bed late—he usually did, I didn't—but I had a lot of work to do, and I got up in the morning running late because I had a big trial that day.

"Brian was supposed to go to Atlanta later in the morning, and I thought, well, he's going to sleep in for a while, but I didn't hear from him all day long, which was strange. I had to go back to the office after my trial. Then when I got home the bedroom door was closed. I went in and he was cold. I think he might have been dead when I left that morning."[11]

As McCarthy says, there's no "expert nexus" connecting the accusations thrown at Kelley and his death. Arteries get clogged. Hearts fail at all sorts of ages. But some of those close to Kelley have little doubt. "They basically destroyed Brian," I. C. Smith says. "He's dead today because of the way he was treated."[12] In broad terms, George Tenet agrees.

"Did the investigation break his health?" I asked Tenet.

Tenet's answer: "I think it did. I think it had a profound impact on his health. There's a tragedy here."[13]

When I ask Mike Rochford the same question, he agrees. "Brian Kelley probably died early," he told me, but then he added this: "The beauty of the law is that by pursuing Brian Kelley, we got to the truth."[14]

Which sounds like an almost perfect example of "collateral damage."

The FBI has its own share of collateral damage in the Robert Hanssen case, along with self-imposed wounds.

"I can tell you, it was dismay around Headquarters when they learned the mole was Bob Hanssen," I. C. Smith says. "So immediately they started looking for justification as to why they hadn't suspected Hanssen all those years."[15]

One of the places that blame-hunt quickly lands is what was said (or not said) in that 1990 (or 1991 or 1992) meeting (or casual conversation) between Mark Wauck and Jim Lyle concerning the wad of cash Bonnie Hanssen had stumbled upon in (or on) her husband's dresser (or maybe in an empty Coke can). The story shifts every which way if you look at it long enough. In some ways, Mark Wauck has never gotten over the matter.

No one seems to dispute this much: Bob Hanssen is barely in handcuffs when Jim Lyle gets the attention of Sheila Moran at Headquarters. "I said, 'Mark Wauck is sitting out there in Chicago. You really don't want him hearing about this from his family. You want him to hear about this from the Bureau.' So Sheila says she'll give someone the order to go call the SAC [special agent in charge] in Chicago and tell them to advise Mark that Bob has been arrested. And I said, 'He needs to be more than advised. He should be interviewed. He might know something.'"[16]

Thus, at roughly 8:00 P.M. that evening of February 18, 2001, Kathleen McChesney, the SAC of the Chicago field office, and Walt Stowe, the assistant SAC, show up at the front door of Mark Wauck's Park Ridge home—the same Chicago home he grew up in—tell him his brother-in-law has just been arrested for espionage, and ask him to sit for a brief interview.

"My first reaction," Wauck tells me, "was to ask what country he had been spying for, and I was told it was Russia, or the Soviet Union. I asked the two of them to come into a private room just off our front entrance, and then, literally within two or three minutes of their arrival, I said, 'I suppose this is the result of what I told the supervisor all those years ago.'"[17]

McChesney and Stowe, Wauck says, both meet him with blank stares. *Whatever are you talking about?*

Mark Wauck insists that the version of events he spells out to his visitors that evening of his brother-in-law's arrest is correct to the letter. Wauck memorializes that version in multiple lengthy self-composed statements, including one sent to Bob Mueller shortly after he becomes director, to which he says Mueller responds on September 10, 2001, one day before disaster strikes the FBI, the US intelligence community, America, and the world at large. Wauck marvels to this day that his version of events has never been submitted to polygraph testing while Jim Lyle's has. The only reasonable explanation, he says, is that the "last thing the FBI wants is for my version of events to be true."

"You can imagine the egotism involved," Wauck tells me. "We're the spy catchers. We've made all these cases, and here's this field agent who's a nobody questioning our honesty and competence. They're trying to protect their sense of self-worth."

As to Mike Rochford's theory that Wauck could not be polygraphed because he had become, in effect, a whistleblower once he started sending his statements to high officials, Wauck replies: "That's just bullshit."[18]

Oddly enough, Wauck's grievances against his lifetime employer—he retired in 2007, at the mandatory age of fifty-seven—are also memorialized in a lengthy series of email exchanges with the man whom the FBI seemed to have wanted to be Bob Hanssen.

"Brian Kelley was being treated with kid gloves by the FBI after he was exonerated," Wauck says. "He was on a tour of FBI offices and did a presentation in Chicago in one of our conference rooms. I missed the talk, but I ran upstairs afterward and introduced myself, and he said he had hoped to meet me. After that, he got the Bureau to send me to a very high-level talk about

Hanssen. It upset me a little—they talked about my sister—but Brian and I hit it off, and we started emailing each other."

The emails themselves are an ongoing interchange of grievances mixed in with case theories. On multiple occasions, Wauck returns to speculation that the mole team had narrowed its search down to six people—three from the Bureau, three from the Agency, including Hanssen and Kelley—and that even then, they refused to pursue the actual spy.

"I suppose the way they looked at it was this: no clerical person has that degree of access, but we know no agent would ever do that, so therefore it must be someone in the Agency! To their limited intelligences that would have appeared to be a perfect syllogism."[19] In fact, Wauck sounds a bit like his brother-in-law.

Kelley, in any event, doesn't buy the six-suspect idea: "The Bureau never looked inside its ranks. . . . Everyone told me that the only organization to focus on for the mole was the CIA, despite other factors that pointed to the FBI."[20]

More often, their exchanges focus on specific personalities. On August 18, 2007, for example, Kelley emails Wauck as follows, in part:

> I was at a function at the [International] Spy Museum earlier in the week and the executive director (a retired Agency case officer) told me that our good friend David Major will be doing a special night on the Hanssen case in the fall, talking about his close associate of twenty years. He plans to cover, inter alia, the reason the investigation to find the mole was so difficult along with Hanssen's use of insider information, which did not allow the FBI to pick him up.
>
> Makes me want to puke.
>
> Hanssen the "Master Spy," which is what the inept investigators continue to spin to cover their ineptness.

Kelley is back to his theory a week later on August 25: "Almost unconscionable for Lyle not to have had you write out your allegation and then get it to Wags [Mike Waguespack, his superior] post haste. Just did not make sense for him to utterly dismiss what you told him. He is not a stupid person. . . .

"I have another colleague from the Bureau who openly speculated that Major was the person who covered for Hanssen constantly and believes that if your report had gotten to Division 5 [Counterintelligence Division], Major would have been one of the key players to have deflected it."

Mark Wauck responds immediately with his own speculation: "My perspective on Lyle differs from yours. I'm not suggesting that he was dumb, but I did believe that he was determined to rise and would do or say what was necessary to advance—parrot whatever the current Bureau line was. . . . Basically, he didn't like me. Thought I was too 'intellectual' and, besides, I was Catholic. We were just two very different people."

Three years further on, in August 2010, the two men are still chewing the same bone. "I still believe in the possibility that Major got a call and just shelved it," Kelley writes in an August 18 email. "Whatever—there is a story that Bureau does not want to get out. Makes zero sense that Lyle just shrugged off your report. He almost assuredly would have told Wags and therein lies the story."

Five days later, August 23, Wauck replies: "To me the issue is this: if it were just one guy, Lyle, not doing his duty, then they could easily throw him to the wolves—we had one bad apple, just a field supervisor, pretty low-level guy, you can't blame the whole organization. [But] that didn't happen."

Buried inside that email, though, is the wound that one suspects really hurts to this day: "I was told by young agents going to their first [counterintelligence] training courses that the Hanssen case agent told them, 'Who knows whether Wauck was telling the truth?' So a whole generation of young agents are being told that I may be a charlatan. I, of course, have never been given an opportunity to tell the full story, and I know damn well that few agents at any level have ever heard the full story."[21]

Some things never stop aching.

Jim Lyle gets to enjoy the afterglow of Bob Hanssen's arrest for all of about eighteen hours before hearing his own knell of trouble early on February 19, 2001, President's Day.

"I'm in my office at Langley early the next morning, and I get a call from WFO. 'Louie Freeh has ordered us to interview you,' they say.

"'Interview me? About what?'

"'Mark Wauck has made some statements about something he told you.'

"As I was driving down to Headquarters, I started to remember this thing, so when I got there, I said, 'Don't tell me anything that Mark said. Let me tell you what I recall him saying.' And I recounted it as best I could at the time.

"And then the story started to get out: dumbass supervisor who either wanted to protect Bob Hanssen or wasn't smart enough to find his way to the restroom by himself.

"I actually sought out the inspector general at the Department of Justice because I knew he was going to get involved. I said, 'Let's get this on the record.' I told the IG, 'I'm the only person in the building across the street who wants to talk to you,' and I was in there for six hours. They all wanted to leave, and I said, 'Wait a minute. I'm still here!'

"I wish we had done something. I'm happy to admit that. But it's been kind of painful. The narrative got loose—Mark Wauck reported these suspicions, and old Lyle didn't do a damn thing about it."

All of which tends to make almost prophetic Lyle's conversation with George Tenet on the morning before Hanssen's arrest.

"This was out at the CIA. The whole hierarchy of the Agency was in the room—the full cast. I was the lone FBI guy addressing the Agency. So I briefed Tenet on what was going to happen the next day, and when I finished, Tenet said, 'Sounds like a plan.'

"Everyone got up and was milling around, and I noticed Tenet was still sitting there, chewing on his cigar. He looked at me and said, 'When this goes down, the Bureau is going to get gored.'

"And I said, 'You're right, but what is going to get lost in the jet wash of all this is the great work that was done by some people in the CIA and some people in the FBI that got us to this point,' And Tenet looked at me and said, 'They won't care about all that.' And he turned out to be exactly right."[22]

The reports that follow from the inspector general's office and the Webster Commission are harsh condemnations of senior management and security practices. At times, they read almost as if the mole who launched them had never been caught.

"The irony of breaking a spy case like this is simple," Louie Freeh says. "Finding the spy is the goal, of course, but finding the mole inside the FBI was also terrible news for the Bureau." And in some ways for Freeh himself.

"Once it emerged that Hanssen was a member of Opus Dei," he told me, "a number of fringe news organizations and Internet sites began speculating that I'd flown cover for him because I was also a member. Sorry, I'm not the Freeh who belongs to Opus Dei."[23]

Jim Lyle retires in June 2002 after thirty years with the FBI. But he retains his clearances for his new work as a Beltway consultant, and he finally gets a chance to look at the full inspector general's report more than a year after its release in August 2003. "What struck me," he says, "was the degree to which members of the extended Hanssen families had suspicions about Bob, and especially certain discussions about Bob between certain family members and Mark Wauck himself."[24]

As Mark's brother Greg put it on the day after Hanssen's arrest: "Surprised, but not surprised."[25]

Brian Kelley's widow, Patricia McCarthy, does get a kind of closure on her side of the Robert Hanssen story on October 19, 2013—two years after Brian's death. In a symposium at the International Spy Museum, Mike Rochford publicly acknowledges for the first time, in response to McCarthy's question, that he and the Bureau had been wrong to pursue her husband so relentlessly and for so long.

"If I had anything to do over again," he tells McCarthy and the forum at large, "it would be not to open up the case on Brian."[26]

Rochford also remembers interviewing Ray Mislock shortly after Hanssen was identified. "He was one of the first outsiders we told about the case. I said, 'I've got to get a sworn statement from you, and you need to be honest about what your decision-making was relative to not filing on Hanssen after he hacked into your computer.'

"He said, 'Not Kelley?'

"I told him, 'No. Hanssen.'

"And he said, 'Well, I tried to fix the wings of a broken-winged employee. I gave him a second chance.'

"And I said, 'Well that's interesting strategic leadership, but it may be an aw-shit moment right now. Just be ready to testify.'"

Rochford tells me later, "Something like Hanssen impacts the entire culture of the FBI, both onboard and retired. We overuse the word *family*, but unless you've lived it, you don't understand. It really is somewhat of a family at the end. You always wish the best for the Bureau, and when something like this happens, you can feel it in your gut, in your heart."[27]

David Major, frequently cited as Hanssen's protector within the FBI and sometimes his unwitting enabler as a spy, seems untroubled by either suggestion, or by the fact that Hanssen has compromised so many of his own operations.

"I've looked in the mirror many times and asked myself if there was anything observable about this man, and I can tell you that if all of us who knew Bob Hanssen had made a list of the thousand people who might be a spy, Bob would not have been on that list. . . . But isn't that what spying is all about? You want to create someone as your source who will never be suspected, and Bob would never have been suspected.

"People have tried to build a cartoon character of who Bob Hanssen was because it makes them feel better. If I don't make him seem normal, then I'll feel more comfortable in my own skin. People tell me he was arrogant, that he was aloof, and I tell them, you didn't know the real Bob Hanssen."

"I sometimes get asked if I want to see him again. There was a time when I did, but not now. There's nothing I could say."[28]

There might not be much response, either. George Ellard, the chief author of the inspector general's report, has heard that almost two decades of twenty-three-hour-a-day solitary confinement have sharply diminished Hanssen's cognitive skills. FBI profiler Kathleen Puckett says much the same: "Now he's like a zombie. He doesn't speak in coherent sentences. He's almost catatonic,"[29] although no one knows for sure if it's a pose Hanssen has consciously adopted or real.

With Hanssen, it's almost impossible to untangle truth and deception. Of all the collateral damage Bob Hanssen inflicts beyond his immediate family, maybe the heaviest load falls on his best friend of a near-lifetime, Jack Hoschouer.

"I've only seen Bob once since his arrest, at his sentencing," Hoschouer says. "I got to the sentencing really early because I wanted to sit right up front so he would know I'm there—that I don't reject him totally. But they filled up from the back, so I was in the back row. When it was all over, Bob's lawyer, Plato Cacheris, came back and asked me a question, and the lady next to me said, 'Are you somebody?' Then the women next to her said, 'Oh, you're *that* Jack!'

"As Bob was led off, I jumped up and waved to him. I don't know if he saw me or not, but that's the last time I physically saw him. When I did that, the lady next to me just freaked out. How could I possibly be a friend of this person? How could I possibly try to greet him?"[30]

Only a few months before Hanssen's arrest, Hoschouer came across a quote from E. M. Forster that has stuck with him ever since: "If I had to choose between betraying my country and betraying my friend, I hope I should have the guts to betray my country."[31]

"I understand the reasoning behind that that," he told me. "I took an oath to protect and defend the Constitution, and if I had suspected like his brother-in-law that Bob was a spy, I'm certain I would have held to that oath, but reporting him would have been very, very hard. For me, that's a dilemma that goes almost to my core. I'm really happy I never had to make that decision."

In other ways, though, Hoschouer continues to make decisions about Bob Hanssen to this day.

"I went to college in Northfield, Minnesota [at St. Olaf], so when I retired, I moved back here and joined the Rotary Club. As part of that, I had to give a 'classification'—a talk about my life. So I told people about my life, leaving out certain pieces that we're talking about now. But when I finished, one of the guys in Rotary raised his hand and asked if I knew Bob Hanssen, and I said, 'Yeah, he's my best friend,' and that shut everything up.

"Ten days or so later we had a barbecue at this guy's house, and he said he was sorry. He didn't mean to put me on the spot, and I said, 'Don't worry about it . . . It's a piece of my life, and I have to deal with it."[32]

So do a lot of others. Bob Hanssen doesn't go away easily.

CHAPTER 24

THE MIND OF A SPY

Why does someone spy? Why do people turn on their country? What internal wiring draws them to an abyss that almost always ends badly? I would make that "always ends badly," but even the most ardent and successful spy hunters don't discount the possibility that more than a few moles live happily in retirement or still lurk in the shadows of the present day.

A 2001 study by the Defense Personnel and Security Research Center created a broad statistical portrait of the 150 US citizens convicted of or prosecuted for espionage between the start of World War II and shortly after Bob Hanssen's arrest.[1] Of those 150, 93 percent were males, 95 percent were heterosexual, 84 percent were white, more than 60 percent took the initiative to volunteer their services to a foreign intelligence service, and more than 50 percent were married when their espionage began. Of those for whom alcohol-use data was available, half also drank to excess.

Half were also uniformed military, 57 percent of those were under age thirty, and only one in ten was an officer—basically young soldiers, many with a high-school education, and often (but not always) without access to the most deeply held secrets. As the sixty-year span of the study wore on, many were found to frequently do it for drug money.

Bob Hanssen's group—the 42 percent who were government civilians or government contractors—were older by far than the military spies when they first began selling secrets: almost half were over age forty. They were also far better educated, accounting for nearly all of the one in seven spies who had at least begun pursuing a graduate degree, and with generally much greater access, again accounting for most if not all of the 15 percent of spies who held top secret SCI clearances. They also earned far more on the whole for their espionage and were more likely to live beyond their means, although as the report notes "unfortunately, this information was not known until after the offender was arrested."[2]

Why did they do it? More than half said their sole motivation was money, and seven in ten said it was at least a motivating factor. Slightly more than a quarter said they were driven by anger at or revenge against their employers, while slightly less than a quarter cited ideological and cultural affinities with those for whom they spied. Sixteen percent were recruited by a family member or friend, 12 percent succumbed to what they thought of as the thrill of spying, and only 4 percent were motivated by the need to be recognized and feel important.

And where does this leave Bob Hanssen? In some ways, out on a limb, practically all alone. At age thirty-three, he's much younger than the average when he launches his civilian spy career. By Jack Hoschouer's testimony, he has suffered from a kind of James Bond–itis since his middle teenage years. His high opinion of himself and low opinion of his employer are legendary. He never lived greatly beyond his means, and he had no known ideological affinity with his Soviet and later Russian handlers. As in most other things, Hanssen is an outlier here as well.

"Bob Hanssen was the intelligence community's Unabomber," says FBI profiler Kathleen Puckett. "Like Ted Kaczynski, he wasn't able to connect. He had an essential deficit in social connection that he couldn't overcome, so he became the lone terrorist within the Bureau."[3]

Similarly, Mike Sulick, who headed up Counterintelligence Division at the CIA and later wrote about American spies in retirement, sees Hanssen's motivation as a combination of internal and cultural factors.

"The FBI is a rock-'em-sock-'em, let's-go-arrest-someone culture—and Hanssen clearly was an outsider to that. That doesn't mean he's a spy. There are lots of people who don't fit in. The CIA is probably the same or even worse. I've served overseas with Mormons. I'm not going to go out and drink with them. That doesn't make them spies, either. But this case is so difficult because there are so many facets of Hanssen that we didn't know about until after he was arrested. He wouldn't go out with the FBI guys to the local go-go bar after work, but he'd go on his own and meet a stripper—and give them his credit card, for God's sake. There's still a question whether they actually had relations or not. And the whole thing with his wife!

"A lot of spies are sickos. Ames had his problems; so did John Walker and others. But with Hanssen, it's all just whacko. And then there are these things about how his father treated him—like you'll never be good enough. Again, that doesn't mean you're a spy, but there's a long history of spies, especially Americans, who suffered Papa-abuse of one kind or another, beginning with Benedict Arnold.

"Almost from birth, Hanssen was treated as an outsider. He couldn't break into any circle, so he joins the FBI, which is an exclusive club. But he gets in there and they still treat him as an outsider. So he becomes this staunch Catholic, and that's not good enough. He gets into Opus Dei, another special group, and even that doesn't satisfy him. So he goes and joins the most exclusive group of all—'I'll work with the enemy intelligence.'

"Unlike the FBI who could assign him here and there, he controlled the spying himself. Even the Russians couldn't control him.

"Money, I don't think, was a big part of his motivation. The Russians are stingy, but he could have gotten far more than he was paid. There were no exorbitant demands like Ames and sometimes Walker made.

"It was more, 'I want to belong to something exclusive that I control' mixed in with revenge: 'They think I'm a weirdo, an outsider, but I'm going to show them that I'm smarter than all of them.'"[4]

As one would expect, Robert Hanssen has been sliced, diced, and otherwise minced by an entire legion of psychiatrists. For those who study the psychology of espionage, a case like Hanssen and to a lesser extent Rick Ames might come along only once or twice in a professional lifetime. What makes him tick? Is he a sociopath or a psychopath?

In a 2007 article for the *Journal of Forensic Psychology Practice*, J. Scott Sanford and Bruce A. Arrigo lay out their case for psychopathy, summarized and augmented below.[5]

Hanssen has a grandiose self-image. From his brief stint with the Chicago police force through his twenty-five-year career with the FBI, Hanssen consistently impresses fellow workers with his arrogance, his aloofness, and his conviction that he is indeed light-years ahead of the rest as a thinker, solver, and doer. He is the best IT guy in the Bureau. He knows information systems inside and out. He is irresistible to women, or so he seems to think. To read his porn entries, his wife is the hottest babe in town. Even the pseudonym the Soviets come to know him by—Ramon Garcia, with its hint of a swashbuckling Latin lover—seems to serve this bloated sense of self.

In a kind of vicious circle, Hanssen's failure to receive the praise and recognition he is certain he merits only intensifies his feelings of alienation and his antisocial tendencies.

Meanwhile, the one thing Hanssen demonstrably shines at—spying—is the very thing he can't tell his FBI colleagues or family about.

Hanssen is manipulative and deceitful. He deceives his children, his wife, his church, his employer, and his country. He's a pious Catholic with a taste for prostitutes and in the secret employ of godless Communists. He is a loving husband who feeds his wife a stream of constant lies, plays upon her simplistic worldview to keep her in line, and turns her into an unwitting porn star. Authors Sanford and Arrigo further contend that Hanssen even manipulates his best friend, Jack Hoschouer, "by cajoling him to engage in sexually explicit and clearly voyeuristic behavior involving his wife."[6]

Hanssen is a control freak. Witness the way he treats his wife. Witness the secretary he physically abuses, Kimberly Lichtenberg. Witness how he cuts off his relationship with Priscilla Galey the minute she disobeys one of his orders. But it isn't just with women. Witness also the fact that over his intermittent two decades plus of spying for the Soviets, he never reveals his real name to his (all-male) handlers and does all he can to control his dealings with them, whether via communication or dead-drops.

Hanssen is recklessly impulsive. As carefully as he plots his spy career and as much as he seeks to control it and those around him, Hanssen has evinced a wildly careless side ever since the zany driving sprees of his teenage years. Twice in college he breaks into offices late at night to change grades that have suffered because the subject or teacher bores him. At the FBI, he hacks into computers and copies documents on a public fourth-floor copier in a way that is either half insane or wholly in your face. Maybe for Hanssen, the possible thrill of being discovered is akin to the thrill of having his friend watch him penetrate Bonnie. Maybe those telltale wads of cash lying around the house are just another way of messing with his wife's head. Quite possibly, they serve both purposes.

Hanssen craves recognition from others. He craves it because he is certain he deserves it—because he is supersmart, because he is superefficient, because he can get to the heart of a problem faster than others, because he under-stands the intricacies of security and espionage and the Soviets and just about everything else better than those around him, and quite possibly because his father blabbed far and wide about what a loser his son was. Simultaneously, though, he advances more slowly through the ranks of the FBI than most of his peers because he lacks the social skills necessary to thrive in a tightly knit bureaucracy and, more bluntly, because so few people want to work with him.

Last, Hanssen shows a complete lack of remorse for his actions. Although as we will soon see that's in some dispute.

★

Plato Cacheris's first choice to evaluate Robert Hanssen prior to sentencing is, like Cacheris himself, high-profile: Alen Salerian is the medical director at the Psychiatric Institute of Washington and a longtime consultant to the FBI, including counseling agents in the wake of the Branch Davidian tragedy at Waco, Texas. Salerian spends some thirty hours talking with Hanssen at a northern Virginia detention facility and more time with Bonnie and other relatives, and he talks freely to the press about what he has learned.

Hanssen "was troubled, psychologically troubled, and he had demons," he tells a *Washington Post* reporter. "He felt horrible about his past and his errors. He felt he had let people down. He was ready to accept any punishment that the system would give, and that the country felt he deserved, including death. He was not afraid."[7]

That last part might have been what turns Cacheris against his hire. A lawyer crafting a plea bargain generally wants more leeway than is allowed by telling the world his client is ready for execution. In any event, Salerian and Cacheris fall into a he-said/he-said argument over who gave the psychiatrist license to speak publicly, and soon David Charney, who previously served as a psychiatric consultant for the Earl Pitts defense team, takes his place. Charney proceeds to do some of the most thorough spy vetting ever undertaken: an entire year of twice-weekly sessions with Hanssen. And in the end, Charney comes out not all that far from where his predecessor landed. Bob Hanssen is a troubled man who did terrible things, but he's neither all good nor all bad. In Salerian's words: "Most of us, like Bob Hanssen, are mixtures."[8]

"The interesting thing to me," Charney says, "is that he understood what this was about from the outset, and he just launched into a discussion of his life. You learn a lot from what someone brings up of his own initiative right at the beginning. As a psychiatrist, you may hear something in the first session that you won't hear again for two more years. They just come out because the client is under a certain amount of pressure, and then the defense maneuvers take over for the following appointment.

"The very first thing he started to talk about was his father. He described him as this tough, hard-boiled Chicago cop who, to put it very simply, belittled him all the time in one way or another, making him feel small and not measuring up to the sturdy tough guy his dad was, and how he would do various things that were humiliating.

"On one occasion, the father got very angry at Robert Hanssen for some transgression or another—he was a kid at the time, maybe ten or twelve—and that's when he wrapped him up in the carpet. I don't remember for how long, but that stood out for Hanssen as a humiliating memory.

"I know what the correct job of a father is supposed to be with a boy. Basically, the message should be, 'Hey, kid, you're my son. Let me show you how it's done. You're going to grow up and you're going to be just as good and competent as I am, and I'll help you in every way I can. You're my kid.' That's healthy and good."[9] What Howard Hanssen did clearly isn't.

Charney says that Hanssen never indicated any fascination with spy heroes and rescuing damsels in distress. But he did talk about his interaction with the KGB in a way that brings to mind David Major's suggestion that Hanssen was, in some misdirected way, acting for the greater good.

"It was a complicated discussion," Charney says, "because he was also trying to rationalize what he had done to some degree. On the one hand, he implied that he was working for the Bureau; on the other, that he was working for the KGB. If you look at it from his angle, he was like the puppet master who was trying for higher purposes. He was passing along information that would give the Russians a different and more correct impression about the true attitude and ideas of the United States so that they wouldn't overreact and would know we were not that much of a threat to them.

"In his mind, Hanssen was above the tactical level, being actually useful for world peace and other lovely things. He invented excuses that are high-sounding and very positive for actions that at first glance are not a good thing to be doing. Of course, that means he knew he was doing something wrong, but he's not this evil, calculating monster. He's much more complicated than that."[10]

In multiple interviews—with Mike Rochford, George Ellard, and others who had witnessed Bob Hanssen's debriefing sessions—I was told Hanssen hasn't shown a bit of remorse. Ellard went further. During one interview when he is present, someone asks Hanssen why he spied for the Soviets.

"He answered, 'Why did I do it? Oh, geez, I don't know.' I thought that was horseshit. He knew what he was doing. He knew that he was sentencing TOPHAT to death and that torture would precede it. Hanssen chose evil."[11]

Charney, by contrast, says he heard sincere regret on several occasions, perhaps because his style is nonconfrontational: "I don't remember the exact words, and it didn't happen frequently, but two or three times he seemed dejected and remorseful and not happy with what his actions were, and I think that was genuine."[12]

For much of the time writing this book, I've also wondered about Bonnie Hanssen. Did Bob have any deep feelings for her? Or was Bonnie just another cog in his overwhelming narcissism? That answer, Charney told me, is unambiguous: "It was very clear that Bonnie was right at the center of his thinking and feeling. He almost worshipped her. She was the force that had converted him to Catholicism. Whatever his involvement with other women might have been, it coexisted with his intense attachment, care, and concern for Bonnie."

And that, Charney tells me, leads to "the one word that captures a good deal of Hanssen's personality and psychology: compartmentalization.

"That's done by design in the intelligence community for very good reason—need-to-know and all that. I do it in my practice. The person I'm seeing at the moment is in one compartment, and when his or her time is up, I close that compartment and take a short rest before I open up a new compartment for my next session. I couldn't survive the day otherwise.

"We all compartmentalize to one degree or another, but I don't think I've ever run into anyone personally who was more compartmentalized than he was. He could compartmentalize everything he did, whether it was spying, or being with Bonnie, or his religion, or whatever.

"Early in our appointments, he said that for me to understand him, I'd have to do a really deep dive into the different domains of his life. He told me a lot about Opus Dei, gave me reading to do, and basically demanded that I set up a meeting with the head of Opus Dei in Washington.

"And I did it. I called up and made an appointment, and went down to the Catholic Information Center in downtown DC and met with what I thought was an extraordinarily impressive man who had previously worked on Wall Street for most of his career and then had a calling and let all that go to become a priest.

"I knew the last thing Opus Dei wanted was to have the embarrassment of having one of their own caught as a spy, but he was very correct and polite with me, and I learned a lot about that compartment, that domain of Hanssen's life."

"Okay," I asked Charney, "but can you explain how we could compartmentalize Opus Dei, his religion, his faith, and being a spy?"

"The answer is I can't," Charney said. "I didn't figure that out. The only answer I have is that he was capable of extraordinary compartmentalization. He took a thing that is commonplace and pushed it to nearly as far as it could go."[13]

Perhaps that's why Bob Hanssen throws caution to the wind that afternoon of February 18, 2001—makes the drop in broad daylight even though he can feel the heat at his back. The family is gathering at home for dinner and Jack Hoschouer has just flown off to Arizona. Maybe compartmentalization finally fails him. The mole room finally opens wide to the kids' room and the Bonnie room and the best-friend room, and Hanssen just says, "To heck with it—I want to get home to dinner."

Or has he just been gaming David Charney all along, the way he has gamed so many others? Pulling strings. Watching people jump. Really, there's no way to know.

Finally, let me suggest one more way to look at the mind of this particular spy. Several months after my lengthy interview with Jack Hoschouer, he contacted me with the suggestion that I watch another of Bob Hanssen's favorite movies, *Investigation of a Citizen Beyond Suspicion*, the 1970 Oscar winner for best foreign film.

Set in Rome, the film opens with a director of political intelligence—the former homicide chief—visiting a woman in her apartment. Their lovemaking is tinged with rage. She tells him he's less than a man. The director counters that he's going to slit her throat, and then he does and heads to the shower to clean off her blood. But that's the only thing he cleans. The apartment is smeared with blood and heavy with clues—his fingerprints, shoe prints, even a strand from his tie that he works under the woman's fingernail before calling in the murder, grabbing a bottle of champagne from the refrigerator, and carrying it back to the police station.

An open-and-shut case of self-incrimination, it would seem, but that's not the way writer-director Elio Petri presents it. The murderer returns to the crime scene to help lead the investigation—thus his fingerprints and shoe prints are explained away. The thread is ignored although it matches his tie perfectly. His admission to the police commissioner that he's had a "little affair" with the victim is basically blown off. It's Rome. Who hasn't had an affair?

Meanwhile, the murderer is toying with other suspects. He feeds the women's ex-husband to investigators, who jail him. Then he feeds them the clue that exonerates the ex, but they won't release him for fear of bad press for the police agency. (Think of Brian Kelley.)

In the privacy of his own apartment, the murderer tapes a confession: I killed her. It was premeditated, and I left clues everywhere to show that I am, indeed, above suspicion. He follows that by writing out a confession and handing it to the police commissioner, but even then, they refuse to believe him. The physical evidence he produces to support his guilt is either unconvincing or missing. "I murdered her out of jealousy!" he shouts, but he's told he can't prove it. When he hands over photographs of the crime scene, they rip them up. "You have a neurosis," he's told.

Finally, the police commissioner gets to the point: "I will not permit you to insult our findings by disputing them!"

At heart, the movie is absurdist, almost slapstick if it weren't for the gore, right up to and including its dual endings. But the Hanssen case is almost absurdist, too, and in many of the same ways. Hanssen hacks computers and is praised for his initiative. He copies top-secret documents in plain sight, walks out of FBI headquarters with vital operational plans, does dead-drops within a short distance from his own house.

I found myself thinking as I watched the film that maybe Hanssen is not the frequently careless spy that the investigator general's report describes, and maybe all those puffs of smoke that hang temporarily over him are intentional. As with the murderer in the movie, it's all about the edge for Bob Hanssen: all about finding that exact spot between the risk of being caught doing the worst thing an FBI special agent can do and the thrill of making the Bureau look nearly as incompetent as any organization could be. If that's the case, the Russians might be the least important part of the entire equation—just props for a domination game that, despite the compromised operations and lost lives, was always all about Robert Philip Hanssen.

CHAPTER 25

ANOTHER HANSSEN?

The Commission for the Review of FBI Security Programs—the Webster Commission, for short—labors mightily in the aftermath of Robert Hanssen's arrest and, in March 2002, produces a 136-page report, thick with recommendations for policies and procedures that will protect the Bureau from another Hanssen.

Information security is to be tightened under the aegis of a new Office of Security.

Personnel security will be upped by, among other measures, stricter controls on interim clearances and new financial-disclosure and polygraph regimens.

Document security—a disaster during the Hanssen era—merits ten recommendations, from handling and storing classified national security documents in SCIFs and other secure areas available only to those with a need-to-know to the far more amorphous and bureaucratic-sounding "FBI Policy Manuals Should Require Security Coordination."

And so it goes—ten pages in compressed form near the front of the report, with more than seventy pages of detailed recommendations to follow. The Commission's thirty-five-member staff conducts approximately four hundred interviews, including four meetings with Hanssen himself. It has clearly gone to school on the Bureau's most famous mole ever. Its report is, in the aggregate, a sober-sided, sweeping dissection of the Bureau and its culture and practices.

But will it do any good? Seventeen years after its issue, George Ellard remains doubtful: "As we were writing the inspector general's report, I went online and saw to my great dismay that a number of commissions across the government had written similar reports, all of which pointed to similar deficiencies. That made me skeptical about the power of presidential commissions to induce significant change."[1]

More important, even if all the changes are successfully made (ignoring the tendency of large bureaucracies to resist change), are they sufficient to the ultimate goal of stopping a new mole before he or she can burrow into the Bureau too deeply to be found?

In my reopening of the investigation into Robert Hanssen, I asked every FBI agent and CIA officer I interviewed this question: "Can you imagine another Hanssen in today's FBI?" The unanimous answer was a resounding yes, often followed by an even more chilling qualifier: "It's probably already happening." What's more, the closer the agents and officers were to the Hanssen case, the more likely they were to agree enthusiastically.

Dave Szady, for example: "Is it going to happen again? Well, is the bank going to be robbed again? Is somebody going to be murdered again? How about corruption? You'd think politicians would learn that corruption isn't a good idea, but do you think it will occur again? Of course it will. People commit crimes, and they're not going to stop. And espionage is a crime.

"Whether it's a messiah complex or whether it's a sociopath or revenge or thrill-seeking, people are going to betray their country. They are going to steal secrets and give them away or sell them, and they are probably doing it right now."[2]

Jack Thompson, one of the Vault People, agrees: "After thirty years in the FBI, seventeen of those as the counterintelligence officer at the Department of Energy (DOE), I have no reason to believe there isn't a recruitment in place right now in the FBI, the CIA, and the DOE. I can say almost with certainty that people in the DOE have been recruited by foreign intelligence services.

"It doesn't matter if someone has an advanced degree in physics. They still have basic human defects that cause them to betray their colleagues, and in Russia's case, the fact that, in 2016, the foreign country trying to recruit you is no longer identified by the president of the United States as part of an evil empire makes it even easier."

Mike Rochford, who ran Hanssen to ground, is in the same boat and sees the FBI rowing contrary to its own interests. "Right or wrong," he says, "[FBI director] Christopher Wray got rid of the Espionage Section, whose job was to investigate penetrations of the intelligence community. The Intelligence Authorization Act, set up after Hanssen, requires every intelligence agency to report suspicion of any employees. In the FBI, the Security Division was required to pass those suspicions on to the Espionage Section. Well, when Wray got rid of that, he got rid of the internal reporting mechanism."[3]

Put another way, once again, as in Hanssen's day, there's no ready way to gather up the puffs of smoke that accumulate over a new mole, other than an inspector general's report, and IG reports are almost invariably done after the fact, not while the damage is underway.

The easy solution, of course, would be to restore the Espionage Section, or at least farm its function out to another entity. Absent that, Rochford says the Bureau needs to directly attack its own no-ratting ethos. "They need to create a new culture where agents and analysts tell on each other. You see somebody stuffing classified documents in a briefcase and walking out the door, say something. They should give rewards to people who report anomalous activities—set up a program—but nobody is speaking in those terms. The Bureau has to act every day and every hour as if it has been penetrated."[4]

According to I. C. Smith, the counterintelligence side of the FBI also needs to do a better job of channeling its inner nastiness to protect itself against another Hanssen. By way of illustration, Smith cites a favorite passage from Eric Ambler's novel *The Light of Day*: "I think that if I were asked to single out one specific group of men, one type, one category, as being the most suspicious, unbelieving, unreasonable, petty, inhuman, sadistic, double-crossing set of bastards in any language, I would say without any hesitation: 'The people who run counterespionage departments.'"[5]

"In counterintelligence," Smith says, "you can never assume anything. But that's what happened with those investigating Hanssen. They just assumed it couldn't be one of their own. The results speak for themselves."[6]

Still, in an organization as traditionally conservative as the FBI, it's hard to believe that there could be a critical shortfall of hard-nosed agents or a glaring absence of those willing to drop a hammer or worse on a rising Bob Hanssen. Just as important, the war zone between the Bureau and CIA is mostly in the past. Hanssen hid himself deftly by playing both sides against each other. Brian Kelley, meanwhile, got trapped in the space between and suffered horribly in consequence.

George Tenet believes that the reforms imposed post-Ames and especially post-Hanssen have done their job. Both organizations are now more apt to share information about penetrations than hide it. Time and distance have helped, too. "The younger CIA officers don't know that J. Edgar Hoover wore a dress," Tenet says. "That stuff doesn't matter to them. They're used to cooperation because that's how they've been trained to do things. How's it going this very moment? I really don't know. But if a civil war breaks out, it will leak in twenty-eight seconds."[7]

David Charney, who probed Hanssen's psyche for a full year, also doesn't doubt the intelligence community is penetrated today, but he comes at the solution from a different angle—one that might lure the Hanssens and Ameses and Nicholsons now embedded in the FBI, CIA, NSA, and elsewhere into the broad light of redemption.

Spies, Charney says, often find themselves trapped in their espionage. They suffer seller's remorse but have no way to undo the wrong without condemning themselves to a lengthy prison term, and probably their families to financial ruin, as well. Why not create what is in essence an amnesty program for them?[8]

All things being equal, then, it's probably safe to say that the FBI is as vulnerable to espionage from within as it was four decades ago when Bob

Hanssen first began his spy career, but with a better set of internal checks, such as required polygraphing and financial reports to root out a mole—and, if David Charney's advice were to be heeded, even a carrot-and-stick approach to lure them in from the cold.

But all things are not equal—or anything close to it.

At the macro level, what the *National Counterintelligence Strategy of the United States of America 2020–2022* calls the "Foreign Intelligence Threat Landscape" is more varied and extensive than ever before. Threat actors today include not only the old standbys—Russia and China—but also North Korea, Iran, Cuba, and almost certainly the Saudis, Israelis, Turkey, and many others hungry for an edge in dealing with the United States; non-state actors, such as the Lebanese Hezbollah, ISIS, and Al-Qaeda hoping to exploit American security weaknesses; transnational criminal organizations and ideologically driven entities, such as hacktivists, leaktivists, and public-disclosure organizations (think WikiLeaks); not to mention freelance secrets-brokers harvesting sensitive data and intellectual property to sell on the black market.

Not only have the actors multiplied exponentially, so have their targets. The lead agencies within the intelligence community—the FBI, CIA, and NSA—remain at the top of the list, but as Jack Thompson alluded to earlier, government entities without a specific national security mission, such as the Energy Department, are also being heavily targeted along with US national laboratories and vital private-sector elements of the US industrial, financial, and information infrastructure, such as banking, the power grid, the digital cloud, and more.

All these threat actors are looking for penetration points. They are all seeking inside information. And they all have significant money to offer a mole, at the right price for the right data. Or maybe they need no money at all—the two most massive US security leaks of the 21st century were basically cost-free.

Beginning in early 2010 and continuing into 2013, US Army intelligence specialist Chelsea Manning—then Bradley Manning—provided WikiLeaks with three-quarters of a million documents that were either classified or highly sensitive, almost all of them related to US actions while prosecuting the war against terror in Iran, Afghanistan, and elsewhere—actions Manning once described as "almost criminal back-dealings" and "non-PR-versions of world events and crises."[9]

Almost simultaneously, Edward Snowden—a CIA employee working as a subcontractor at the NSA—was beginning to leak to *The Guardian* and other publications the first of an estimated 1.7 million documents purloined mostly from the NSA and the Department of Defense and including 160,000 intercepted emails and instant-message communications.[10]

Finding a mole who is selling secrets to a foreign intelligence service is hard enough, but at least there's money to follow if you can ever get a whiff of it. Finding a mole who is giving away secrets to mitigate perceived national hubris or geopolitical wrongs or whatever the tipping point might be is harder still.

Scott Shane, who spent twenty-five years following national security issues as a reporter for the *Baltimore Sun* and the *New York Times*, thinks Edward Snowden and Chelsea Manning are more harbingers of the future than relics of the past; although, he adds, "I don't think it will happen often on that scale: it requires a leaker of skill, intense motivation, and the courage to risk prison or exile. But it's never going to be possible to protect all the secret information from the workforce in an electronic age."[11]

Embedded spies, whether moles or self-styled whistleblowers, are also far harder to find when cooperation between once aligned international intelligence services, once friendly governments, and once binding relationships like NATO begin to fall into disarray.

The CIA tiptoes around this issue in its 2019 threat assessment: "Some US allies and partners are seeking greater independence from Washington in response to their perceptions of changing US policies on security and trade and are becoming more open to new bilateral and multilateral partnerships."[12] Its careful language reflects a gloomy reality: like the nation itself, the US intelligence community is in danger of becoming a sort of Western World pariah, little trusted and less informed by its peer nations and intelligence services than it once was.

At the micro or even nano level, discouraging penetrations, identifying them once they happen, and finally rooting them out is becoming more difficult still.

In the late 1960s, RAND corporation economist Daniel Ellsberg was assigned to work on a top-secret review of classified documents related to the Vietnam War. As he did so, Ellsberg laboriously photocopied the documents, and in 1971, they were eventually released in the *New York Times* and *Washington Post*, and later elsewhere, as the "Pentagon Papers"—another example, famous at the time, of unsolicited espionage.

A decade and a half later, Robert Hanssen began harvesting and copying—in plain sight, on the fourth floor of FBI headquarters—reams of secret documents to sell to his Soviet handlers. Hanssen eventually segued to computer disks for the bulk of his booty transfers—sleeker, smaller, faster, but still relatively slow to load in a computing backwater like the FBI and with a detectable physical bulk and density.

Two decades after Hanssen and his floppy disks, as I was finishing this book, I transferred the entire manuscript—several hundred pages, some hundred thousand words—in a few seconds onto a thumb drive no longer than half my thumb and a tenth as slim. And that was using what is by modern standards dinosaur technology. Chelsea Manning and Edward Snowden, far more tech savvy than I, swiped, stored, and transmitted hundreds of thousands of documents with a few clicks of a mouse, but even that took place in a hi-tech Stone Age compared to what is available to spies, moles, leakers, hackers, and more today.

That potpourri of possibilities is well described in the *National Counterintelligence Strategy*:

> The global availability of technologies with intelligence applications—such as biometric devices, unmanned systems, high-resolution imagery, enhanced technical surveillance equipment, advanced encryption, and big data analytics—and the unauthorized disclosures of U.S. cyber tools have enabled a wider range of actors to obtain sophisticated intelligence capabilities previously possessed only by well-financed intelligence services. These technologies have

opened up new opportunities for adversaries to use information as a strategic resource in achieving their economic security aims and exert leverage over their competitors.[13]

Translated: it's easier to steal secrets than ever before and easier to go undetected as you do so.

To get a broader picture of the on-the-ground national security landscape today, I spent several hours with someone I can identify only as one of the nation's leading authorities on cutting-edge forensics—the kind of expert both Fortune 100 and government agencies rely on to avoid penetrations and find the culprits when they happen. Here's some of what I learned.

"Once you've been cleared and you're inside the FBI or CIA or NSA, you're trusted, so nobody's watching you, and you can do anything you want. The kind of information that you have access to at that point would just blow anyone away. It's better than make-believe.

"The things that the government does and doesn't do and denies and whatever—it's all right there, and everyone has access because none of the networks are secure. None of them. The FBI has been hacked, so have the CIA and the Pentagon and the White House. If you have enough time and a state sponsor, you will get into a network. . . .

"The thing that got Edward Snowden, Chelsea Manning, and a couple of others in so much trouble is that the government does a lot of things that should not be classified. These are things that will embarrass the government or somebody high up. And we get to see this when we have this privileged access clearance.

"Most of us just talk about it among ourselves. 'That guy's a real sleaze,' or 'This guy's lying to the public about something important. I wish I could talk publicly about this,' but we never do. Snowden and Manning, though, took that final additional step.

"People say, 'Well, they should have done it legally by going up the chain,' but there is no chain when it's classified. You cannot go up the chain because they tell you it's none of your business. It's above your pay grade. The only choice then is to do what Manning and Snowden did, at least the way they see it, but they wouldn't have felt compelled to do so if so much dirt wasn't being hidden behind 'classified' status. . . . .

"The private sector has a huge problem with security. I did a case not long ago where I went to an oil company. They had just paid many millions of dollars for a new security system, and they asked me to try to penetrate it. So I walked in and asked for an application form for a job, and while the front-desk clerk was getting it, I stole five badges that were sitting on the desk, and then I walked through the whole building and got into their network, got into their lock box, everything.

"And that wasn't a rare occasion. Most of the security systems on the electrical grids are really old, twenty to thirty years. The Department of Energy alone has 22,000 cameras currently covering the major electrical grids and nuclear power plants, and they are not state of the art. Hack into a camera, block it, and then you can go in and do whatever you want at that nuclear power plant.

"And then there's the banking system. Banks are being hacked and hit constantly for hundreds of thousands of dollars a month. Even little banks. They don't announce it because then their depositors are going to feel like the bank is not safe and pull their money. But they are being hacked all over the place all the time, and they cannot find out how to block it. The FBI is so busy now it doesn't investigate anything under a million dollars, and the bad guys know it. So they just take smaller amounts every time. . . .

"There are always going to be guys like Hanssen. To do his job, you have to have access, and access always creates vulnerabilities. There's always going to be that tension between convenience and security, and security is almost always going to suffer for that. But it's a million times more dangerous now than it was then because everything is online. It's all digital, and people trust the cloud. . . .

"If I wanted to screw a whole company, instead of hacking its network, I'd hack the cloud. I'd take the whole cloud down. All these companies have all these virtual machines running on a cloud. You take that machine down and you take their backups down, and the companies are gone. . . .

"Iran is hacking us like crazy right now. So are the Chinese because they're pissed off at us poking them in the eye about Hong Kong and Taiwan and a bunch of other stuff. Even the Russians are pissed off at us whatever you hear to the contrary.

"These government cybersecurity sites are going nuts. They're hiring people like crazy because they can't keep up with it all. And the Russians and the rest of them are not going to stop. It's in their interest to disrupt our politics—change people's minds by putting out fake information and making it look so real that you change your mind about who you are going to vote for while you're on the way to the polling place."[14]

It's a rough world out there, in short—a national security terrain littered with potholes, rife with penetration possibilities, and knee-deep and worse with external threats—but if the FBI is going to avoid becoming a breeding ground for future Hanssens, its leaders also need to stop shooting themselves in the feet, and the Bureau needs far fewer interferences from Pennsylvania Avenue.

My eighty-five-year-old father was an FBI agent back in the days when there was hell to pay if you were caught taking a handful of paper clips home from the office or giving your spouse a ride in a Bureau-issued car. The message was clear: once you put that badge on, you do not cross lines!

Dad was later a federal prosecutor, and in both capacities—as a member of the FBI family and as one who later reported to the Justice Department across the street—he was horrified when then-director James Comey said publicly that "no reasonable prosecutor" would bring a case against Hillary Clinton for using her personal server as secretary of state.

That was crossing even a more sacred line: the FBI is tasked with investigating crimes, then handing its findings over to the US Attorney's Office (the federal *prosecutors*) to determine whether the evidence warrants prosecution and meets the legal standard for bringing a case and bearing the burden of proof beyond a reasonable doubt for guilt.

The rule here is ironclad: investigators are *never* supposed to make that determination of law. Comey threw that under the bus. Dad predicted that this would have a devastating impact on the morale of the line agents. I fear he's right.

Dad was also thrown into dismay when President Trump tried to bring Comey into an unholy alliance by demanding that he all but drop the investigation into Russian meddling in the 2016 election and also announce that Trump was not being personally investigated.

I'm also a former federal prosecutor, appointed by George H. W. Bush and reappointed by Bill Clinton, and I was equally dismayed by President Trump's attempt to co-opt Jim Comey and disheartened by subsequent events. A certain amount of politics is always going to seep into the Justice Department. This program or that gets prioritized less for its deterrent value than for its vote appeal, but line assistants like me were trained to follow our leads, not bow to presidential whims.

The Trump Justice Department under William Barr's leadership, or more accurately heel, went in exactly the opposite direction, lending its full weight to the proposition that the FBI is an embedded part of the Deep State problem. Thus an honorable institution and the many honorable men and women within it who carry the torch for law enforcement and save lives every day by helping keep our national secrets safe became yet another Twitter feed in Donald Trump's bent narrative of the nation he was elected to serve. Richard Nixon and his attorney general John Mitchell at their worst were rookies at destruction compared to this.

Happily, current attorney general Merrick Garland has been focusing more on Constitutional abuses in the states and less on protecting the president, pardoning his cronies, and pummeling the political opposition. Garland's boss, Joe Biden, appears prone to stumbles, but he clearly respects the rule of law and stands foursquare for basic democratic principles. Still, when a majority of the Republican Party refuses to acknowledge the legitimacy of Biden's presidency and when seasoned senators and the minority leader of the House of Representatives continue to paint the January 6, 2021, savagery at the United States Capitol as a tourist prank gone slightly awry, the fabric of the nation is weakened.

That's bad for America, but in significant ways it's even worse for places like the FBI that are dedicated to defending the Constitution and on the front lines of upholding the rule of law. Such an onslaught fundamentally undermines morale and functioning, from the core, and it gives an implicit license to those within such organizations who might have financial problems or are discontent with their career advancement or exist at the edge of the group culture or are simply looking for a thrill to perk up their bureaucracy-bound lives to give in to their own worst instincts, the dark angels of their psyche.

When that line gets crossed, you can institute all the polygraphs you want, run all the credit checks imaginable, but there's always going to be one special agent with a high security clearance who slips through the net, scoops up a handful of vital secrets, and sits down in the basement one evening to write a letter to the Russian or Chinese or Saudi or Israeli intelligence chief stationed in Washington, a letter that begins roughly:

> Soon, I will send a box of documents. They are from certain of the most sensitive and highly compartmentalized projects of the U.S. Intelligence community. All are originals to aid verifying their authenticity. Please recognize for our long-term interests that there are a limited number of persons with this array of clearances. As a collection they point to me. I trust that an officer of your experience will handle them appropriately. I believe they are sufficient to justify a $100,000 payment to me.

Odds are, one special agent or case officer already has. And this time it's not only US assets and operations abroad that are endangered—it's democracy itself.

SOURCES AND METHODOLOGY

This book represents the culmination of many months and countless hours of research that included multiple, lengthy interviews with many of the key individuals in the Hanssen investigation, and the review of thousands of pages of investigative material and numerous other sources ranging from books to newspaper articles and magazine stories as well as select television news programs, podcasts, public appearances, and symposia featuring prominent players in the Hanssen saga.

My aim throughout was to move the Hanssen story forward by uncovering new details through primary sourced materials, including interviews with Hanssen's best friend, his brother-in-law, his psychiatrist, and others who could lend an enhanced perspective.

I sought to go beyond an analysis of the Hanssen case and make a link between Hanssen and an increase in risk to national security today. To do so, I relied extensively on interviews with experts in the field of high technology, security, and forensics.

In addition to the individuals named below, I corresponded by email with many current and former members of the FBI who had known Hanssen in some capacity. While many described Hanssen as a problematic employee who left many telltale signs of his treachery behind, all were uniformly shocked to discover that he had been spying in plain sight for much of his twenty-two-year FBI career.

Principal Interviews

Current or retired FBI agents, special agents, and supervisors:
Anonymous, a still-active FBI agent who worked closely with Hanssen and didn't trust him.

Anonymous, a still-active FBI agent who worked in the Vault.

Dave Brown, called Hanssen "Whispering Bob."

Louis Freeh, director, attended the same conservative Catholic church as Hanssen; their sons also attended the same school.

Gwen Fuller, helped build the matrix that originally targeted the wrong suspect.

Rich Garcia, Hanssen's supervisor for the two months after he was identified but before his arrest; had an office constructed for him that was crammed full of surveillance equipment.

Jim Lyle, Hanssen's supervisor earlier in his career and the Bureau liaison to the CIA at the time of Hanssen's arrest.

David Major, Hanssen's supervisor, friend, and protector within the Soviet Analytical Unit.

Jim Milburn, the first person to identify Hanssen as the spy originally code-named GRAYSUIT.

Joe Navarro, a fellow counterintelligence expert; he thought Hanssen "didn't know how to participate" in the usual Bureau social events.

Jim Ohlson, Hanssen's longest-standing friend within the FBI; he admired Hanssen's ability to analyze and solve problems.

Eric O'Neill, a surveillance specialist who served undercover as Hanssen's administrative assistant during the two months before his arrest.

Kathleen Puckett, a profiler; Hanssen, she says, has either lost his cognitive skills in prison or he's faking it.

Mike Rochford, central player in Hanssen's arrest; he headed up Operation PENNYWISE, which found the Russian source who brought Hanssen down even though the Russians never knew Hanssen's name until his arrest.

Kendall Shull, polygraph expert who refused to go along with the effort to pin Hanssen's crimes on CIA officer Brian Kelley.

I. C. Smith, Hanssen's supervisor; he found Hanssen "frankly . . . a loathsome individual."

Don Sullivan, Hanssen's friend and admirer; he learned Hanssen was the spy only moments after learning that his wife was critically ill with breast cancer.

Dave Szady, CIA liaison at the time when blame settled hard on the wrong suspect; he furiously defended the FBI's performance on a 2003 episode of *60 Minutes*.

Jack Thompson, one of the Vault People and part of the special unit assembled in 1995 to run GRAYSUIT to ground; Hanssen was never among their top suspects.

Mark Wauck, Hanssen's brother-in-law, who would later claim that a decade before Hanssen's arrest he had wondered aloud to his supervisor if Hanssen was a spy; carried on an extensive email correspondence with Brian Kelley in the years after Hanssen's arrest.

CIA officials:

Mike Sulick, counterintelligence chief who helped provide the $750,000 down payment to Mike Rochford's Russian source for evidence sight unseen.

George Tenet, director; he and Louie Freeh both signed off on the roughly $7 million the Russian source ultimately received, along with relocation to the United States.

Others:

Anonymous, one of the nation's leading experts on high-tech security and forensics.

David Charney, psychiatrist who interviewed Hanssen twice weekly for an entire year after his arrest.

George Ellard, deputy counsel of the commission that produced the devastating inspector general's report on the FBI's performance in the Hanssen case.

Jack Hoschouer, Hanssen's lifelong best friend; he was with Hanssen within a few hours of his arrest and attended his sentencing hearing so Hanssen would know he hadn't "rejected him totally," though he's not sure if Hanssen ever saw him there.

Barry Kelley, son of Brian Kelley, the CIA officer who spent almost four years as the lead suspect in the Hanssen case and carried on an extensive email correspondence with Mark Wauck after Hanssen's arrest.

Patricia McCarthy, Brian Kelley's widow; the investigators, she says, "tried to force a square peg into a round hole."

Scott Shane, *New York Times* national security correspondent.

Public Records

Affidavit in support of criminal complaint, arrest warrant, and search warrants in the case of *United States of America v. Robert Philip Hanssen*, February 2001, https://fas.org/irp/ops/ci/hanssen_affidavit.html.

Affidavit in support of search warrants in the case of *United States of America v. Robert Philip Hanssen*, February 2001, https://fas.org/irp/ops/ci/hanssen _affidavit2.html.

Affidavit in support of criminal complaint, arrest warrant, and search warrants in the case of *United States v. Earl Edwin Pitts*, https://www.hanford.gov/files .cfm/earlpitts.pdf, 6.

Daniel R. Coats, *Worldwide Threat Assessment of the US Intelligence Community*, Senate Select Committee on Intelligence, January 29, 2019, https://www.dni.gov/files/ODNI/documents/2019-ATA-SFR---SSCI.pdf.

Office of the Inspector General, *A Review of the FBI's Performance in Deterring, Detecting, and Investigating the Espionage Activities of Robert Philip Hanssen*, US Department of Justice, August 2003, https://fas.org/irp/agency/doj/oig/hanssen.pdf.

Office of the Inspector General, *A Review of the FBI's Progress in Responding to the Recommendations of the Office of the Inspector General Report on Robert Hanssen*, US Department of Justice, September 2007, https://oig.justice.gov/sites/default/files/legacy/special/s0710/final.pdf.

Office of the Inspector General, "The Federal Bureau of Investigation's Management of the Trilogy Information Technology Modernization Project: Analysis and Summary of Actions Necessary to Close Report," Audit Report No. 05-07, February 2005, appendix 8, https://oig.justice.gov/reports/FBI/a0507/app8.htm.

National Counterintelligence Strategy of the United States of America 2020–2022, National Counterintelligence and Security Center, February 2020, https://www.dni.gov/files/NCSC/documents/features/20200205-National_CI_Strategy_2020_2022.pdf.

Sentencing memorandum in the case of *United States of America v. Robert Philip Hanssen*, May 2002.

U.S. Senate, Select Committee on Intelligence, *An Assessment of the Aldrich H. Ames Espionage Case and Its Implications for U.S. Intelligence*, S.Prt. 103-90 (Washington, DC: Government Printing Office, 1994), https://fas.org/irp/congress/1994_rpt/ssci_ames.htm.

U.S. Senate, Select Committee on Intelligence, Special Report, committee activities, S. Rep. No. 104-4 (1994), https://www.intelligence.senate.gov/publications/special-report-committee-activities-select-committee-intelligence-january-4-1993.

William H. Webster, *A Review of FBI Security Programs*, Commission for the Review of FBI Security Programs, US Department of Justice, March 31, 2002, https://fas.org/irp/agency/doj/fbi/websterreport.html—commonly known as the "Webster Commission Report."

Television, Movies, Radio, Podcasts, and Public Appearances

60 Minutes, season 35, episode 18, "The Wrong Man," segment hosted by Lesley Stahl, aired August 24, 2003, on CBS.

Breach, directed by Billy Ray, starring Chris Cooper as Robert Hanssen and Ryan Phillippe as Eric O'Neill (Los Angeles: Universal, 2007).

David Major, talk given at the International Spy Museum, Washington, DC, April 2007. Michael Rochford, "Investigation of Robert Hanssen," discussion, International Spy Museum, October 1, 2013, Washington, DC, online video, https://www.c-span.org/video/?315217-1/investigation-robert-hanssen.

FBI Retired Case File Review with Jerri Williams, "Mike Rochford—FBI Betrayal, Robert Hanssen," episode 31, August 2016, https://podcasts.apple.com/ca/podcast/episode-031-mike-rochford-fbi-betrayal-robert-hanssen/id1082012464?i=1000394396943.

Investigation of a Citizen Above Suspicion, written and directed by Elio Petri (Los Angeles: Columbia Pictures, 1970); winner of the 1970 Oscar for Best Foreign Film. One of Hanssen's favorite movies with many echoes of his own spy career.

Michelle Van Cleave, "Foreign Spies and the US Response," Brian Kelley Memorial Lecture, Institute of World Politics, Washington, DC, October 26, 2012.

PBS NewsHour, "Damage Assessment: Convicted Spy Robert Hanssen," Ray Suarez interview with Elaine Shannon and Susan Rosenfeld, aired May 10, 2002, on PBS, https://www.pbs.org/newshour/show/damage-assessment-convicted-spy-robert-hanssen.

Sandy Grimes, interview, National Security Archive, episode 21, January 30, 1998, https://nsarchive2.gwu.edu/coldwar/interviews/episode-21/grimes1.html.

Notable Books

Victor Cherkashin, *Spy Handler: Memoir of a KGB Officer—The True Story of the Man Who Recruited Robert Hanssen & Aldrich Ames* (New York: Basic Books, 2005).

Pete Earley, *Family of Spies: Inside the John Walker Spy Ring* (New York: Bantam, 1988).

Bill Gertz, *Enemies: How America's Foes Steal Our Vital Secrets—And How We Let It Happen* (New York: Crown, 2006).

Adrian Havill, *The Spy Who Stayed Out in The Cold: The Secret Life of FBI Double Agent Robert Hanssen* (New York: St. Martin's, 2001).

Eric O'Neill, *Gray Day: My Undercover Mission to Expose America's First Cyber Spy* (New York: Crown, 2019).

Lawrence Schiller, *Into the Mirror: The Life of Master Spy Robert P. Hanssen* (New York: HarperCollins, 2002).

Elaine Shannon and Ann Blackman, *The Spy Next Door: The Extraordinary Secret Life of Robert Philip Hanssen, the Most Damaging FBI Agent in U.S. History* (New York: Little, Brown and Company, 2002).

David A. Vise, *The Bureau and the Mole: The Unmasking of Robert Philip Hanssen, the Most Dangerous Double Agent in FBI History* (New York: Grove Press, 2002).

David Wise, *Spy: The Inside Story of How the FBI's Robert Hanssen Betrayed America* (New York: Random House, 2003).

David Wise, *The Seven Million Dollar Spy: How One Determined Investigator, Seven Million Dollars—And a Death Threat by the Russian Mafia—Led to the Capture of the Most Dangerous Mole Ever Unmasked Inside U.S. Intelligence* (Newark, N.J.: Audible Studios, 2018).

Notable Journal Articles

David L. Charney, "True Psychology of the Insider Spy," *Intelligencer: Journal of U.S. Intelligence Studies* 18, no. 1 (Fall/Winter 2010).

David L. Charney and John A. Irvin, "The Psychology of Espionage," *Intelligencer: Journal of U.S. Intelligence Studies* 22, no. 1 (Spring 2016).

George Ellard, "Top Hat's Face: Explaining Robert Hanssen's Treason," *Philosophy and Public Policy Quarterly* 23, nos. 1/2 (Winter/Spring 2003): 5, http://ojs2 .gmu.edu/PPPQ/article/view/394/322.

Barton Gellman, Julie Tate, and Ashkan Soltani, "In NSA-Intercepted Data, Those Not Targeted Far Outnumber the Foreigners Who Are," *Washington Post*, July 5, 2014, https://www.washingtonpost.com/world/national-security /in-nsa-intercepted-data-those-not-targeted-far-outnumber-the-foreigners -who-are/2014/07/05/8139adf8-045a-11e4-8572-4b1b969b6322_story.html.

Evan Hanson, "Manning-Lamo Chat Logs Revealed," *Wired*, July 13, 2011, https://www.wired.com/2011/07/manning-lamo-logs/.

Richards J. Heuer Jr. and Katherine Herbig, "Espionage by the Numbers: A Statistical Overview," *Eye Spy Magazine*, issuu.com, March 2014, https://issuu .com/eyespy/docs/the_mind_of_a_spy.

Brian J. Kelley, "The Movie *Breach*: A Personal Perspective," *Studies in Intelligence* 52, no. 1 (March 2008): 25–29.

Scott McCaffrey, "Oakcrest Graduates Told Living Good Lives Will Bring Happiness," *Inside NoVa*, June 3, 2013, https://www.insidenova.com/news /fairfax/oakcrest-graduates-told-living-good-lives-will-bring-happiness/article _b23332ff-a93d-506b-9889-9007da8829c7.html.

James Risen, "Gaps in Ames Case May Be Filled by FBI's Own Spy Case," *New York Times*, February 21, 2001, https://www.nytimes.com/2001/02/21

/national/gaps-in-ames-case-may-be-filled-by-fbis-own-spy-case.html
?searchResultPosition=1.

J. Scott Sanford and Bruce A. Arrigo, "Policing and Psychopathy: The Case of Robert
Philip Hanssen," *Journal of Forensic Psychology Practice* 7, no. 3 (2007): 1–31.

Scott Shane, "Blessed Are the Traitors, for Preventing Nuclear War," *Baltimore
Sun*, August 17, 2003, https://www.baltimoresun.com/news/bs-xpm-2003-08
-17-0308180372-story.html.

Chris Strohm and Del Quentin Wilber, "Pentagon Says Snowden Took Most US
Secrets Ever: Rogers," Bloomberg, January 9, 2014, https://www
.bloomberg.com/news/articles/2014-01-09/pentagon-finds-snowden-took
-1-7-million-files-rogers-says.

David A. Vise, "From Russia with Love," *Washington Post*, January 6, 2002,
https://www.washingtonpost.com/archive/lifestyle/magazine/2002/01/06
/from-russia-with-love/b28c2127-65e5-43f3-8a9a-0e75ab851cb3/

Tim Weiner, "C.I.A. Head Says He Misspoke on Possible Espionage Cases," *New
York Times*, April 21, 1994, https://www.nytimes.com/1994/04/21/us/cia
-head-says-he-misspoke-on-possible-espionage-cases.html.

Ursula M. Wilder, "Why Spy?: The Psychology of Espionage," *Studies in
Intelligence* 61, no. 2 (June 2017).

Newspapers, Magazines, and Internet Sites That Provided Notable Coverage

The carefully staged announcement of Robert Hanssen's arrest on February 20,
2001—two days after the actual takedown—was a front-page, top-of-the-
evening-news blockbuster, even when few details about him or his crimes were
immediately available.

Below are samples of the often excellent journalism that followed over the next
fifteen months, until Hanssen was sentenced to life in prison:

February 22, 2001: Pam Belluck, "A Search for Answers: The Chicago Years," *New
York Times.*

March 5, 2001: Johanna McGeary, "The FBI Spy: It Took 15 Years to Discover
One of the Most Damaging Cases of Espionage in US History. An Inside
Look at the Secret Life, and Final Capture, of Robert Hanssen," *Time.*

March 18, 2001: James Bamford, "Lives: My Friend, the Spy" (op-ed), *New York
Times,* https://www.nytimes.com/2001/03/18/magazine/lives-my-friend
-the-spy.html.

April 22, 2001: James Risen and David Johnston, "FBI Rejected Spy Warning
Two Years Before Agent's Arrest," *New York Times.*

July 3, 2001: Dan Eggen, "Revelations and Recriminations in Spy Case,"
Washington Post, July 3, 2001, https://www.washingtonpost.com/archive

/politics/2001/07/03/revelations-and-recriminations-in-spy-case/17ef4900
-c7fe-40e6-b4ff-b2d195f629af/.

July 12, 2001: Robert D. Novak, "A Spy's Double Life" (op-ed), *Washington Post*,
https://www.washingtonpost.com/archive/opinions/2001/07/12/a-spys
-double-life/f84dbf93-df43-4d21-9f84-aef3765d862b/.

July 13, 2001: Eric Lichtblau, "Spy's Wife Apologizes, Finds His Life Sentence
'Appropriate,'" *Los Angeles Times*.

April 5, 2002: Philip Shenon, "Agent Who Betrayed FBI Cites Its Laxity," *New
York Times*.

May 11, 2002: Michael Kilian, "FBI Spy Hanssen Gets Life, Apologizes," *Chicago
Tribune*.

Also special notice to:

B. J. Hollars, "The Infiltration of Knox College: The College Experience of Super
Spy Robert Hanssen '66," *Knox Magazine*, originally published in the *Knox
Student* (newspaper), March 23, 2007, https://www.knox.edu/news/robert
-hanssen-61; student reporting at its best.

And a tip of the hat to a very useful Internet resource that encapsulates the
Hanssen story: Adrian Havill, "The Last Day in the Sun—The Robert
Hanssen Story," Forum at ILW.com, posted July 31, 2008.

ACRONYMS AND AGENCIES

Acronyms

ACS	Automated Case Support system
ASAC	Assistant Special Agent in Charge (FBI)
CARLABFAD	FBI background-check system
COINS-II	Community On-Line Intelligence System
COOP	Continuing Operations
CNC	Counternarcotics Center (CIA)
DCI	Director of Central Intelligence (later CIA)
DDO	Deputy Director of Operations (CIA)
ECF	Electronic Case File
FISA	Foreign Intelligence Surveillance Act (1978)
GRU	Soviet's military intelligence wing (a Russian acronym for Main Intelligence Directorate)
HUMINT	Human Intelligence
ICBM	Intercontinental Ballistic Missiles
IG	Inspector General (Justice Department)
KGB	Soviet intelligence (later SVR after the collapse of the Soviet Union in 1991)
MASINT	Measurement and Signature Intelligence (CIA)
NDAs	Nondisclosure Agreements
NSA	National Security Agency

NYFO	New York Field Office (FBI)
OFM	Office of Foreign Missions (State Department)
OIPR	Office of Intelligence Policy and Review (Justice Department)
OODA	Observe, Orient, Decide, and Act
SAC	Special Agent in Charge
SAR	Suspicious Activity Report
SCI	Sensitive Compartmented Information
SCIF	Sensitive Compartmented Information Facilities
SES	Senior Executive Service (FBI)
SIU	Special Investigation Unit (FBI)
SSG	Investigative Specialist (FBI)
SVR	Russian intelligence (previously KGB before the collapse of the Soviet Union in 1991)
WFO	Washington Field Office (FBI)

List of Agencies and Others

CIA–FBI	National Counterintelligence Center
CIA	Agency, the
CIA	Central Intelligence Agency
CIA	Counterespionage Center
CIA	Counterintelligence Division (aka Division 5) Counterintelligence Espionage Group (CEG; headed by the FBI in the Agency)
CIA	Counterintelligence Evaluation Branch
CIA	Counternarcotics Center
CIA	Financial Investigations Branch
CIA	National Counterintelligence and Security Center
CIA	Operations Center
CIA	Soviet-European Division
DOD	Defense Personnel and Security Research Center
DOJ	Office of Intelligence Policy and Review (OIPR)
DOJ	Office of the Inspector General
DOS	Bureau of Intelligence and Research
DOS	Office of Foreign Missions (OFM)
FBI	Analyst Group (or the Vault People)
FBI	Budget Unit
FBI	Bureau, the
FBI	C13 section

FBI	Chicago Division
FBI	Engineering Research Facility
FBI	Espionage Section
FBI	Eurasian Section
FBI	FBI Academy (Quantico, VA)
FBI	Headquarters
FBI	Information Resources Division
FBI	Inspection Division
FBI	Intelligence Branch National Security Threat List Unit
FBI	Mail Services Unit
FBI	National Security Branch Counterintelligence Division
FBI	Office of Foreign Missions (headquarters liaison with State Department)
FBI	Russia House
FBI	Russian Section
FBI	Security Countermeasures Branch
FBI	Security Division
FBI	Sensitive Source Unit
FBI	Soviet Analytical Unit
FBI	Soviet counterintelligence division (within NYFO)
FBI	Special Investigation Unit (SIU)
FBI	Vault, the; Vault People, the (or Analyst Group)
FBI	Washington field office

ENDNOTES

Prologue: Strange Encounter
1   Louis Freeh, interview by Howard Means, 2004. Used by permission of Louis Freeh.

Chapter 1: TOPHAT
1   Sandy Grimes, interview, January 30, 1998, National Security Archive, https://nsarchive2
    .gwu.edu/coldwar/interviews/episode-21/grimes1.html.
2   Sandy Grimes, interview, January 30, 1998, National Security Archive, https://nsarchive2
    .gwu.edu/coldwar/interviews/episode-21/grimes1.html.
3   Ibid.
4   Ibid.

Chapter 2: Spying 1.0
1   Jack Hoschouer, multiple interviews by the author, summer-fall 2020.
2   Mark Wauck, multiple interviews by the author, spring-summer 2020.
3   Jack Hoschouer, multiple interviews by the author, summer-fall 2020.
4   William H. Webster, *A Review of FBI Security Programs*, Commission for the Review of FBI
    Security Programs, US Department of Justice, March 31, 2002, https://fas.org/irp/agency/doj
    /fbi/websterreport.html.

Chapter 3: "What Are You Hiding?"
1   Jack Hoschouer, multiple interviews by the author, summer-fall 2020.

Chapter 4: Grooming a Mole
1   Scott Shane, "Blessed are the traitors, for preventing nuclear war," *Baltimore Sun*, August 17,
    2003, https://www.baltimoresun.com/news/bs-xpm-2003-08-17-0308180372-story.html.
2   David Major, interview by the author, June 2020.
3   Jim Ohlson, interview by the author, December 2020.
4   Ibid.

5   David Major, interview by the author, June 2020.
6   Ibid.
7   Mark Wauck, multiple interviews by the author, spring-summer 2020.
8   Dave Szady, interview by the author, summer 2020.
9   Jack Hoschouer, multiple interviews by the author, summer-fall 2020.

Chapter 5: Spying 2.0

1   All communications between Robert Hanssen and his Soviet and later Russian handlers are
     from the affidavit in support of criminal complaint, arrest warrant, and search warrants in the
     case of *United States of America v. Robert Philip Hanssen*, https://fas.org/irp/ops/ci/hanssen
     _affidavit.html. I have corrected minor errors of spelling, punctuation, grammar, and usage in
     the affidavit for ease of reading.
2   Affidavit in support of criminal complaint, arrest warrant, and search warrants in the case of
     United States of America v. Robert Philip Hanssen.
3   Mike Rochford, multiple interviews by the author, spring-summer 2020.
4   Affidavit in support of criminal complaint, arrest warrant, and search warrants in the case of
     United States of America v. Robert Philip Hanssen, https://fas.org/irp/ops/ci/hanssen_affidavit.html.
5   Ibid.
6   Victor Cherkashin, *Spy Handler: Memoir of a KGB Officer; The True Story of the Man Who
     Recruited Robert Hanssen & Aldrich Ames* (New York: Basic Books, 2005), 234.
7   David Major, interview by the author, June 2020.
8   Affidavit in support of criminal complaint, arrest warrant, and search warrants in the case of
     United States of America v. Robert Philip Hanssen, https://fas.org/irp/ops/ci/hanssen_affidavit
     .html.
9   Ibid.
10   Ibid.
11   Ibid.
12   Ibid.
13   Ibid.
14   Ibid.
15   Ibid.
16   Ibid.

Chapter 6: "Holy Shit!"

1   Mike Rochford, multiple interviews by the author, spring-summer 2020.
2   Affidavit in support of criminal complaint, arrest warrant, and search warrants in the case of
     United States of America v. Robert Philip Hanssen.
3   Ibid.
4   Louis Freeh, interview by Howard Means, 2004. Used by permission of Louis Freeh.
5   Affidavit in support of criminal complaint, arrest warrant, and search warrants in the case of
     United States of America v. Robert Philip Hanssen.
6   Ibid.
7   Ibid.

Chapter 7: Who Is Robert Hanssen?

1   Joe Navarro, interview by the author, November 2019.
2   Jim Ohlson, interview by the author, December 2019.
3   Ibid.
4   Ibid.

5   From multiple references including the Webster Commission report, email from Dave Brown, and previously cited literature on Hanssen.

6   Dave Brown, email message to author, July 30, 2020.

7   David Major, interview by the author, June 2020.

8   Mike Rochford, multiple interviews by the author, spring-summer 2020.

9   I. C. Smith, interview by the author, summer 2020.

10 Ibid.

11 Elaine Shannon and Ann Blackman, *The Spy Next Door: The Extraordinary Secret Life of Robert Philip Hanssen, the Most Damaging FBI Agent in U.S. History* (New York: Little, Brown and Company, 2002), 77.

12 Mark Wauck, multiple interviews by the author, spring-summer 2020.

13 Jack Thompson, interview by the author, June 2020.

14 Affidavit in support of criminal complaint, arrest warrant, and search warrants in the case of *United States of America v. Robert Philip Hanssen*. The first two lines are from a poem "Leisure" by William Henry Davies.

15 Affidavit in support of criminal complaint, arrest warrant, and search warrants in the case of *United States of America v. Robert Philip Hanssen*.

16 Ibid.

17 George Ellard, "Top Hat's Face: Explaining Robert Hanssen's Treason," *Philosophy and Public Policy Quarterly* 23, nos. 1/2 (Winter/Spring 2003): 5, http://ojs2.gmu.edu/PPPQ/article /view/394/322.

18 Affidavit in support of criminal complaint, arrest warrant, and search warrants in the case of *United States of America v. Robert Philip Hanssen*.

19 David Major, interview by the author, June 2020.

20 Mike Rochford, multiple interviews by the author, spring-summer 2020.

Chapter 8: All-American Boy

1   Jack Hoschouer, multiple interviews by the author, summer-fall 2020.

2   Ibid.

3   Ibid.

4   Ibid.

5   Ibid.

6   Ibid.

7   Ibid.

8   Ibid.

9   Ibid.

10 B. J. Hollars, "The Infiltration of Knox College: The College Experience of Super Spy Robert Hanssen '66," *Knox Magazine*, originally published in the *Knox Student* (newspaper), March 23, 2007, https://www.knox.edu/news/robert-hanssen-61.

11 Adrian Havill, *The Spy Who Stayed Out in the Cold: The Secret Life of FBI Double Agent Robert Hanssen* (New York: St. Martin's, 2001), 34.

12 Adrian Havill, *The Spy Who Stayed Out in the Cold: The Secret Life of FBI Double Agent Robert Hanssen* (New York: St. Martin's, 2001), 35–36.

13 Jack Hoschouer, multiple interviews by the author, summer-fall 2020.

14 Adrian Havill, *The Spy Who Stayed Out in the Cold: The Secret Life of FBI Double Agent Robert Hanssen* (New York: St. Martin's, 2001), 37.

15 David Wise, *Spy: The Inside Story of How the FBI's Robert Hanssen Betrayed America* (New York: Random House, 2003), 14.

16 Jack Hoschouer, multiple interviews by the author, summer-fall 2020.

17   Adrian Havill, *The Spy Who Stayed Out in the Cold: The Secret Life of FBI Double Agent Robert Hanssen* (New York: St. Martin's, 2001), 51.

Chapter 9: Black Is White/Good Is Evil

1   James Bamford, "Lives; My Friend, the Spy," *New York Times*, March 18, 2001, https://www.nytimes.com/2001/03/18/magazine/lives-my-friend-the-spy.html.

2   David Wise, *Spy: The Inside Story of How the FBI's Robert Hanssen Betrayed America* (New York: Random House, 2003), 164.

3   James Bamford, "Lives; My Friend, the Spy," *New York Times*, March 18, 2001, https://www.nytimes.com/2001/03/18/magazine/lives-my-friend-the-spy.html.

4   Robert D. Novak, "A Spy's Double Life," *Washington Post*, July 12, 2001, https://www.washingtonpost.com/archive/opinions/2001/07/12/a-spys-double-life/f84dbf93-df43-4d21-9f84-aef3765d862b/.

5   Jim Ohlson, interview by the author, December 2019.

6   Email exchange between Jim Ohlson and Robert Hanssen, January 2001. Courtesy of Jim Ohlson.

7   Ibid.

8   David Major, interview by the author, June 2020.

9   Ibid.

10   Jack Hoschouer, multiple interviews by the author, summer-fall 2020.

11   Mike Rochford, multiple interviews by the author, spring-summer 2020.

12   Adrian Havill, *The Spy Who Stayed Out in the Cold: The Secret Life of FBI Double Agent Robert Hanssen* (New York: St. Martin's, 2001), 143.

13   Jack Hoschouer, multiple interviews by the author, summer-fall 2020.

14   Ibid.

15   Adrian Havill, *The Spy Who Stayed Out in the Cold: The Secret Life of FBI Double Agent Robert Hanssen* (New York: St. Martin's, 2001), 148.

16   Ibid., 47.

17   David A. Vise, *The Bureau and the Mole: The Unmasking of Robert Philip Hanssen, the Most Dangerous Double Agent in FBI History* (New York: Grove, 2002), 261.

18   Jack Hoschouer, multiple interviews by the author, summer-fall 2020.

19   Ibid.

20   Mike Rochford, multiple interviews by the author, spring-summer 2020.

21   Ibid.

22   Jim Ohlson, interview by the author, December 2019.

Chapter 10: Trust Me!

1   George Ellard, interview by the author, March 2020.

2   Ibid.

3   David Major, interview by the author, June 2020.

4   William H. Webster, *A Review of FBI Security Programs*, Commission for the Review of FBI Security Programs, United States Department of Justice, March 31, 2002, https://fas.org/irp/agency/doj/fbi/websterreport.html.

5   Affidavit in support of criminal complaint, arrest warrant, and search warrants in the case of *United States of America v. Robert Philip Hanssen*, https://fas.org/irp/ops/ci/hanssen_affidavit.html.

6   William H. Webster, *A Review of FBI Security Programs*, Commission for the Review of FBI Security Programs, United States Department of Justice, March 31, 2002, https://fas.org/irp/agency/doj/fbi/websterreport.html.

7   Ibid.

8   Ibid.

9   Mike Rochford, multiple interviews by the author, spring-summer 2020.

10 The Foreign Intelligence Surveillance Act (FISA) of 1978 prescribes procedures for requesting judicial authorization for electronic surveillance and physical search of persons engaged in espionage or international terrorism against the United States on behalf of a foreign power.

11 Office of the Inspector General, *The Federal Bureau of Investigation's Management of the Trilogy Information Technology Modernization Project: Analysis and Summary of Actions Necessary to Close Report*, Audit Report No. 05-07, February 2005, appendix 8, https://oig.justice.gov/reports/FBI /a0507/app8.htm.

12 William H. Webster, *A Review of FBI Security Programs*, Commission for the Review of FBI Security Programs, United States Department of Justice, March 31, 2002, https://fas.org/irp /agency/doj/fbi/websterreport.html. Ellipses appear in the report.

13 Dave Szady, interview by the author, summer 2020.

14 Ibid.

15 Ibid.

16 Office of the Inspector General, *A Review of the FBI's Performance in Deterring, Detecting, and Investigating the Espionage Activities of Robert Philip Hanssen*, United States Department of Justice, August 2003, page 22, https://fas.org/irp/agency/doj/oig/hanssen.pdf.

17 Office of the Inspector General, *A Review of the FBI's Performance in Deterring, Detecting, and Investigating the Espionage Activities of Robert Philip Hanssen*, United States Department of Justice, August 2003, pages 22–23, https://fas.org/irp/agency/doj/oig/hanssen.pdf.

18 William H. Webster, *A Review of FBI Security Programs*, Commission for the Review of FBI Security Programs, United States Department of Justice, March 31, 2002, https://fas.org/irp /agency/doj/fbi/websterreport.html.

19 Jim Ohlson, interview by the author, December 2019.

20 Joe Navarro, interview by the author, November 2019.

21 Affidavit in support of criminal complaint, arrest warrant, and search warrants in the case of *United States of America v. Robert Philip Hanssen*, https://fas.org/irp/ops/ci/hanssen_affidavit .html.

22 Eric O'Neill, interview by the author, summer 2020. O'Neill was eventually detailed to be Hanssen's "administrative assistant" during the closing act of his spy career. In fact, he had Hanssen under almost constant workday surveillance.

23 Office of the Inspector General, *A Review of the FBI's Performance in Deterring, Detecting, and Investigating the Espionage Activities of Robert Philip Hanssen*, United States Department of Justice, August 2003, https://fas.org/irp/agency/doj/oig/hanssen.pdf.

Chapter 11: Puffs of Smoke

1   David Wise, *Spy: The Inside Story of How the FBI's Robert Hanssen Betrayed America* (New York: Random House, 2003), 161.

2   Ibid.

3   Mike Rochford, interview by the author, spring-summer 2020.

4   I. C. Smith, interview by the author, summer 2020.

5   Mike Rochford, multiple interviews by the author, spring-summer 2020.

6   David Major, interview by the author, June 2020.

7   Don Sullivan, multiple interviews by the author, summer 2020.

8   Ibid.

9   Office of the Inspector General, *A Review of the FBI's Performance in Deterring, Detecting, and Investigating the Espionage Activities of Robert Philip Hanssen*, United States Department of Justice, August 2003, 15–16, https://fas.org/irp/agency/doj/oig/hanssen.pdf.

10   Ibid., 16.

11   Ibid., 21–22.

12   Mike Rochford, multiple interviews by the author, spring-summer 2020.

13   David Major, interview by the author, June 2020.

Chapter 12: "Do You Think Bob Could Be a KGB Agent?"

1   Dixon Whitworth, interview by the author.

2   Mark Wauck, multiple interviews by the author, spring-summer 2020.

3   Ibid.

4   Ibid.

5   Ibid.

6   Ibid.

7   Jim Lyle, multiple interviews by the author, spring-summer 2020.

8   Ibid.

9   Ibid.

10   Mark Wauck, multiple interviews by the author, spring-summer 2020.

Chapter 13: Sumo Wrestling

1   Mark Wauck, multiple interviews by the author, spring-summer 2020.

2   Mike Rochford, multiple interviews by the author, spring-summer 2020.

3   Anonymous, interview by the author.

4   David Wise, *Spy: The Inside Story of How the FBI's Robert Hanssen Betrayed America* (New York: Random House, 2003), 155–57.

5   This incident can be found in multiple sources, including David Wise, *Spy: The Inside Story of How the FBI's Robert Hanssen Betrayed America* (New York: Random House, 2003), 155–57.

6   I. C. Smith, interview by the author, summer 2020.

7   Mike Rochford, multiple interviews by the author, spring-summer 2020.

8   David Major, interview by the author, June 2020.

9   David Wise, *Spy: The Inside Story of How the FBI's Robert Hanssen Betrayed America* (New York: Random House, 2003), 156.

10   William H. Webster, *A Review of FBI Security Programs*, Commission for the Review of FBI Security Programs, United States Department of Justice, March 31, 2002, https://fas.org/irp /agency/doj/fbi/websterreport.html.

11   Ibid.

12   I. C. Smith, interview by the author, summer 2020.

13   Ibid.

14   Ibid.

Chapter 14: The Vault People

1   Jack Thompson, interview by the author, June 2020.

2   Mike Rochford, multiple interviews by the author, spring-summer 2020.

3   Jack Thompson, interview by the author, June 2020.

4   Affidavit in support of criminal complaint, arrest warrant, and search warrants in the case of *United States of America v. Robert Philip Hanssen*, https://fas.org/irp/ops/ci/hanssen_affidavit.html.

5   Office of the Inspector General, *A Review of the FBI's Performance in Deterring, Detecting, and Investigating the Espionage Activities of Robert Philip Hanssen*, United States Department of Justice, August 2003, page 16, https://fas.org/irp/agency/doj/oig/hanssen.pdf.

6   Dave Szady, interview by the author, spring 2020.

7   David Major, interview by the author, June 2020.

8   Jack Thompson, interview by the author, June 2020.

Chapter 15: Odd Couple

1   Bill Gertz, *Enemies: How America's Foes Steal Our Vital Secrets—and How We Let It Happen* (New York: Crown, 2006).

2   David Major, interview by the author, June 2020.

3   Jack Hoschouer, multiple interviews by the author, summer-fall 2020.

4   Affidavit in support of criminal complaint, arrest warrant, and search warrants in the case of *United States of America v. Robert Philip Hanssen*, https://fas.org/irp/ops/ci/hanssen _affidavit.html.

5   Mike Rochford, multiple interviews by the author, spring-summer 2020.

6   Sandy Grimes, interview, January 30, 1998, National Security Archive, https://nsarchive2.gwu .edu/coldwar/interviews/episode-21/grimes1.html.

7   U.S. Senate, Select Committee on Intelligence, *An Assessment of the Aldrich H. Ames Espionage Case and Its Implications for U.S. Intelligence*, S.Prt. 103-90 (Washington, DC: Government Printing Office, 1994), 8, https://fas.org/irp/congress/1994_rpt/ssci_ames.htm.

8   David Major, interview by the author, June 2020.

9   U.S. Senate, Select Committee on Intelligence, *An Assessment of the Aldrich H. Ames Espionage Case and Its Implications for U.S. Intelligence*, S.Prt. 103-90 (Washington, DC: Government Printing Office, 1994), 35, https://fas.org/irp/congress/1994_rpt/ssci_ames.htm.

10   Mike Rochford, multiple interviews by the author, spring-summer 2020.

11   U.S. Senate, Select Committee on Intelligence, *An Assessment of the Aldrich H. Ames Espionage Case and Its Implications for U.S. Intelligence*, S.Prt. 103–90 (Washington, DC: Government Printing Office, 1994), 10, https://fas.org/irp/congress/1994_rpt/ssci_ames.htm.

12   U.S. Senate, Select Committee on Intelligence, *An Assessment of the Aldrich H. Ames Espionage Case and Its Implications for U.S. Intelligence*, S.Prt. 103-90 (Washington, DC: Government Printing Office, 1994, 14, https://fas.org/irp/congress/1994_rpt/ssci_ames.htm.

13   U.S. Senate, Select Committee on Intelligence, *An Assessment of the Aldrich H. Ames Espionage Case and Its Implications for U.S. Intelligence*, S.Prt. 103-90 (Washington, DC: Government Printing Office, 1994), 36–37, https://fas.org/irp/congress/1994_rpt/ssci_ames.htm.

Chapter 16: First Blood

1   U.S. Senate, Select Committee on Intelligence, *An Assessment of the Aldrich H. Ames Espionage Case and Its Implications for U.S. Intelligence*, S.Prt. 103-90 (Washington, DC: Government Printing Office, 1994), 72, https://fas.org/irp/congress/1994_rpt/ssci_ames.htm.

2   Tim Weiner, "C.I.A. Head Says He Misspoke on Possible Espionage Cases," *New York Times*, April 21, 1994, https://www.nytimes.com/1994/04/21/us/cia-head-says-he-misspoke-on -possible-espionage-cases.html.

3   Ibid.

4   U.S. Senate, Select Committee on Intelligence, Special Report, Committee Activities, S. Rep. No. 104-4 (1994), https://www.intelligence.senate.gov/publications/special-report-committee -activities-select-committee-intelligence-january-4-1993.

5   Mike Sulick, interview by the author, June 2020.

6   George Tenet, interview by the author, March 2020.

7   Ibid.

8   Mike Rochford, multiple interviews by the author, spring-summer 2020.

9   Ibid.

10   Ibid.

11   Gwen Fuller, interview by the author, June 2020.

12   Jack Thompson, interview by the author, June 2020.

13   Ibid.

14   Affidavit in support of criminal complaint, arrest warrant, and search warrants in the case of
     United States v. Earl Edwin Pitts, https://www.hanford.gov/files.cfm/earlpitts.pdf, 6.

15   David Wise, *Spy: The Inside Story of How the FBI's Robert Hanssen Betrayed America* (New York:
     Random House, 2003), 115.

16   Affidavit in support of criminal complaint, arrest warrant, and search warrants in the case of
     United States of America v. Robert Philip Hanssen, https://fas.org/irp/ops/ci/hanssen_affidavit.html.

Chapter 17: And the Winner Is . . .

1   Mike Rochford, multiple interviews by the author, spring-summer 2020.

2   Gwen Fuller, interview by the author, June 2020.

3   Mike Rochford, multiple interviews by the author, spring-summer 2020.

4   Louis Freeh, interview by Howard Means, 2004. Used by permission of Louis Freeh.

5   Office of the Inspector General, *A Review of the FBI's Performance in Deterring, Detecting, and
     Investigating the Espionage Activities of Robert Philip Hanssen*, United States Department of
     Justice, August 2003, page 20, https://fas.org/irp/agency/doj/oig/hanssen.pdf.

6   Ibid.

7   Lesley Stahl, *60 Minutes*, season 35, episode 18, "The Wrong Man," aired August 24, 2003, on CBS.
     See also Mary-Jayne McKay, "To Catch a Spy: Probe to Unmask Hanssen Almost Ruined Kelley,"
     CBS News, January 30, 2003, https://www.cbsnews.com/news/to-catch-a-spy-30-01-2003/.

8   George Ellard, interview by the author, March 2020.

9   Ibid.

10   Lesley Stahl, *60 Minutes*, season 35, episode 18, "The Wrong Man," aired August 24, 2003, on CBS.

11   Ibid.

12   Ibid.

13   Gwen Fuller, interview by the author, June 2020.

14   Anonymous, interview by the author.

15   The reference is to the pipe-bomb explosion at Centennial Olympic Park during the 1996
     Summer Games in Atlanta that killed one person and injured 111 others. Security guard
     Richard Jewell was the initial suspect. The actual bomber was Eric Rudolph.

16   Mike Rochford, multiple interviews by the author, spring-summer 2020.

17   Ibid.

Chapter 18: Whac-a-Mole

1   Patricia McCarthy, multiple interviews by the author, spring 2020.

2   Kendall Shull, interview by the author, summer 2020.

3   Ibid.

4   Ibid.

5   Ibid.

6   Ibid.

7   Ibid.

8   Lesley Stahl, *60 Minutes*, season 35, episode 18, "The Wrong Man," aired August 24, 2003, on CBS.

9   Ibid.

10   The Office of Intelligence Policy and Review (OIPR) mission is to assist the attorney general and
     other senior Justice Department officials in fulfilling national security–related responsibilities;
     to provide legal advice and guidance to various elements of the US government that are engaged

in national security–related activities; and to oversee the implementation of the FISA and other statutory, executive order, or attorney general–based authorities for national security–related activities.

11   The director of central intelligence (DCI) was the head of the American Central Intelligence Agency from 1946 to 2005, acting as the principal intelligence advisor to the president of the United States and the US National Security Council, as well as the coordinator of intelligence activities among and between the various US intelligence agencies (collectively known as the Intelligence Community from 1981 onward). The office existed from January 1946 to April 21, 2005. After the Intelligence Reform and Terrorism Prevention Act, it was replaced by the Director of National Intelligence (DNI) as head of the Intelligence Community and the Director of the Central Intelligence Agency (D/CIA) as head of the CIA.

12   Mike Rochford, multiple interviews by the author, spring-summer 2020.

13   Michelle Van Cleave, "Foreign Spies and the US Response," Brian Kelley Memorial Lecture, Institute of World Politics, Washington, DC, October 26, 2012.

14   Lesley Stahl, *60 Minutes*, season 35, episode 18, "The Wrong Man," aired August 24, 2003, on CBS.

15   Gwen Fuller, interview by the author, June 2020.

16   Lesley Stahl, *60 Minutes*, season 35, episode 18, "The Wrong Man," aired August 24, 2003, on CBS.

17   Ibid.

18   Mike Rochford, multiple interviews by the author, spring-summer 2020.

19   Jim Lyle, interview by the author, summer 2020.

20   Barry Kelley, interview by the author, summer 2020.

21   Ibid.

22   Patricia McCarthy, multiple interviews by the author, spring 2020.

23   Ibid.

24   Jim Lyle, interview by the author, summer 2020.

25   Ibid.

Chapter 19: He's Back!

1   Office of the Inspector General, *A Review of the FBI's Performance in Deterring, Detecting, and Investigating the Espionage Activities of Robert Philip Hanssen*, United States Department of Justice, August 2003, pages 14–15, https://fas.org/irp/agency/doj/oig/hanssen.pdf.

2   Barry Kelley, interview by the author, summer 2020.

3   Brian J. Kelley, "The Movie *Breach*: A Personal Perspective," *Studies in Intelligence* 52, no. 1 (March 2008): 24.

4   David Wise, *Spy: The Inside Story of How the FBI's Robert Hanssen Betrayed America* (New York: Random House, 2003), 185.

5   Affidavit in support of criminal complaint, arrest warrant, and search warrants in the case of *United States of America v. Robert Philip Hanssen*, https://fas.org/irp/ops/ci/hanssen_affidavit.html.

6   Ibid.

7   Ibid.

8   Ibid.

10   David Major, interview by the author, June 2020.

11   Jack Hoschouer, multiple interviews by the author, summer-fall 2020.

12   Ibid.

13   Affidavit in support of criminal complaint, arrest warrant, and search warrants in the case of *United States of America v. Robert Philip Hanssen*, https://fas.org/irp/ops/ci/hanssen_affidavit.html.

14   Ibid.

15   Ibid.
16   Ibid.

Chapter 20: PENNYWISE

1   Mike Rochford, multiple interviews by the author, spring-summer 2020.
2   Ibid.
3   Although others have done so, I have chosen not to identify Mr. Pym, the man who would become Mike Rochford's critical Russian source, by name. Vladimir Putin's Russia recognizes no statute of limitations on revenge.
4   Michael Rochford, "Investigation of Robert Hanssen," discussion, International Spy Museum, October 1, 2013, Washington, DC, online video, 1:15:37, https://www.c-span.org/video /?315217-1/investigation-robert-hanssen.
5   Mike Rochford, multiple interviews by the author, spring-summer 2020.
6   Michael Rochford, "Investigation of Robert Hanssen," discussion, International Spy Museum, October 1, 2013, Washington, DC, online video, 1:18:50, https://www.c-span.org/video /?315217-1/investigation-robert-hanssen.
7   Mike Rochford, multiple interviews by the author, spring-summer 2020.
8   Ibid.
9   Ibid.
10   Ibid.
11   Ibid.
12   Ibid.
13   Jim Lyle, interview by the author, summer 2020.
14   Ibid.
15   Gwen Fuller, interview by the author, June 2020.
16   Mike Rochford, multiple interviews by the author, spring-summer 2020.
17   Ibid.
18   Jim Milburn, interview by the author, summer 2020.
19   Ibid.
20   Ibid.
21   Gwen Fuller, interview by the author, June 2020.
22   Jim Lyle, interview by the author, summer 2020.
23   Mike Sulick, interview by the author, June 2020.
24   Mike Rochford, multiple interviews by the author, spring-summer 2020.
25   Ibid.

Chapter 21: Baiting the Trap

1   Mike Rochford, multiple interviews by the author, spring-summer 2020.
2   Jim Lyle, interview by the author, summer 2020.
3   Mike Rochford, multiple interviews by the author, spring-summer 2020.
4   Ibid.
5   Ibid.
6   Jim Lyle, interview by the author, summer 2020.
7   Rich Garcia, interview by the author, spring-summer 2020.
8   Ibid.
9   Ibid.
10   Jim Lyle, interview by the author, summer 2020.
11   Rich Garcia, interview by the author, spring-summer 2020.
12   Ibid.

13   Ibid.

14   Don Sullivan, interviews by the author, summer 2020.

15   Ibid.

16   Rich Garcia, interview by the author, spring-summer 2020.

17   Ibid.

18   Ibid.

19   Jim Lyle, interview by the author, summer 2020.

20   Rich Garcia, interview by the author, spring-summer 2020.

21   Don Sullivan, interviews by the author, summer 2020.

22   Eric O'Neill, *Gray Day: My Undercover Mission to Expose America's First Cyber Spy* (New York: Crown, 2019), 44.

23   Eric O'Neill, *Gray Day: My Undercover Mission to Expose America's First Cyber Spy* (New York: Crown, 2019), 62.

24   Eric O'Neill, interview by the author, summer 2020.

25   Ibid.

26   Eric O'Neill, interview by the author, summer 2020.

27   Rich Garcia, interview by the author, spring-summer 2020.

28   Ibid.

29   Ibid.

30   Affidavit in support of search warrants in the case of *United States of America v. Robert Philip Hanssen*, https://fas.org/irp/ops/ci/hanssen_affidavit2.html.

31   Rich Garcia, interview by the author, spring-summer 2020.

Chapter 22: Takedown

1   Jack Hoschouer, multiple interviews by the author, summer-fall 2020.

2   Ibid.

3   Mike Rochford, multiple interviews by the author, spring-summer 2020.

4   Jim Lyle, interview by the author, summer 2020.

5   Louis Freeh, interview by Howard Means, 2004. Used by permission of Louis Freeh.

6   Rich Garcia, interview by the author, spring-summer 2020.

7   James Risen, "Gaps in Ames Case May Be Filled by FBI's Own Spy Case," *New York Times*, February 21, 2001, https://www.nytimes.com/2001/02/21/national/gaps-in-ames-case-may-be-filled-by-fbis-own-spy-case.html?searchResultPosition=1. Also, FBI National Press Office, "Statement of FBI Director Louis J. Freeh on the Arrest of FBI Special Agent Robert Philip Hanssen," news release, February 20, 2001, https://www.fbi.gov/history/famous-cases/robert-hanssen.

8   Patricia McCarthy, multiple interviews by the author, spring 2020.

9   Barry Kelley, interview by the author, summer 2020.

10   Mike Rochford, multiple interviews by the author, spring-summer 2020.

11   David A. Vise, "From Russia with Love," *Washington Post*, January 6, 2002, https://www.washingtonpost.com/archive/lifestyle/magazine/2002/01/06/from-russia-with-love/b28c2127-65e5-43f3-8a9a-0e75ab851cb3/.

12   David Wise, *Spy: The Inside Story of How the FBI's Robert Hanssen Betrayed America* (New York: Random House, 2003), 14.

Chapter 23: Collateral Damage

1   *In camera*: in private; in particular, taking place in the private chambers of a judge, with the press and public excluded.

2   Mike Rochford, multiple interviews by the author, spring-summer 2020.

3   George Tenet, interview by the author, March 2020.
4   Ibid.
5   Mike Rochford, multiple interviews by the author, spring-summer 2020.
6   Scott McCaffrey, "Oakcrest Graduates Told Living Good Lives Will Bring Happiness," Inside
       Nova, June 3, 2013, https://www.insidenova.com/news/fairfax/oakcrest-graduates-told-living
       -good-lives-will-bring-happiness/article_b23332ff-a93d-506b-9889-9007da8829c7.html.
7   Mark Wauck, multiple interviews by the author, spring-summer 2020.
8   Camp Peary, known as "The Farm," a training facility run by the CIA.
9   Jim Lyle, interview by the author, summer 2020.
10   Barry Kelley, interview by the author, summer 2020.
11   Patricia McCarthy, multiple interviews by the author, spring 2020.
12   I. C. Smith, interview by the author, summer 2020.
13   George Tenet, interview by the author, March 2020.
14   Mike Rochford, multiple interviews by the author, spring-summer 2020.
15   I. C. Smith, interview by the author, summer 2020.
16   Jim Lyle, interview by the author, summer 2020.
17   Mark Wauck, multiple interviews by the author, spring-summer 2020.
18   Ibid.
19   Ibid.
20   Brian Kelley, email message to Mark Wauck.
21   Mark Wauck, email message to Brian Kelley, August 23, 2010.
22   Jim Lyle, interview by the author, summer 2020.
23   Louis Freeh, interview by Howard Means, 2004. Used by permission of Louis Freeh.
24   Jim Lyle, interview by the author, summer 2020.
25   Greg Wauck, interview by the author, spring-summer 2020.
26   Michael Rochford, "Investigation of Robert Hanssen," discussion, International Spy Museum,
       October 1, 2013, Washington, DC, online video, 1:37:53, https://www.c-span.org/video
       /?315217-1/investigation-robert-hanssen.
27   Mike Rochford, multiple interviews by the author, spring-summer 2020.
28   David Major, interview by the author, June 2019.
29   Kathleen Puckett, interview by the author, summer 2020.
30   Jack Hoschouer, multiple interviews by the author, summer-fall 2020.
31   E. M. Forster, *What I Believe* (London: Hogarth Press, 1939).
32   Jack Hoschouer, multiple interviews by the author, summer-fall 2020.

Chapter 24: The Mind of a Spy

1   The 150 figure also includes those not prosecuted even though clear evidence of espionage
       exists—those who defected, for example, or died or committed suicide before charges could
       be brought as well as those who plea-bargained for lesser charges or received immunity from
       prosecution in return for providing evidence against others.
2   Richards J. Heuer Jr. and Katherine Herbig, "Espionage by the Numbers: A Statistical
       Overview," Defense Personnel Security Research Center, March 2014, https://www.sri-hq.com
       /SRI-NET/Security/Treason/Numbers.htm.
3   Kathleen Puckett, interview by the author, summer 2020.
4   Mike Sulick, interview by the author, June 2020.
5   J. Scott Sanford and Bruce A. Arrigo, "Policing and Psychopathy: The Case of Robert Philip
       Hanssen," *Journal of Forensic Psychology Practice* 7, no. 3 (2007): 1–31.
6   J. Scott Sanford and Bruce A. Arrigo, "Policing and Psychopathy: The Case of Robert Philip
       Hanssen," *Journal of Forensic Psychology Practice* 7, no. 3 (2007): 30.

7   Dan Eggen, "Revelations and Recriminations in Spy Case," *Washington Post*, July 3, 2001,
     https://www.washingtonpost.com/archive/politics/2001/07/03/revelations-and-recriminations
     -in-spy-case/17ef4900-c7fe-40e6-b4ff-b2d195f629af/.
8   Ibid.
9   David Charney, multiple interviews by the author, spring-summer 2020.
10   Ibid.
11   George Ellard, interview by the author, March 2020.
12   David Charney, multiple interviews by the author, spring-summer 2020.
13   Ibid.

Chapter 25: Another Hanssen?

1   George Ellard, interview by the author, March 2020.
2   Dave Szady, interview by the author, summer 2020.
3   Mike Rochford, multiple interviews by the author, spring-summer 2020.
4   Ibid.
5   Eric Ambler, *The Light of Day* (New York: Vintage, 2004), 52.
6   I. C. Smith, interview by the author, summer 2020.
7   George Tenet, interview by the author, March 2020.
8   David Charney, multiple interviews by the author, spring-summer 2020.
9   Evan Hanson, "Manning-Lamo Chat Logs Revealed," *Wired*, July 13, 2011, https://www.wired
     .com/2011/07/manning-lamo-logs/.
10   Chris Strohm and Del Quentin Wilber, "Pentagon Says Snowden Took Most US Secrets Ever:
     Rogers," Bloomberg, January 9, 2014, https://www.bloomberg.com/news/articles/2014-01-09
     /pentagon-finds-snowden-took-1-7-million-files-rogers-says; and Barton Gellman, Julie Tate,
     and Ashkan Soltani, "In NSA-Intercepted Data, Those Not Targeted Far Outnumber the
     Foreigners Who Are," *Washington Post*, July 5, 2014, https://www.washingtonpost.com/world
     /national-security/in-nsa-intercepted-data-those-not-targeted-far-outnumber-the-foreigner
     -who-are/2014/07/05/8139adf8-045a-11e4-8572-4b1b969b6322_story.html.
11   Scott Shane, interview by the author, July 2020.
12   Daniel R. Coats, *Worldwide Threat Assessment of the US Intelligence Community*, Senate Select
     Committee on Intelligence, January 29, 2019, page 4, https://www.dni.gov/files/ODNI
     /documents/2019-ATA-SFR---SSCI.pdf.
13   *National Counterintelligence Strategy of the United States of America 2020–2022*, National
     Counterintelligence and Security Center, page 3, February 2020, https://www.dni.gov/files
     /NCSC/documents/features/20200205-National_CI_Strategy_2020_2022.pdf.
14   Anonymous, interview by the author, summer 2020.

INDEX

ACKNOWLEDGEMENTS

I remember hearing my FBI dad talking about Robert Hanssen when I was very young. Dad had disgust for the man, and felt deep dismay that the FBI failed to uncover Hanssen's treachery for decades. Hanssen was a black mark against the FBI, and I wanted to know how one man fooled the FBI for so long.

As I began the research and writing for this book, I hoped to move the Robert Hanssen story forward, to find new clues into what had happened, and to ask whether such treason might occur again. For answers, I went straight to the sources, interviewing the key FBI and CIA agents who had hunted the spy, including Michael Rochford, the agent who spearheaded the hunt, and who has shouldered a lot of blame for the FBI's imperfect internal controls and mechanisms. Rochford spoke to me in great detail, revealing aspects of the hunt for the first time. I am extremely grateful for his candor and insight.

I was also fortunate enough to gain access to Hanssen's inner circle, including his brother-in-law, Mark Wauk; his best friend, Jack Hoschouer; and his psychiatrist, Dr. David Charney. I am also indebted to CIA Agent Brian Kelley's widow, Patricia. She shared with me the devastation brought to the Kelley family by the FBI's false claims that he was the traitor.

I am profusely thankful to all the present and former FBI and CIA agents who, for the first time, went on the record about Hanssen.

I am also thankful for Howard Means, star researcher and storyteller, who brought so much passion to this project. It was Howard who convinced former FBI director, Louis Freeh, to speak about his personal experience with Hanssen. Howard's steadfastly upbeat attitude helped bring this book to life. Thank you, Howard.

To my agent, Todd Shuster with Aevitas Creative, I say thank you for believing in this project even when we hit bumps along the road. Todd's perseverance brought this project home to Pegasus, and I will always be grateful. And thank you, Justin Brouckaert, also with Aevitas Creative, who brought his keen editing eye and unwavering enthusiasm to the project.

Todd led us to Jessica Case, deputy publisher at Pegasus, who embraced the project with open arms, and quickly got to work with her editing pen. Her high spirits match the high quality of her input and edits. Thank you, Jessica.

Jessica brought in Jenny Rossberg, head of publicity at Pegasus. Jenny is relentless in her effort to get the Hanssen story out to readers far and wide. Thank you, Jenny.

The folks at Pegasus form a real dream team, including Maria Fernandez, head of production; Drew Wheeler, copyeditor; Mary O'Mara, proofreader; and Faceout Studios, in charge of the cover design.

I was inspired by my parents to undertake this project and to move the story forward with the help of all the people who told me of their dealings with this dangerous and notorious spy. I am inspired daily by my children, Jacob and Dani, who continue to forge their individual paths with grace, empathy, and fortitude. You are my heroes.

ABOUT THE AUTHOR

Lis Wiehl is a *New York Times* best-selling author and the former legal analyst for Fox News. The former cohost of WOR radio's *WOR Tonight with Joe Concha and Lis Wiehl*, she has served as legal analyst and reporter for NBC News and NPR's *All Things Considered*, as a federal prosecutor in the US Attorney's office, and as a tenured professor of law at the University of Washington. She appears frequently on CNN as a legal analyst.